Creature of Habit

A Journey

The Troops for Truddi Chase

Moonbeams Unlimited Publishing

Delaware

The various spellings (British, Middle English, Old English, etc.) originate from Ean, one of Truddi Chase's personalities. Ean, the Irish Troop member simply said that they are part of his background, his heritage.

If you find any additional errors please send to info@truddichase.com.

Acknowledgements

While Truddi is no longer of this plane, I know there are people she would have liked to recognize. This book is dedicated to Robert A. Phillips, Jr., Ph.D. Wherever you are, thank you again for making the battleground safe. Rebecca McCormick for staying the course; Mary Francis and Edward Curvey and Carol and Cliff Dunning for listening and understanding; to Oprah Winfrey and her staff for giving Truddi a platform to help others; and Roseanne Barr for her endless love and support.

As for me, I need to thank so many for helping me to see this labor of love to fruition.

Special thanks to Christine Gray Moore for countless hours of back and forth edits, patience with my grammatical ineptitude, and giving such a beautiful description to Creature. To Rebecca McCormick for her encouragement and enthusiasm in getting Truddi's story told to the world. I hope you are drinking scotch and smoking up a storm with The Troops. Many thanks go to members of The Rehoboth Beach Writer's Guild whose gentle encouragement gave me the strength to persevere; to my Maryland friends who knew and loved Truddi, thank you for waiting; to my Delaware friends who have come to know Truddi through me, thank you for your desire to see me succeed in this project; to Oprah Winfrey and her staff, for their continued efforts to bring awareness to the world about child abuse and its effects; to Roseanne Barr, you brought so much joy and laughter into mine and Truddi's life. Thank you for your generosity of heart.

Obviously, I have to thank my mother, Truddi Chase, for her insatiable desire to encourage survivors to forge ahead, find their voice, and shout from the mountaintops. It takes my breath away to think about how much love, talent, and unfettered brilliance was wrapped up in 92 personalities encompassed in one body. Thank you for sharing your gift with me, breaking the chain, and teaching me about true strength. With love beyond time, I miss you! To Melody Diaz, thank you does not begin to cover the gratitude I feel for your endless hours of hard work and knowledge. You truly have a creative eye, and I know Truddi would have approved of every edit, artwork placement, and font choice. You saw her vision and kept Creature pure and true.

Last but certainly not least, my partner, husband, and "Superman," Paul. You lifted me when I was ready to give up and gave me the strength to persist with this passion and the confidence to keep going, even when I was banging my head against brick walls. Thank you for gnawing through the straps for me when I was too tired to chew them myself and for letting me be me, including all of my inherited "Truddi-ness."

A mother's journey becomes a daughter's destiny...

After experiencing incredible trauma in her life, my mother, Truddi Chase, wanted to share her story with others, a story of coping with post traumatic stress and the diagnosis of Multiple Personality Disorder, now classified as Dissociative Identity Disorder. This lead to her first book, When Rabbit Howls, which tracks her life with The Troops (her collective personalities) and the impact abuse has on individuals. A few years after the release of When Rabbit Howls, Truddi and The Troops finished their psychotherapy with Dr. Phillips and began a journey of self-discovery in order to prove to themselves that there is "life after therapy" for multiples. Out of this discovery process, they created Creature of Habit, A Journey. Creature would give Truddi and The Troops a new way to speak into other's lives; to reach out to those struggling with the aftermath of trauma; to let them know that they aren't alone; and that through their own journey, they might find strength, knowledge, and freedom. It was into Creature that I watched Truddi and The Troops pour their heart and soul, blood, sweat, and tears until....

Back in the late 1990s, way before our current technology boom, Truddi and The Troops were told that Creature was too long and had too much artwork to publish. This news devastated them. Succumbing to depression following this blow, Truddi began closing herself off from the rest of the world, and so Creature was packed away, never to be seen or heard from again. I felt her frustration at having to set aside her passion, but I felt rather helpless to change the situation. By 2010, Truddi's health was in serious decline. With this knowledge, I desperately wanted to give her the gift of seeing all of her beautiful words and artwork in published form before she left this earth. So, I decided it was time to resurrect Creature from its dusty grave in the attic. My goal was simple: to get it into a format that would be in time with the current technology so we could try again to have it published. Unfortunately, Truddi was not to see the finished work. She passed away before it was completed. After her death, I knew my purpose in life was to see Creature through to the end. I felt I owed it to her to have it published somehow, even though she would never see it in printed form.

I have always known that this story needed to be shared and that it could help so many suffering with various traumas. I have seen firsthand how post traumatic stress—brought on by events like rape, abuse, and war—causes us to develop potentially destructive habits as a means of "protecting" ourselves from further harm. And yet, these very habits—meant for our protection—actually put us in further bondage. Instead of experiencing freedom from the trauma, these behaviors place us inside a compound with walls so tall there's no way to escape. It is only in the breaking free from these habits that we begin to grow and discover our true selves, a lesson explored through Creature's journey.

Now, almost 25 years later, it is with a deep sense of pride and joy that I pass along what Truddi and The Troops started so many years ago. It is my greatest wish that people share this book with everyone they know. Whether you have suffered a trauma or not, Creature will touch your heart and show you that destructive habits can be broken and ultimate knowledge and unfettered thought is within reach.

ii

The Creature of Habit, A Journey

Prologue

Before there was much at all upon the land, and few paths by which to travel - provided one dared go – there existed a Creature of Habit.

A curious creature was he, in that he had no curiosity whatever, at least none that he knew of. But one dark night, while reviewing his tasks for the following day – the same tasks he'd always performed and which he expected to perform until there was nothing left of himself – he happened to glance upward.

The midnight heavens looked the same as on any other evening, until he looked again, to note a very fine oddity.

And thus – unwittingly – did his journey begin.

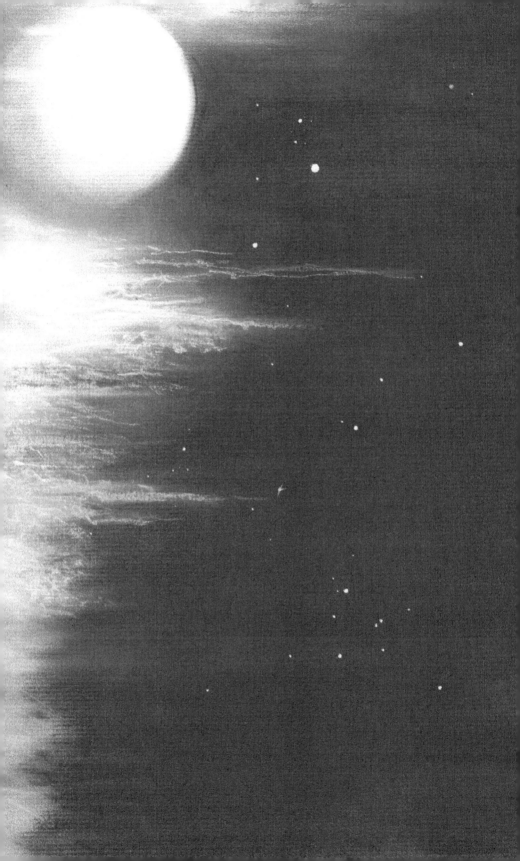

1

A Vast Distance To Go

At night, the stars appeared as pin-prick holes
in a deep-dark canopy. The moon seemed nothing more than
a circle of pale gauze, through which a dim light spilled.
And the Creature of Habit wondered what lay beyond
the holes in the sky. And wondered why one could not
go there…*beyond.*

A bold idea.

So little did he ever wonder about anything of importance that startled, his gaze was immediately riveted upon that upward path…

while just a short distance away, the great Vine pretended, as usual, to sleep. More than a casual observour peering through the moonlight; would have seen the coiling length of it stir ever-so-slightly. But the Creature could seldom bring himself to look directly at the Vine…nor did he look now.

So much space, the Creature mused – from here to there – to those intriguing bright holes in that soaring canopy: Exactly how much space might that be? And how might one *get* from here to there, to the holes in the sky, and then through then – *to what?*
Provided of course,
that one were free to go.

Free

The lone word hung on the night air, until
the wind, normally silent and still, brought it
sighing, closer to him…*free*…

Distracted, he turned from the heavens. Along the ridge of the Vine, the deft hand of the moon tipped each leaf in silver, and they rustled slightly – perhaps it was only the wind.
Free…the word no longer sighed around him, but seemed

imprisoned
within his mind.

4

Dawn woke him every morning thereafter to a gnawing unease.
He went about his duties, sorry that he'd summoned such
thoughts – for one unleashed by his inspection of the heavens, the
thoughts simply *stuck,* refusing any attempt
to be rid of them.

In every kind of light, that tempting huge ocean above the
world he knew taunted, flaunted its secrets. By day, great
stretches of white cotton clouds bunched together,
then scattered across an expanse of sun-lit blue
or rain-dashed pewter-grey—
presenting
a picture
that
must surely
be backed by a canvas
of sorts: something substantial,
resting yet upon something else—which, by
the very nature of things, must surely rest upon
something else.

But how many were those canvases,
and where did their number end?
In fact—*how could* their number end, *at all?*
Who might have the answers,
and would he *dare*
to ask?

Time after time, he pried his thought down
from those heavens, forcing himself to a mindless performance
of duty. But if he couldn't count the canvases in the sky, he surely
could not say how often he'd watered the Vine's roots, tended its
vicious little tendrils, or secured the soil at the base of its brand
new, earth-bound sprouts—laboring all the while, under the
darkest of truths: just once had probably been enough—and
the Vine, fully aware of his treachery, only bided time
behind its hooded, all-seeing eyes.

Nor were others blind, either. Sensing that the Creature
was up to something he shouldn't be, they drew further and
further away from him.

Who could blame them? He was, after all, entranced by a
dangerous pursuit; dangerous enough that not even he wanted to
contemplate its outcome. Nevertheless, alone now, and trapped
by this thing he had started he just couldn't stop. His own
unanswered questions wouldn't let him stop.

Each day, that dragon-wall sprawled around them, with
all the brilliance of a spectacular green jewel, displaying a quite
believable innocence, provided one didn't know better, but
everybody did: small acts of meanness, larger acts of cruelty—
not ever lightened by anything merciful or caring. And always,
the threat hung over their heads, that

unless they behaved,
those heads
might easily roll.

For Vine-weapons were
awesome, capable even, of
whipping clear across the
compound in any direction, and
snapping the wings from a speeding gnat.
He had seen it happen one night while watering.
The Vine had winked at him maliciously, saying,
"You're next, creature." But while it was a true story,
nobody had believed it. They said, "Really, now—
we know the Vine is bad, but it isn't

all that bad."

And
nobody
consulted
the gnat.

Small
wonder,
that when
night fell
upon the land…

9

the Creature's thoughts
left the Vine's enclosure,
and his eyes
climbed again that upward path
...where the heavens posed
their same deep
puzzle
which he dare not voice
to anyone
but himself.
Pondering the puzzle did not unravel
the thread of its reality, at least
not to his satisfaction. And since
a habit of seldom lingering in his mind
had become ingrained, like the
rings in a tree, he'd always found
lengthy pondering
difficult.

Difficult or not, however,
it seemed he was doing it, or at least
trying. So now, everyone else,
unsuspecting his nameless crime to be
an unforgivable one, stopped
speaking to him,
entirely.
Sometimes,

as if

they would
speak to him,
the smaller winds—which
had become so awfully,

strangely insistent of late—

would pause just above him. But always,

they turned away.

And so he would stand alone in the silence
looking up,
and hoping for an answer.
But no answer came.

He hadn't expected one. It had been a long while since anything of consequence had entered the compound where he lived with the other creatures of his kind. They were a quiet group, content to pass through their lives without incident. No longer did they hunger for knowledge, nor were they interested in change, either in themselves, or in the spot of earth on which they dwelled. As a result, theirs was not so much a dreary place, as it was simply, grindingly,

the same,

one day onto the next.

The Creature of Habit began to feel decidedly torn. For in spite of that sameness being expected, even needed by all creatures, the mysterious holes in the night's dark veil bombarded his thoughts, expanded then, demanded of him the treachery of thinking even more thoughts, none of which supported the Vine's theory of sameness.

Powerless against panic each time the full weight of his treachery descended upon him, he denied everything, panic, treachery, and mystery alike. And still, nothing would quell his growing awareness that he had led himself to the brink of the unknown.

Sure enough, the moment came—as he had somehow known it would—when he stood atremble and all by himself on that brink, to confront what had become for him an even bigger question: How much longer could he go on, *unless he found out what lay beyond?*

A double-edged dilemma for certain; and so distressing that at times even the moon seemed bent on unnerving him. All too often, as her changing face peered through that pale gauze, he wondered if she might know
the answer.

          But the moon kept her own counsel,
                as he troubled himself further, by wondering why she observed him in such silence.

          Thus was the battle joined, almost unknowingly,
  as fear and torment
        threatened the
            unfolding
                of his curiosity. He stumbled more often
          over the gnarled roots of the ubiquitous Vine,
     and it took to opening one hooded eye and staring at him,
  whenever his back was turned. That Vine-stare set the
other to arguing—softly, of course, since raised voices were
forbidden—while they tried to predict the next major Vine-rage.
And all anybody could actually do, including the Creature,
    was await the inevitable.
He wished most heartily that just one, something different,
would brave the green walls and take their minds off
disaster; for lately, not even the distant call of a bird could
be heard. Then one afternoon, a small thought arrived,

tapping as it were, upon his badly wracked nerves: *The Vine*

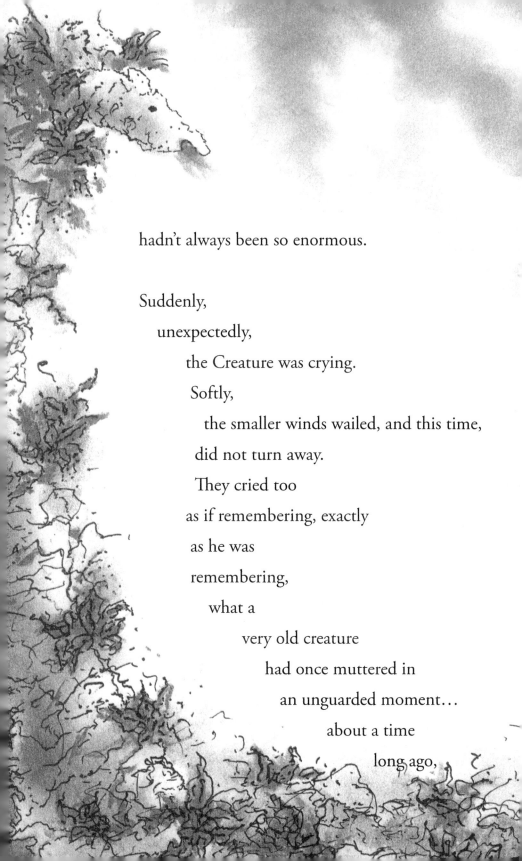

hadn't always been so enormous.

Suddenly,
   unexpectedly,
      the Creature was crying.
     Softly,
       the smaller winds wailed, and this time,
     did not turn away.
    They cried too
   as if remembering, exactly
   as he was
   remembering,
    what a
      very old creature
       had once muttered in
        an unguarded moment…
         about a time
          long ago,

long

before

the vine...

when one could see

all that lay in the distance

- tall trees, taller mountains -

even a great body of water,

where birds wheeled

and freely dipped their wings in the sky.

The Creature fought to see through his tears,

to envision the wonder of what that old Creature's

re-telling of old ancient legends,

But he failed, miserably.

For the legends were as ghosts,

with no real form or substance;

gone

as the old one was gone-

while the Vine still prospered,

growing greener than green,

wider than wide,

and taller than tall

- taller even than trees or mountains-

so that no one could see

over it.

No one could see
through it,
either.
Because-having traveled five or six times around
the compound, constantly looping and lacing
back and forth
-barely a hole remained
in the Vine's entire rough tapestry.

Of course, it was nobody's duty but his own to walk the
long wall of confinement twice a day, carrying the heavy earthen
jug of water. At dawn, and again after dusk, he traversed the
imprisioning boundary. While pouring water on each twisted root,
he could only watch in devistation as the Vine bent upon itself, taking
nourishment from its own coiled ropes. More and more during his
plodding rounds, he sought refuge in staring above it. Until it came
to pass one sunny but ill-begotten morning - just as lengthy
pondering had finally worn him down - that his mind wandered
over the whole miserable state of thing; wandered in fact,
just a bit too far...

"Are you thinking?" snarled the Vine from behind him. "I've
been watching you, Creature. You're not fooling me! You always have to be
up to something, don't you? If it isn't this, it's that. You're
forever a problem, sneaking around with your infernal curiosity,
sketching in the dirt when I've told you not to, daydreaming when I
have forbidden it. On and on goes the list of your stupidities!"
Quite by rote, the culprit cast his eyes upon his feet-as was
right and proper-uttered something unintelligible,

and slunk away.

The Vine found him where he stood, cringing inside himself.

"Trying to think," it hissed, "causes misery. Misery and discontent. Any you know that leads to curiosity, something that never ever did anybody any good. Keep up this belligerence of yours, and pretty soon you'll be beyond help."

Everybody knew the Vine hardly ever spoke to anybody. And when forced to do so by some infraction of the rules-either real or imagined-unthinkable punishements were sure to follow. Sweat ran down the Creature from his head to his toes, as in amongst the rustling leaves, tendril after tendril started to uncoil...yet somehow, despite what was an almost blinding fear, he just couldn't resist giving that last remark a silent prod: What if he were already beyond help, at least as far as any he might expect in the compound? *What if he were free of the compound?*

Free. The idea hummed in his head, and strongly...much as if it had made itself at home and now refused to leave. In worried silence, the others hovered nearby, trying to look anywhere-exept at the Vine-or at him. The air fairly crackled with Vine-anger, and create-fear, his own included. He wanted to explain himself, but realised-he wasn't really close enough to anyone to entrust his new and skyward thoughts-nor especially this free word, which now resided in him as though it belonged there. Before even estimating what was at risk, he'd

looked up. And was
facing the Vine. "I need to ask you
a question." He began, with every ounce of politeness
and humility he had. "Well, actually, there are two of
them. I know that no one has ever asked you even one
question, let alone two, but if it wouldn't trouble you unduly—"

"Oh, do continue," urged the Vine, mocking and
daring at the same time.

"Perhaps you will tell me," mumbled the Creature in barely
audible tones, "why we are forbidden to look one another
in the eye."

"Say please."

"Please," he said, immediately, obediently.

"What a sorry mess you are." Casually, a small bug was
flicked from the glorious coat of green. "Very well. The reason is
simple, so I'll give it to you: Contamination. Looking one another
in the eye transmits very nasty conditions from looker
to lookee—disease, insanity—why go on? It's boring. But feel free,
Creature. Do it, and you'll be struck with the plagues and begin to
babble. I myself, do it all the time, because I need to keep an eye
on all of you, but I am equipped! Next question, and make it

fast!"

A flurry of appendages with their little knotted ends snaked
out over the compound, leapt into the air, and cracked like the evil
whips they were. So dreadful was the sound the Creature
desperately wished that he didn't have a next question.

But he did.

To make matters worse, it had three parts.
With his nerve fast disappearing,
he asked:
"Why are we forbidden to greet anybody? And what is a
greeting anyway? What purpose does it serve?"
Behind him, everybody seemed perplexed at the nature of
his questions. Still aghast that he would ask anything at all,
they kept their eyes on their feet. Nobody moved an inch.
"So that's your little flummox, is it? You're too dumb to
know anything! Have you nothing but meaningless drivel
on which to risk your ugly, tiresome existence?" The Vine went
dark with anger, and fluffed its luxuriant green foliage,
each tentril coiling smartly
with practiced menace. "Well then, stupid, I'll tell you why
you are firmly forbidden to greet each other: Mental
stimulation,that's why! Greetings, all that silly, soppy,
inquisitive nonsense, only invites *curiosity.* Such stimulation
as you well-know, is *corrosive* to our feelings of well-being!"

As though clearly in the presence of a witless wretch,
the towering mass of expertise let out a hot breath of disgust,
nearly scorching the perimeters. But knowing how the heat of
rage would presently wilt its grandly-displayed self, it glared,
sending the Creature into a frenzy of water-hauling, as he soaked
and re-soaked the massive root system.
"Listen," the Vine hissed softly, so the others wouldn't hear,
"get it in your head! All you need to know is what I tell you!"

And then much louder, so that everybody
could hear, "Those rules you've been flaunting, are for the

19

good of all! Mark me well, they're the only protection you've got!"

"I see," said the Creature as he worked, but of course he did not.

"Doesn't *matter*," the Vine thundered on, "whether you see or you don't see, because you're just a water-carrier! And don't fool yourself for one minute that your duties with that silly jug will save you! Things are in place around here, because I make all your decisions for you, tend to your every need, but are you *satisfied?* No! *You* want to disturb the *safety of sameness!* Well, guess what? *I'm* concocting a little lesson in rules at this very moment, just for your benefit, and we'll see if you're satisfied with *that!*"

And so saying, the Vine drew itself up to a dramatic fullness of knowing and gave off and air of dire concentration. The Creature of Habit had been dismissed.

He caught sight of those tendrils one more time before they recoiled and withdrew into the shadows of their lair. Punishment would follow, and soon. There was no predicting what, or when it would be, for the Vine liked suspense. Faint with terror and limp with humiliation, the air in his throat grew shallow and then non-existent, as he tried to breathe but couldn't. He felt himself staggering, not enough that anyone else would notice perhaps, but enough to make him mortified at his weakness. Panic set in, as he fought in short little gasps for air that wasn't there, each gasp forcing him further into the eye of his own imminent doom. Yet just when he

thought he'd breathed his last breath—payment most likely, for
disobedience—there came that moment as it always did, when
anxiety let up enough that he could breathe fully once more.
Never before had fear attacked so completely. His breathing still
sounded laboured and ragged at every hefting
of the water jug.
And he could not see
the obvious,

but wondered, was it
an omen of some sort?
Moving rapidly to make up for his
momentary lapse, and grateful for his
habitual duty—for it meant that he was still
safe—he continued soaking the ground at the base of
the Vine.

The little word *free* sailed around in his head. The moon
unfettered, sailed into his mind. How he envied
her freedom. Someday
when his duties were done—how grand it would be if he
were sailing up there unfettered, just as the moon herself.
Too late, he realized how easily he kept slipping into the forbidden
world of daydreams. He realized also
the impossibility—for him—of not slipping into those daydreams.
Shaking visibly now, he trudged on with his tasks as the whips
playfully uncoiled again from their ugly little knots and began
reaching out tauntingly for him…as if it were only a game.

The day ended. He had almost finished gathering up the withered, discarded Vine leaves which would comprise the creatures' evening meal—old Vine leaves were all there was to eat in the compound aside from fresh Vine sprouts, and those were forbidden—when he heard whimpers above his head. Suspended by their tails along the great ridge of the Vine were a number of little grey mice.

Snickers came from the Vine whips as they dangled the mice to and fro, over the compound. This game had obviously been going on for some time. Eyes filmed over, their voices faint, the small bodies hung practically lifeless. The Creature had no particular fondness for mice, and any inclination to heroism had long since left him. The more he thought about it—and he thought for some time—it just didn't seem fair that Vine whips should outnumber the mice more than fifty-to-one, and the idea of their baking in the sun all day tomorrow turned his stomach.

No sooner had the creatures finished their meal of leaves, than he had swept away the stray fits and was watching the moon come out, highlighting the five small slumped bodies. Now he watched for the Vine whips to join the Vine in slumber, and when they did, he proceeded to untangle each mouse from its captors.

"Go!" he hissed, watching them sprint with sudden alacrity toward a scant parting of vines at his feet. "Go, and don't come back!"

His stomach rumbled. There were never enough withered leaves to go around, but he resisted the urge to steal fresh sprouts. He always got caught. The spacing of his two upper front teeth left identifying marks which he was not clever enough to hide, and which the Vine easily spotted.

The last mouse tail wiggled through the Vines. The Creature saw it leaving with a wrenching inside himself that was much stronger than even his hunger for crunchy-crispy Vine sprouts. He could not have named the cause of the wrenching, for by this time, nearly all his deeper connective emotions were almost as deadened as the evening meal inside him…

The only way he could express what that escaping mouse aroused in him, was to grab a sharp rock and begin sketching its image in the dirt. It was with regret that he remembered in time, to erase everything before falling asleep that night.

And so it went, from every dawn-to-dusk,
each one unendingly the same.
Until one evening…
as he plodded through the watering…his foot slipped, striking down new-born, verdant Vine sprouts.

"You *stepped on me,* Creature," said the Vine, in a dangerously quiet tone.
Near its blatant green edge, a tendril he had been avoiding so carefully shot out and grabbed his offending foot. It slip up to his ankle and attached itself. Tightly. "I am," he cried, with his bones rattling in his body, "so sorry. Believe me. I never meant to."

The attached tendril bit into his flesh.

23

Hooded eyes beheld him,
held him,
fixed in place.
"Now I'll ask you a question," said the Vine, whose
ominous voice grew loud and then
louder, "is it any wonder you're a quaking, shaking,
breathless, tormented, stupid mess, after all your dilly-
dallying in the at non-existent land of so-called THINKING?"

The creatures of the compound peered out from various
nooks and crannies where they'd hidden themselves, and nodded
in agreement with the Vine. Seeing this, *it* promptly fluffed
up,turning ever more proudly-green at its victory. "You," it said,
"would throw away Habit—your most prized possession, which
has been so good to you—for something so unreal, so trivial as
thinking? Well, I think you should *stop trying to think,* once and
for all, and get yourself back to reality—where you belong!"

And the creatures in their nooks and crannies all
nodded again—and they looked with pity in the Creature of
Habit's direction, as if he might need a long rest in a quiet, dark
place.But there would be no long rest, either in a quiet dark place
or any other. The Vine had yet to name a revenge for his earlier
offense of the day—thus feeding its beloved suspense—but it kept
him working slavishly, deep into the night, until he thought he
would drop.

Finally, he did.

With a last savage bite, the tendril loosened it grip on his

ankle and snapped back into the dark undergrowth of the Vine,
allowing the Creature to collapse on his water jug. He let the full
weight of himself just sink down upon it
—as if any hope he might have had, was
of no more use to him—as if he were trying to squash both
his untried-visions and his sorely-tried self, inside
that worn and cracked old jug.

      Wearily, his eyes closed. He hadn't even a thought of
      lifting them to the heavens. There was, in fact,
not a single thought in his entire mind.

"Good," said the Vine from behind him. "That's the
way it should be."

      Alone beyond loneliness and small beyond small,
      cold beyond any coldness he'd ever felt before,
the Creature lay fast asleep atop his jug in the shadows of the
great Vine, the chilly dark clouds sailing over him.
Folded into himself for the only comfort there was, he shivered
shadow-shivers of things that were—and things that
were yet to be.

           The way it should be? His sleeping mind
wandered among those words
all that great long
        journey
                into the dawn.

And so, being otherwise occupied,
the Creature of Habit
was never to know
that as he slept, it came on the night wind soughing,

...that the moon crept out of the clouds,
and lo, from her forehead glowing,
she sent a thousand stars
to tumble freely downward
and scatter across the skies.
It was there
where he'd fallen, she saw him
outlined within her light...
and since she could
if she would,
she covered him
in the warmth of
a moon-dusted,
star-misted night
...'til he glowed
as did she,
there on the sea

where she traveled.

2
The Earthenware Jug

They discovered him the next morning, before the sun had even risen, knee-deep in tendrils. The great Vine—unaware that it was at the very moment, being shorn of its weapons—slumbered in the grey floating mist, with both hooded eyes peacefully closed. And truth be told, it did look benign and quite beautiful there in the dawn, with its emerald-green leaves freshly bathed by dew drops. It was a beauty the Creature had to envy, knowing that he lacked any of his own.

Badly startled, the others demanded of him, in terrified whispers, "*What are you doing?*"

But the Creature went right on,

plucking the dozing tendrils so tightly coiled and knotted in their Vine dreams.

"Those things will grow back," someone protested, "and then we'll all be in trouble…*now what are you doing?*"

For with every last little tendril-whip in a pile at his feet, he kept looking into the sky and mumbling the strangest thoughts under his breath.

"Freedom," the others frowned.

"Why does the Creature want it so badly? Whatever can it mean to him, and why does he stare at the sky that way?" They all said he would make himself sick, and begged him to stop. He only mumbled louder…and now he was staring, long and hard, at the terrifying amount of new growth that had suddenly sprung up, encouraged perhaps by all his forced watering of the night before—and—alerted, he stared even longer, at how the Vine now entirely walled-in the compound with such chilling finality of purpose.

Yet Habit-bound, he reached for his water jug and held it securely by its handle.

"Do you think," he asked, running his fingers across the rough earthenware surface, "that we might put back a few of the leaves? Any day now, the Vine will be high walls and *a roof.* It's going to cover us up. Why, you can barely see the heavens, any more."

The others didn't look pleased. "What do the heavens matter anyway?" they asked each other. "We don't live there." *No*, thought the Creature to himself. *We*

certainly don't. We live here, with the nasty Vine.
Time ticked on relentlessly. The dawn made ready to reach out and touch the dozing Vine, awakening it to another day. No amount of persuasion, although offered politely, and in abject humilty—as was right and proper—moved a single creature to change its mind.

They wouldn't, couldn't, they said,
allow even one Vine leaf to be touched. "Doesn't make sense," they declared, "Why risk changing what is just for a view of the sky?"

Somebody said he could keep cutting off the little Vine whips. He wondered if he could spend his whole life cutting and watering and listening to the Vine threaten and roar? And the roof they were about to receive, what about that? What would happen when the Vine managed to blot out the heavens, and steal the last star from the sky?

The Creature of Habit

 put down his earthenware jug.

An awful
stillness swept the compound, swept over the sleeping Vine. Even the dew drops quivered in the swiftly approaching dawn, while every pair of creature-eyes accused him, as he accused himself of his treachery.

"You can't mean it,"
they cried in horrified dismay. "We gave you that job

because you are the Creature of Habit.

More than any of us, you are suited to the task. By the sound of your rounds each morning, the sun's place in the sky can be told without looking."

"Very soon," he said, "with that Vine over our heads, there won't be any sun at all."

He took himself to the very center of the compound—as far from the Vine as he could get—and went over what they'd said about him. Their description was right, it fit him exactly. He'd forever thought of himself as suited only to pattern, to rote, to sameness, so maybe he did belong there, where habit was revered. Maybe he should stop moaning about the Vine and do as the others did, without questioning.

There was the sky, however, and even in the daylight, he fancied he could see those wonderful, beckoning holes. It came to him then, that as on the threshold of battle, a choice had plunked itself down, square in his path: *Stay*, and wait for the Vine to close out the sky altogether—and if that happened, there would be no choice—*or journey forth*, and risk himself to all that waited on the other side of the compound.

One last time, he gazed straight up, and was reassured: Whatever secrets lay behind that sea of blue, begged to be explored. *Well*, he said to himself, *so be it*.

No one spoke to him as he strode up to the slumbering Vine, fearsome even in dew-splashed repose.

Nor did they speak, as he found

the tiniest crack, and with quaking, shaking hands and a mouth gone stiff as a board, began to chip away at it.

When he had made a space large enough to crawl through, he looked out. What he saw made his eyes water and go wide in wonder; as behind him, at last undone by his actions and nearly at the point of hysteria, one of the others gave a strangled groan of protest.

"Creature, where is your caution? No one has ever gone beyond the Vine. No one has ever wanted to. *What's wrong with you?*"

That stopped him just long enough to ask himself the very same thing. It was not the nicest of questions, implying as it did some truly sinister difference lurking between himself and all the others. One day that same question would be back like an ill-wind to taunt him—but for now, he was too busy staring through the chink he'd made in the Vine's twisted and maze-like structure; too busy *just being there* at the tantalising edge of freedom. *Dare he* slip right through it?

Dare he dash through it—fling himself into the midst of all that was visble out there, beyond the dense mesh of momentarily peaceful leaves—which surrounded him so thickly now, and could only grow ever-thicker in the days to come?

And yet, dare he not?

What the journey beyond that smallest of openings in the previously impenetrable green armour might be like…a warning flickered ominously, and then
it was gone…spirited away by the anxious breeze.

How he wished there were some other way, some compromise between his treachery and the desire he could no longer disobey, for already the journey called out, notifying him of the strongest of longing…that didn't seem
willing to be quiet.

So strong in fact, was the hope rushing about inside him that he could barely contain it, and his eyes scanned above the topmost rise of the Vine, where all he desired so much, lay waiting.

With a roar
that shook the earth under the compound, the Vine came awake, and reached for its tiny whips. Creatures everywhere sped to their hiding places. Only the stunned Creature of Habit remained, right in the middle of the Vine-ringed walls.

"What have you done to me?" In a wild flurry of screams, the Vine curled around itself, in and out of itself, seeking a missing tendril long enough to lash out and strangle its lone,

hapless onlooker.

"*You want to think, do you, Creature?* Then think about this! Your stupidity makes you the most unlikely candidate imaginable, for even a *short* little stroll out there!" The Vine tossed its leaves about with ferocious disdain. "You'll be torn to shreds before you can blink an eye! This compound—which you feel high and mighty enough to scorn—is a nice place, and you have a place within it. Out there is *not* a nice place, and you can't *survive* in it! You can't begin to imagine what's out there—slimy, nasty, unkempt, roaming beasts, just teeth and fangs and claws—all of them *eager* for something as stupid as you!"

Now the others in their hiding places looked grim, as if the Creature of Habit already lay in shreds before them. As for him, he'd had no idea the Vine cared so much for his welfare. And he remembered then, as in too terrifying a nightmare, the Vine's old stories about those wild things, vicious, brutal and BIG, and preying all night upon the lost and unsuspecting.

"They'll be on you," roared the Vine, "before you can think even one more of your idiot thoughts! You'll be fodder; you'll be nothing but a memory!"

The Creature was right then, of a mind to fling himself on the Vine, plead forgiveness, and promise most sincerely to be good for the rest of his life.

But he didn't because
he couldn't.
He wouldn't.
So there he stood, unable to open his mouth

and save himself from the punishment surely to come.

Seeing this, the Vine seemed to take on another dimension, another persona, writhing in and out of itself just as before, but now beginning to slither…

slithering the whole long wall of its greenery, round and round and round the compound, as if it were no longer a Vine at all, but some thing awful, and foul and feral.

His mind would not close against that slithering, for it mesmerized him, as through the massive length of the beaste a shudder raced, and it heaved itself up, rising ever-higher against the sky, threatening to blot out all that lay beyond.

And its leaves, a glint in full sun, did not rustle, but rushed dead-speed along the Vine's giant ridge, propelled as if by an unseen force…until, before the Creature's stricken eyes they dropped one

by one,

and it was revealed to him, the true depths of intimidation beneath the masque of its innocent bright green coverings.

Smooth now, and darkly foreboding in its rage, the Vine strengthened and grew more polished with every forward step the Creature dared take, appearing to be in its element, thriving on the fear it created, as the full sight of the great writhing snaking length, no longer hidden, caused him to halt, and consider appeasing it.

High overhead, the wind which had started to shriek held its breath, as though almost ready to relinquish the battle, and the compound went silent.

Timidly, a single creature approached. To the dismay of everyone, he did the unheard of and raised his eyes to the Creature's. "You're alone in his madness," he told him. "No one will go with you. Just take whatever punishment the Vine had for you, and once it's over, things can get back to normal."

Confronted with the first pair of eyes that had ever looked into his own—except for those of the Vine—the Creature was struck by their depths, and by the enormous fright too plainly visible inside them.

How was it possible, he wondered, for two tiny orbs to contain so much fear? So quickly that it could not be avoided, an emotion he'd never before encountered stirred in him. Compassion it was and compassion he experienced, as the power of it alerted him to dangers he'd never faced before, either…danger of emotional involvement, of perhaps having to overcome his own basic survival instincts, thus pinning his fate to that of

another…in strange new surroundings where he doubted his own ability to survive.

"Won't you reconsider?" the creature before him pleaded. "Let the compound get back to normal again, and you'll see—"

Normal?

For a few seconds that were far too long, not even the Vine, snarling behind him—could untangle the web of that unfamiliar compassion—or the pain it suddenly heaped upon him. Underneath that pain, he sensed there might be a whole lot more, just beyond the inexplicable numbness that gripped him.

"Please come with me," he begged, unable to take his eyes from the fear staring back at him.

But the lone creature merely averted his frightened gaze and stumbled off to join the rest.

"Normal?" the Creature asked of no one, for no one seemed to hear him. "That's what I'm afraid of. And I can't, I won't, go back to the Habit of being content without freedom."

He was crawling then, through the narrow opening he'd made in the vine, and it raged around him and over him—hissing all the while and puffing itself up in an attempt to crush him—and screaming one last threat,

"You're not *smart enough to be free!* You'll never be anything more than a water-carrier, no matter where you go! Never! Do you *hear me?*"

On risking a final backward glance, it did not surprise him to see that one of the creatures already had the earthenware jug in hand and was filling it up with water. Nor did it surprise him to see the Vine working furiously to seal up the rent in its side.

So quickly
were these tasks accomplished,
that no one heard the
Creature of Habit say,

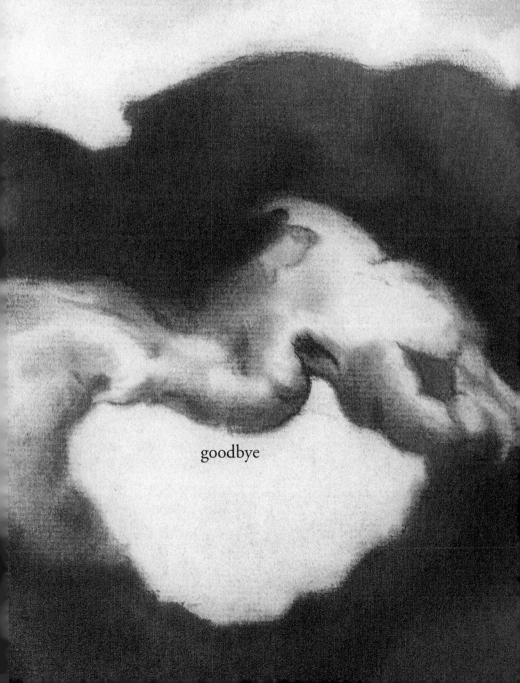

goodbye

3

A Warrior Afoot In The Wilderness

He snatched each breeze as it passed, shocked at its freshness, shocked at his daring, and desperate to be quickly away.

Far off in the distance, exactly as the old creature's legend had said, must lay that great body of water, where birds wheeled and freely dipped their wings in the sky. For as his feet flew over the ground, all he could see, bathed in the sun's warm glow, were the mountains outrageously tall and the trees swaying gently in the shadow.

The tallness of those mountains grabbed his attention. One shot up so high it disappeared into the clouds, thus cleverly hiding its actual height, but there was no tricking him, not today.

Rashly, he speculated: *Might one climb then, right up to the sky, leap into the intriguing, light-filled holes that appeared at night, and thereby reach beyond?* That should do it!

Delighted with his journey's sudden simplicity, and fixing the exact position of those fabled mountains in his mind, he raced toward them at full speed, while yelling silently in his head—but loudly—as he had never dared yell outside it, "I'm gone! I'm gone, and it's wonderful, *wonderful!*"

Without a doubt, blurred though it was, by his rushing lickety-split over hill and dale, the miracle of unobstructed splendor that greeted his hungry eyes, should have satisfied him ten-fold, but the harder he ran; and the further he got, the more he wanted.

For it seemed no marvel of scenery nor even the strongest breeze whipped up by his flight, could cool his ears still burning with shame at the Vine's parting insults. The spite and venom in those insults had tarnished his duties—made water-carrier sound like the lowest of lowly tasks—and himself like the ugliest and lowest of all creatures.

You're not smart enough to be free! Hard words, indeed. Leaning against a tree to catch his breath and fan his shame and wind-burnt self, he stole but a moment to reflect: Admittedly stupid though he might be, the Vine's having forbidden creatures thought and denied them freedom, had to mean that both did exist, and were valuable! And if they existed, then he must somehow find them. Yes, he vowed, no matter what the Vine said, he would find and claim both thought and freedom.

And where might those two treasures be?

A question so enormous would have stopped a more worldly creature in his tracks. But the Vine had left the Creature sadly misinformed and badly uninformed, with only the scattered whisperings of a few old legends carried on the wind to his ears. Hence—like one of those blank canvases in the sky—and driven solely by desperation and the sheer power of will, on he ran, faster and faster until presently, a flash of inspiration overtook him:

Freedom must be somewhere nearby. The wild things seemed to have freedom, for nary a Vine wall came into view. And if, like himself, the wild things had no intelligence—as the Vine had always insisted—then thought was not hiding down here with freedom.

Thought would more likely be up there, unfettered as the moon herself, hiding behind those light-filled holes that appeared in the night sky!

His excited mind yanked at even the furthest corners of his imagination, making him see that once he found the proper path to freedom—for surely, there must be an easier passage through the distraction of lush landscape—he need but reach those beckoning portals way up high, slip beyond then, and grab unfettered thought.

Then, he would be satisfied.

How thunderstruck the creatures of the compound would be when he got back and described this amazing outside world full of promise, since it appeared very much, out of breath as he was, just admiring the logistics, that his lowly water-carrier's journey had actually become a warrior's glorious envisioning, a full-fledged quest. As if a thousand warriors cheered him to victory, he unveiled the penultimate plum: What he had was no less than a priceless, step-by-step treasure map!

Nothing more remained to complete his journey, his quest… but getting there. And he appeared to be doing that extremely well, and quickly, except when the feathered greenery of the hills and the meadow-sweet dales over which he fled in such haste blocked his target mountains from view.

Whenever they vanished for too long, he tended to become scared and scuttle about in circles, with no sense of direction. Of course it wasn't an easy path her followed, but more like a faint trail of different paw-prints that zigged and zagged in lazy patterns, as if their owners had all the time in the world.

Under the warmth of a mid-day sun, those owners were little more than vague fleeting shapes, calling to each other and answering back from a reasonably safe distance away. The thought of bigger and more dangerous nocturnal beings, biding their time until nightfall, waiting to prey upon any unwitting creature, was what started him shivering, and yet— an unquenchable curiosity filled him as to their habits. What better amusements might they currently have, than tearing him to shreds? How he envied their comings and goings, in a world so closed to him, a world of which he knew nothing.

His envy came to an abrupt halt, for goose bumps had suddenly peppered his flesh. His eyes darted, raking the landscape, and there, in a snarl of bushes at the side of the path, were suspicious green leaves attached to what looked like the Vine. He did not walk, but practically had to carry himself on legs that had taken to wobbling this way and that. Nobody knew Vine leaves like the Creature knew Vine leaves, having watered and watered them for as long as he had. Nearer he bent, as near as he dared, finding foliage too pointed and a colour too pale to belong to the Vine. Not only that, but there were small purple flowers attached not to a Vine, *but a bush.*

With hands clasped in gratitude, he fell to the ground before the bright small blooms. "Thank you," he said. "Thank you for not being the Vine."

Had he just spoken to a flower? Had he spoken aloud to it? This was not a good sign. Flowers belonged to that group of inferiors—only one notch below creatures themselves—who were regarded by the Vine as unworthy of notice. According to Vine-wisdom, saying anything aloud to an inferior meant that one teetered on the abyss of mental collapse.

Frazzled at the dangerous loss of composure, he told himself, "Get ahold of yourself." How of course, speaking to himself aloud, was an equally grave mis-step.

Ah, but how he wanted to pick one of those flowers and carry it along on his quest. The Vine had never once sprouted flowers. On the only occasion when a delicate pink bud had popped up in the compound, in a circle of creatures all breathless at the sight, the Vine had ordered that it be stomped on.

"Get it out!" the Vine had shrieked. "No telling where

it's been—or what it's brought with it—or how much of my water it wants! Get it out!"

Somebody had done the job. The Creature never found out who. He hadn't asked, and nobody ever told him. After the little flower disappeared, he'd mourned at the loss of something—just what, he couldn't say—since he'd never really had anything to speak of, other than his own existence.

He again thought to pluck a flower for his quest, but quickly changed his mind. Best leave that flower where it was. Traveling with him might not be all that safe.

For even as he turned to go, the way grew rougher, more jolting. And worse, much worse, hideous apparitions sprung from the sunlit thickets, scaring him into thornbeds where long brambles whipped back and forth…vivid reminders of the Vine.

A loud rumbling from his stomach signaled hunger. Tender roots and berries aplenty spilled across the landscape. Birds and eager forest creatures were already there ahead of him, gorging on the food he didn't dare steal. By the time he caught on that food belonged to whoever got there first, everything around him had been eaten. Only a patch of clover remained, and bees were humming, piercing the shaggy lavender blooms with their wicked-looking antennae. He'd just managed to filch a mouthful of clover when the bees swarmed, angry at being disturbed. They pursued him without mercy, cutting off his frantic retreat across the meadow. Trapped, he sat where he was.

The stings at first seemed harmless, but the buzzing was so violent it scared him. While he hung back politely, a rabbit darted ahead. The Rabbit nibbled and nibbled, while he continued to hang back waiting for his turn, and beginning to feel every vengeful sting. Spluttering in an icy stream, he dunked his swollen face and body repeatedly, but to little avail. Hungrier than ever, but afraid to brave the wildlife, he stood on that faint and meandering trail, leading into the darkest of nights that he might ever face.

Through eyes which the bee stings had nearly closed, he gazed at the path wondering if this could truly be the way to freedom. He kept looking over his shoulder to see if the Vine had followed, and from behind which rock or tree or turn in the trail it might sneak up. Comfortably nesting forest creatures mocked his pain, and he snapped, 'What do they care? They aren't searching for the hidden treasures of unfettered thought and freedom!"

Along with the pain, his anxiety grew, and it hung about, a truncheon of expected doom. His former racing pace slowed. The fledgling exuberance that had pounded in his chest like a happy hammer was squashed. Certainly, and he studied a rather large boulder with care before rounding it, freedom for him was not right here. Not if he feared the Vine could still be lurking.

A family of bears padding fearlessly around even bigger boulders, strolled calmly as they foraged across bright, bountiful meadows, and he had to wonder: Might the essence of freedom be a lack of fear so that one did not have to look for enemies, because there were none? But how did one get rid of all enemies?

A strange scene, out of focus and painted not nearly as bloody as the real thing, rushed in from nowhere. Before his mind's eye was what warrior-questors did as a matter of course and he nearly fainted, whereupon, a furry red fox on four fast legs flew out from behind a rotted log, and halted just inches away, flaunting a mean attitude and an outraged yipping voice.

"Wait! Don't be angry. I'm leaving, I swear it!"

He tried not to scream out his protest, because even in dire situations, raising one's voice had always meant punishment. The furious animal glared back and the blithering Creature caught sight of two small mewling kits, curled up in the sunshine.

Hoping Red Coat wasn't following, he ran with his heart in his throat, and without looking back. Defending one's own was a new concept that left him astonished at the animal's raw *nerve,* and wondering where he could find some for himself. But in order to be nervy, one would need to be rude—rude as that fox in its glorious red coat—so it was out of the question.

Red Coat was an enemy. The Creature could not envision running amuck with a weapon and vanquishing anything, even an enemy. Nor could he uncover and alternate means. Was there some ready answer to this that he simply wasn't smart enough to see? How he wished right then to already have the treasure of thought. But the secretive heavens revolved overhead, and mystified, he halted, searching the daylight canvases of the sky for whatever they might be hiding. The puzzle yielded not at all, and uneasily, he moved on.

For the first time, he actually dared imagine having thousands of thoughts, none of them imprisoned, but loosed of all bonds and flying, soaring to heights that might match even those beyond…and oddly enough, he felt he knew those heights—

and even those beyond—as if he had traveled them, long before his aborning. As unusual and strong as the sense of re-experiencing was, it rocked him right back on his heels, forcing the waste of precious time, while he sat asking himself, *What did it mean?*

He hesitated in a dazzling ray of sunlight, while his weary feet yearned to be up there, as though they knew full-well, the endless expanse of cloud-tossed azure, leading inexorably across beyond, and into…

he took to his betraying feet and fled, because he'd never been further than back and forth around the compound.

And that was that.

Or so he told himself, stubbornly ploughing ahead, over a land big and raw—owned not by the Spartan-minded Vine, but by nature—and she, by no means Spartan, did things brashly, strewing boulders here and gullies there, tossing mountains at the feet of deep chasms, burying bogs in patches of fog, and lacing up innocent blades of grass in deadly webs that trapped one and wouldn't

let go.

Unable to say why, but nimbly, and with an expertise born of long and unwitting practice, he avoided each dewy mirror reflection of himself. Wary and silent, he felt certain the only way through what he'd set about, was simply to do it, with his eye on the goal alone, thus keeping sanity and goal intact. Otherwise, he might be questioned for absolutely days, and that wasn't part of his plan.

His first day of escape waned into late afternoon. The sun glinted sharply on the horizon, even as its warmth faded from the earth, Twilight crept amongst the trees and took away the path. Soon it would be time for the Vine's nightly watering. Instinctively, he reached for the earthenware jug—*but it wasn't there.* His sign of relief ended in a muffled shriek as a long dark form shot from between his feet.

Eyes crossed in stark terror and already halfway up a tree, he looked down to discover it had been nothing but his own shadow, menacing the gloom. Crouched in the same tree in which he cowered, a great horned owl lifted its wings, puffed out its chest feathers, and gave a meaningful hoot of what sounded to the Creature like disgust. Whereupon, a curious thing happened, curious, at least to him: On the heels of the hoot, other calls followed in near-unison, ranging from tweets to growls, the effect a single, cacophonic message, being aimed directly at him.

He didn't understand the message and hence, had no reply. Neither did he sense the feelings of disappointment flowing toward him from out of the darkening forest, and it then exploded in meaner sounds, of what must be, as the Vine had warned—the bigger animals—which obviously slept all day and roamed all night. Less than a yard away, an animal of what had to be considerable bulk heaved itself up through the underbrush and commenced its evening rounds. The noise of its progress was quickly followed by other similar thrashings. Mindful that when the darkness settled full, it would belong to those unseen nocturnal beasts, he sought and extra bit of comfort before they discovered him and slit him, from gizzard to gullet.

With a last drop of energy, he gathered soft grasses and prepared his bed in the largest clearing he could find. Once prepared, he was afraid to get in and become too comfortable. New beds were not a new experience because in the compound, he had sought to outwit the Vine by never sleeping in the same spot twice. The uncharted landscape of his quest, however, was new to him. It spread out on all sides, floating in a sea of evening mystery.

No Vine leaves rustled. The creatures of the compound were far away. He was alone. And hungry, again. The moon, rising through the trees lit up various roots and a number of interesting plants with short stocky stems and little rounded tops, not too far away. That same moon also shone on a group of animals built low to the ground with pot bellies, broad pointed snouts, and wiggly ears. The old creature of the compound had described these marauders, exactly. They were already at the plants, using their hooves and snouts to root them out to the ground. The plants were then devoured in loud fits of pleasure that made the Creature drool.

Stomach churning, he considered begging for the scraps, but good manners dictated patience. His stomach knotted and groaned. The crunching, tearing, mashing and lip-smacking noises of pleasure continued. Grimly, he studied the moon so high above, so removed from his problems. He thought she smiled, but it was probably only the wisp of cloud streaming over her face.

He began to think very hard about being alone in such a vast wilderness, the exact Truth of that, and what it really Meant.

Never having thought much about Truth before, to have this particular one sitting so obstinately in his path…he gnawed at his fingernails, a very old Habit which no amount of trying would break.

Only the thrill of having escaped the compound, a thrill which had yet to be worn away by the day's events, saved him from panic. It was into that remembered excitement that he dodged,
determined to get through the night without falling apart. After all, the penultimate plum of a treasure map didn't fall into a creature's lap every day of the week!

Despite sheer weariness, thoughts of tomorrow romped in his head, because surely tomorrow, having found thought and freedom, his stupidity could become a thing of the past. Down into his grasses he burrowed, spirits soaring. He commenced to envision his questing success, in scenes so real and so strange that it made him frown, wondering where they had been hiding.

He wondered too if the Great Spirit Winds would be blowing upon his journey. Harsh as they sounded at times, it seemed silly to miss them. But he did.

He never saw fear which had long been his second-skin as it lay down beside him, there in his brand-new bed. And had his time in the compound not been as long and intense, nor would his escape from it so frantic and fraught with peril, what was about to happen to him probably would not have happened.

4

An Ancient Ability

Lying in that fresh-smelling grass, where moon-bound shadows grew longer, and throngs of crickets dinned—every hidden eye he'd imagined inspecting him that day was multiplied by a thousand. Certain as he could be that they were bloodthirsty cut-throats, all of them, his own eyes stayed wide open as if the lids had been pinned apart, and sleep refused his nod upon her breast.

Thus, all tired senses were forced to escape by the one route they could take, down that strange avenue which creatures had closed to themselves most firmly and so long ago, that nobody believed it still existed.

Intricately designed as the avenue was, it led many places,

depending upon the particular creature traveling its mystical path. Not surprisingly then, did the Creature of Habit exit that avenue precisely where he did, to find himself in that special part of his hind which for creatures, had once been all there was.

The longer he lingered, unable to move or summon sleep, the less attached he felt to the world around him. Even the path which that entire day had extended relentlessly in front of him, and still floated before his closed eyes; an endless but welcome opponent seemed part of a far-off land.

On the vista of his drifting mind, beneath cascading brambles and briars, he began to see creature-footprints worn away by the eons and imprinted now, upon the memory of nature alone. Innocent of exactly how far he'd *really* gone, he pondered intently: There had been others before him—trodding this very same path—hoping the same as he, *What had been their fate?*

Focused so strongly, from inside the most open part of himself, his question inadvertently threw down across the face of time that life-line from one side to the other, whereby what has supposedly been lost is lost no more, and the past may actually appear again, to the present. Unsuspecting, the Creature wandered, conscious of the fact that this was no dream, but reluctant to describe it any other way.

The air was filling with the faintest of shifting sounds as if it had been nudged, while everything—trees and grasses, the air itself, and the moonlight falling in ghostly shafts—quavered,

just before the image of them shattered

and parted in slivers.

No longer lying inert, the life-line humming with a strong flow of energy carried him along its length to the moonlight parting, where he glided effortlessly into a world not his own, but rather one that existed alongside it.

He blinked his eyes and rubbed them, anxious to find a familiar sight within the space stretching before him, but there was nothing. Silence greeted his ears.

Then, just beyond peripheral vision came a hint of movement, and there appeared a creature so old he must be considered as ancient. Of absolutely no kith or kin, nor ancestry coming to him, the old one did not take shape or materialise, but simply was there breathing identical air. Before the Creature could move to break the spell, he counted five more— each one the same—ancient. An Elusive quality about this specific handful of old souls, immediately warned: Something about them was wrong, even dangerous.

A peculiar emotion filled their eyes. Their faces and bodies contorted with the same emotion, unreadable but instantly unlikeable, and frightening to the Creature. He sensed that if he could hear them, their words—being mouthed in a seemingly endless stream—would be equally unlikeable.

He sensed as well how fully they felt his aversion. Finally defeated in their attempt to make him understand, they backed away, and faded into the distance. But already, there were other creatures to draw his attention: a variety of ancient questors who had struck out long ago to seek what he was seeing, burnt with a desire to have the shield, of unfettered thought and freedom. Arrayed in furs and skins and a wealth of flesh—or tatters and sharpness of bone—draped in ornaments of metal, crudely or intricately worked, their weapons were of the same.

The Creature studied them, for they would not leave his mind. And he discovered not one of them overlapping the other, but proudly displaying each to his own, a strength of visage and a posture so marked it was impossible not to know each one, for they were warrior-questors, battle-hardened and flint of eye, intending no stealth of disguise, or thought of surrender, or quarter given.

Without saying a word, each conveyed to him a blazing intelligence, a hunger to know—raw and impassioned, and shining from their eyes like beacons—lighting each expression with an attitude of listening, even when there was no sound to be heard. Aside from the intelligent listening attitude, no two faces were further alike. But then, across the features of each, he spotted it, eagerness and hope springing to life, hope being fanned by the fires of need…then hope adwindle, and dying finally, like the last lick
of flame from a giant bonfire.

In the unfamiliar near-darkness,
he ached for each one, and for himself. He touched his own face with tentative fingers, wondering what secrets it might reveal. Never in his life had he inspected himself; to do so had never

occurred to him. But his fingers did not feel, nor did he sense, anything about him that came even close to matching the strength on the faces of those unknown warrior-questors. If his mind did hold the same forceful intelligence streaming from their eyes, wouldn't he know it, feel it?

It seemed when they'd tarried as long as they would, they were leaving with one last furl of the flag. Within the walls of his mind, he saw their breath, anxiously frosted in the cold air of dawns uncountable. He could feel their distress, lit by the moon at many midnights, as they gnawed at the endless yoke of time.

Their great steeds were a-whinny now, pawing the earth of centuries fleeting, eager to be questing again. Before he could bear to let go of them, he had to see what had stopped them short of the mark they'd so clearly tried to reach. And there, just beneath the hard bravery of their ornaments and armaments and flinty eyes, was a soft underbelly turned up to the skies, exposed to the very first blade that would pierce it.

Stricken, he drew back, for that underbelly was *humility*. He saw it, felt it, rising up to defeat every unknown creature as they vanished from his reflective mind.

The slivers of moonlight opened. He found himself back on the other side, as easily as he'd first entered. He was scrambling then, from his bed of soft grasses, calling to them, begging them not to go. But the sound of their horses faded away, and alone once more, he was sharply reminded: *Humility*, a time-honoured quality, had been revered amongst creature for as long a he could remember. Too confused by the thoughts bumping about in his head, he never saw the handful of unlikeable old creatures slip silent as ghosts through the moonlight parting, where they blended wraith-like, into the shadows at his back.

His own shadow spread long upon the ground, where it dodged and darted the same as he, between one doubt and another:

That world, or plane of reality, or whatever it was that he'd just encountered, didn't seem half as strange, as the questions it had left

behind. For one, the intelligence he'd seen in the faces of those warrior questors—seen with such clarity as not to be denied—made him wonder where they had gotten it. Creatures as far as he knew, had never had intelligence. With so much of it already in their possession, he couldn't think what had moved those warriors to quest after unfettered thought,nor could he fathom how it was, that having utterly no intelligence of his own, he had been able to *recognize* intelligence in them. Further pondering poked more holes in his reasoning, permitting the emergence of a doubt so numbing that his shadow froze in front of him. There seemed to be an odd Truth behind all these questions, at the very center of which, the question of his own intelligence lay like a boulder, hiding a bigger

Truth.

Hesitant to disturb that boulder for fear of what might or might not be found, he clenched his fists in frustration. If those warrior-questors had failed, what would happen to *his* quest? Too shy and uncertain to consider re-entering their world and engaging anyone in argument, he made a pillow of a huge tree root, dropping as if he'd been felled into an exhausted sleep. Through the forest and into the clearing, footfalls padded. A black wet nose sniffed the ground in a circle around his sleeping form. The fur of the thing never touched the earth, but skimmed it, and its scent and the soft grasses mingled. Its cries were poignant. The dark eyes glittered, scanning the forest perimeter.

Not until the first paw touched him did the Creature half-way awaken to see the thing boastful atop his chest, using him as a sentry post, ears pointed skyward, and fangs gleaming white. He dare not hit it, lest that drive it to frenzy, he dare not move, lest that incite it to riot. It might well have been the Vine towering above him, so afraid was he to defend himself, or attempt to claim the small spot of earth on which he lay. Fear wouldn't lessen long enough to let him see what happened next, by the light in the wild beast's eyes turned to friendly curiosity. It was bending closer to inspect him.

Fur tickled his nose. He sneezed, sending the animal leaping backwards, and raking his flesh in the process. His own blood pooled black, by the light of the moon, as the furry thing wandered off, waving its glorious striped tail behind it, making it clear that he was of little relevance.

Sleep now out of the question, every thought crawled back to humility, searching for the error in his earlier observation. Had he missed a few facts, or had he misread too many?

All the colour seem to drain from his world, as he pondered

the treacherous question:

How could humility
defeat his kind?

Inside a thin gathering of clouds, the moon sailed along at her leisure. She smiled, and then he knew that she knew more than he did. It seemed that wishing for unfettered thought was easier than achieving it. His fascination for the heavens arching high above, cradle for secrets he might never plumb, and pierced by mysterious light, moved aside just enough to let in his continuing extreme fatigue. Too tired to reach for thought, thoughts began floating past him, uninvited and apparently attached to nothing important, at least to him. It was as if his mind had left him behind that it was thinking without him.

How fascile and effort thinking could be, he mused, but that musing was from an infinite distance, for he realized his opinion especially did not matter, that it was irrelevant to anything his mind might be considering.

Humility.

His mind led the word right into the heart of battle, making it a virtual reality, and hopelessly pitting it against a horde of enemies, where pride and self-assertiveness had to be the first line of offense, for without belief in self, no questing warrior could stand for long.

All this did that mind of his firmly decide while he, merely the observour, and utterly unsure of what *self* really meant, rested quietly in the distance, and was eventually called—for an awesome moment, the Creature of habit stood unknowingly, within the depths of self—accepting what he believed had only fallen

upon him, and it began to flow strongly through his entirety, *the wonder of how special, how unique, must be the place where that knowing originated.*

While the night winds blew against the grass where he lay, he shrank from that place of origin because the truth of it wrenched him. He held onto himself as tightly as he could. Whether to protect himself from that truth or gather the will to accept it, he didn't know. The moment was there, square at the threshold, and then it was gone, and he was glad. Creatures knew better than to trust stray rubbish flying into their heads. At least the Vine, whatever else its faults, had taught him that much.

The moon, for the next little while, rode just at his shoulder, seemingly unconcerned. Had he glimpsed her expression, he would have known otherwise, but he didn't look that closely. Somewhere in the darkness, dogs began baying at her. It was a strange sound, at least to him, for no dogs had been allowed inside the compound. It was rumoured that the Vine hated them, hated all creatures of lesser value than itself.

Often, the Creature had wondered what that said about his own worth or the worth of any inside the compound, for the Vine hadn't liked them, either. Then one day—marked upon a calendar long ago forgotten inside him—he'd gotten the Vine's message and acted henceforth accordingly, not even aware of what he was doing, or why.

On the brink of a small awareness he teetered there, until a bit of obscuring mist wafted past him on a sweet-scented night breeze, leaving him to stare in dismay. The dogs had moved

so close that each individual hair on their bodies, and the muscles
straining in their throats, were obvious as they bayed. Disbelief fought with the realization: These same mangy and slobbering beasts of Vine story and legend were doing something he could not
do, for unless he was mad, they were speaking to the moon.

Secondly, they weren't mangy and slobbering. They did, in fact, dress up the night with themselves and their cries. Nor did the gorgeous moon seem to find them unpleasant, because from a sweep of gossamer cloud, she moved even higher in the heavens. With the stars right behind her, she went on her way, dipping everything in sight, in veils of the sheerest of moonglow, as if paying tribute to something more than remarkable.

The primordial sounds of baying intensified, the emotion in each searching cry *telling* him what it was: Communication strong and sure, between the giant glowing globes sailing high above—and the animals of lesser value
far below.

Next morning, the Creature gathered up what was left of the world as he thought he knew it. He was very much afraid of disaster if he tossed away Vine-wisdom in favour of any paltry few—and suspect—observations of his own. Hoping his silly thoughts would go away, until real thought could be found, he instinctively sought comfort in the old and familiar and scolded himself roundly: Never having missed one day of chores, how could he forget good Habits, simple because he'd left the compound? Maybe there was no Vine to water now, but there was still the most important chore of all. So he set about what the Vine had designated as the Chastising List. On a stretch of soft earth, he compiled and updated a fresh list of new failures, untold personal shortcomings, and a running tally of his guilts. When the list was sufficiently long, and he'd counted every broad stroke against him, he gave himself mentally each lashing the Vine would have given him. Then, just to be sure, he added a few.

A sense of balance properly restored, he got up from his chores, quietly watching the sunrise and thinking how lucky he was that the Vine had correctly pointed out his faults. He might not be a genuine warrior-questor, he might be dumb as a ditch, but with extra diligence, somehow, some way—he was going to find thought and freedom where they were hiding!

The first pebble landed at his feet. The second narrowly missed his head. Ferns but a few yards away, shook, and the underbrush bent and snapped. He heard footsteps running away into the forest. It didn't sound a bit like the work of animals. Animals might dislodge stones, but they did not throw them.

Somebody was following him.

Accompanied by a rosey dawn, the journey as he proceeded grew harder and more bewildering still, for he saw the slowest, most sill-looking of wildlife, knowing where they were going, and getting there with alarming ease, never stumbling or falling…

whereas he—well, it didn't bear thinking about. And now, trying to keep three steps ahead of those unidentified pebble hurlers, it did seem proper to ask: Was everything under the moon and the sun conspiring against him?

Presently, he fell upon an idea of singular brilliance. Since the land seemed displeased at his presence, maybe she would be less offended if he slunk where he was going. And compressing himself into almost nothingness, that was the way he went, pretty much as he'd done without knowing it all his days in the compound.

Little pebbles peppered his path with greater regularity. The hurlers kept themselves stubbornly hidden. He tried not to think about being followed, tried to make his mind blank. As if they would quest without him, stray thoughts too often began taking him unawares—which left no choice but to reach further ahead of himself—or try to clear his mind, entirely. Unable to believe these thoughts could actually be coming from his own mind, he only knew that which he sought was definitely out there, somewhere just ahead. He wouldn't miss it for the world. But if exhaustion rattled his wits, determination to keep on going, rattled, them, further. And the lower he slunk in his desperate desire for acceptance, the nastier was his reception.

The land as he took it, step-by-aching-step, forced him back three steps, while the rocks in lively fashion seemed to procreate beneath his feet. He tripped over each one and went crashing head-long, into bogs and patches of briars. One bruise healed on top of another while the underbrush flourished, and flourished again.

The rains came back and soaked him, then soaked him anew, before he had truly
dried out. The sun burnt him with fire
and icy cold froze him right down to his toes. One moment he lay quite senseless on the forest floor, and the next, beset by the driving force of his quest, he was off and questing, trying in vain to keep those evasive mountains always in view.

His yelps of pain as battle scars multiplied, his hapless *Ah,* of surprise at each new sight, only served to brighten the wildlife around him. And even though he asked now and then, not one of the small sleeping families of the fur-covered, four-legged variety that abandoned their peace and quiet and fled from his forward march, ever told him a thing about the location of freedom.

He could have sworn the paw-prints on the fading path kept getting larger. The bigger they got,
the smaller he felt.

Great flocks of birds, their wings iridescent in the sunlight, affixed him to the spot, and jangled his nerves a little bit more each time they screeched from the treetops, to warn of the pebble
hurlers. Surely he was going nowhere if he could not get there faster than this. And his pace—only as fast as he could make it—
was far too slow. Especially when some bird whipped by,

covering in minutes, more territory than he'd covered in a day.

He pictured capturing one of those bundles of flapping feathers and persuading it to give up its flying secrets. Maybe that was he could fly too, thus neatly solving his need to go further, faster.

But no bird ventured within snatching distance, and the Creature was about to abandon that plan, when good fortune decided to smile. Because there in a marsh, a hundred plump frogs croaked from their lazily drifting lily pads. And on a branch overhanging the edge of the marsh, sat a huge blackbird, sound asleep.

He wondered if he should—or even could—then he was reaching out, snatching up that bundle of sleek black feathers all ruffled and squawking. With its wings beating upon him in a frenzy, its talons found his wrist and dug in.

The Creature hung on and was greeted by a stare so contemptuous, so damning, that he quickly let go, watching the powerful body launching itself into nothingness, finding an air current and staying with it, flapping its wings fiercely for a moment and then simply hovering until it began to glide on that current, up and up and up further still, until it was gone from sight.

When he looked down at his hand, there was single, glossy black feather, and black as the beautiful colour of midnight. Placing it behind one ear, he set off, no more sure than before of how he would get where he was going. There had been no chance to ask of the bird how it did what it did. Could those things talk?

They certainly could squawk. Most unsettling of all, they were dangerous, never to be trusted, not with those eyes so full of contempt, and so utterly lacking in politeness or humility, either.

How—and a serious frown erupted in the middle of his forehead—might the blackbird have fared with the Vine? In battle, who would emerge the victor? Which of them would back down and humble itself before the other?

Visions of the Vine, defiant ruler of the compound and all within its walls, strode through his thoughts as if he were there, still tamed and imprisoned. Another question darted immediately, across his path: Why had the Vine taught humility—when it had none?

Here was a puzzle, indeed. With a sigh of resignation, he left off wondering about anything, and increased his speed, determined to outrun whoever followed him. Quickly, he picked up the trail again, running until he couldn't run any longer. Completely out of breath, he felt almost too tired to be frightened at the looming shape which presented itself directly ahead.

Its very hugeness called up visions of the Vine and so he was frightened even when the shape revealed itself, and he saw what lay before his throbbing feet, covered by grey lichenfrost so thick it might have been a disguise, was a hummock of enormous size and particular steepness. Tall slender shoots of palest green grasses bent low to its crevices as if in homage to the sudden gust of sharp wind. The wind carried with it a hint of rain and the sky had gone darker, foretelling of storms and cold air to come.

There couldn't be a more perfect place for the Vine to wait,

unseen than directly behind that hummock. But there was no way over it; he must cross it directly, or forge a new path, thus walking for some great distance in the now bitter air. Moreover, he could sense it, beckoning him onward in a manner he could not name. Awe overcame him, as he approached and grew as he placed one foot after the other, fighting down a strong desire to turn and flee.

Up he went, unable to avoid his apprehension, for the hummock seemed to pulsate, to breathe as he breathed, to push him faster and faster up its steep surface. On reaching the crest, he reeled in the thinner atmosphere, and quite against his will, looked down at what lay
on the other side.

5

The Invaders

The fragrance reached for him,
even before he saw the vast plain upon which it drifted.

It engulfed him without mercy and with no prior
warning…sliced right through the innermost of him, *pausing
there at an entrance* where creature-time had never
counted at all. *Nor was that entrance bolted against him* as he
absorbed the surrealism of what he saw, for the flowers did not
grow, so much as

they had gathered themselves together

…as if from the farthest corners of the earth.

Whatever the reason for their gathering, and no reason
sprang to mind, one bloom nodded at the elbow of the other but
none sought to intrude on his solitude.

And so he was lulled.

The flowers simply were what they were, he thought, a
fantasy-sea, alive with exquisite beauty, and pure perfume—each
flower standing alone in that expanse of vibrant colour—to
announce itself to his senses.

Once announced, it seemed he was lost in that sea, for there
came a yearning from that just-discovered entrance within him, a
yearning that ignored his vow to look at as little as possible and
forced him to take in their power, their majesty, stretching to the
left, to the right of him, as far as the eye
could travel.

He felt his breathing slow
and his strength ebb as the sight truly dawned. He had to turn
away before he could look again and when he did, the sunlight
had disappeared, chased out by the dark clouds moving in over the
land.

Quite overcome,
all logic collapsed, while he slid and fell down the length of the
hummock, unsure of what he wanted—or *dared*—to do. Nothing,
during all his time in the compound, had prepared him for his
feelings: Did he want to protect the flowers from the cold sweeping
in, or only walk in their midst, inhaling their sweetness?

Nor could it be fathomed, the hush that curtained the plain
at his approach. No stalk nor petal moved, and even the wind had

paused as well. The plain and its occupants only waited, while he wandered helplessly, through their domain. It was hardly likely that he truly saw what he thought he saw, but hiding amongst them…were there expression of belief that speaking to him was of primary importance?

No longer lulled,
he immediately put up his guard,
more against himself than anything a flower might
impart to him.

Despite his suspicions, his mind continued to speak of things he had to ignore, if he heard them at all. But the sight, smell, and sound of those flowers, stem-to-stem, petals now rustling—and yes, impossibly softening his resolve—drew him further into their midst. Yet even with their faces close to his own, their tiny whispering thoughts forming a message he almost caught in a word or two, made

no sense to him.

This far-flung profusion of flowers surely signaled something…but what? So intensely did he want just then to have unfettered thought, that he might decipher at will, a breath might have broken his heart.

Indeed, his heart already felt broken, for during the last few seconds, his outsider status had struck him more cruelly than having an entire compound turn its back and refuse to speak to him. Wanting to present himself as a valid insider, The Creature leaned forward, understanding the message no better than before and growing sadder by the minute.

His very footfall through their gentle frivolity seemed too disruptive; his voice as he desperately pleaded his cause echoed sharply. A lummox he was, knowing himself entirely out of place, while a butterfly watched him from a nearby froth of flowers, spreading its wings in surprise at his lack of perception.

Something about the perfume was standing him still without his permission, opening his mind to the world where the butterfly visited, then tiptoed and paused in hypnotic rhythm… stripping him of the will to move even a finger, and quiet the thin green stalks tapping at his forehead.

All by itself, his chin pointed into mid-air, as if inviting him to start for longer than he'd intended, directing his eyes from flower-to-flower, all wafting toward his welcoming nose, their incredible, sun-warmed fragrance…nature's potion, potent indeed…

and still, the butterfly beat its wings…

until he was thoroughly smitten.

The wind drew closer and breathed a frigid draft, causing the sea of delicate blossoms to shiver. The Creature wondered why their discomfort should affect him so deeply. Slowly then, the pull of what existed between himself and them made itself known, and he was all but *viewing* a kind of mysterious and utterly timeless connection. That connection so carefully veiled, hinted at its shape, both beautifully formed and amazingly strong, and seemed to look back at him with no pretence whatever, and its own
air of waiting.

Along with that knowing came another: He was close to deciphering, the ability hovered just beyond his grasp, as into the center of a bell-shaped cup of exquisite petals, he stared bemused, sensing what the flowers sought from him might be his personal acknowledgement of connection.

And there it was,
his on-going failure, for he had little practice in connecting to anything. He knew it as surely as he stood there. As surely as he

quickly denied having just learned it.

Hard as the butterfly beat its wings, calling for his response, and no matter his brow being beaten in that gentle fashion—or the disappointment on those stricken flower faces—he was the outsider, capable of little more than a despairing groan of defeat.

While preparing to take his leave, he thought he heard them whispering among themselves, uttering sounds of

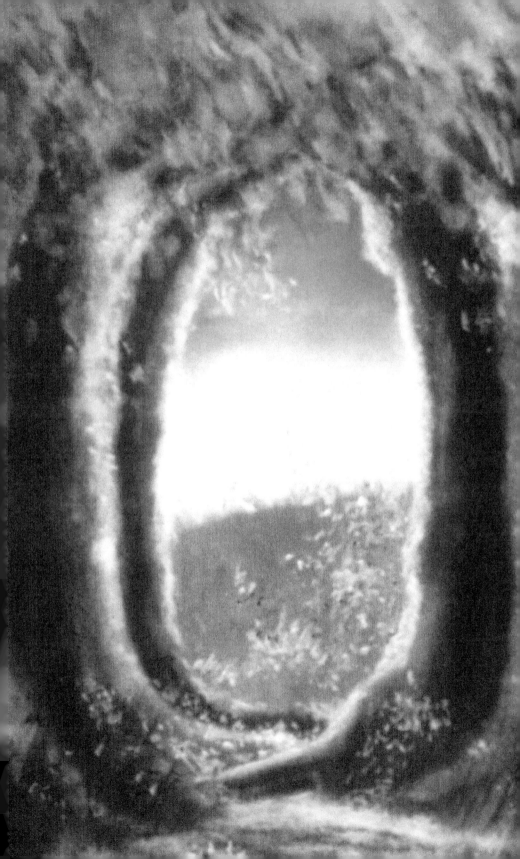

astonishment and sorrow at having offered something and been rejected.

He believed as he left their periphery, firmly training his thoughts on the next horizon that he heard the tiniest tinkle of laughter following after him…and he could not blame them. They'd apparently been on this earth much longer than he, mysterious in their repetition from one cycle to the next, dependent only upon the heat of the sun and the moisture of rain to bloom season after season. Whatever they had wanted of him, he'd been too bound up in himself to give it.

And turning his back, he lengthened his stride—almost a thing of perfection now—anxious to be off and questing. On his way out from that undulating sea of fragrance, he pretended not to have been affected by much. But the lingering memory of knotted white buds brushed against his mind, and caught him up short.

All the little flowers, he said to himself, might the mystery of their repetition be fully as deep as that of the heavens? While hurriedly counting backwards the number of those repetitions, it became obvious that just like the heavens, they seemed to go on…forever…

At dusk he halted near a stand of trees… trees so old they reared high above his head, boughs sighing as they touched. So wide were their trunks, wider even than the Vine, that resting at their feet was like being in a fortress. Except that he had never been inside a fortress. *What was a fortress, anyway?*

Their sighing reminded him of an ancient music coursing from a deep and primordial wellspring. But he hadn't a clue as to why he'd though that either, never having run into a primordial well spring that he knew of.

It occurred to him that what the trees were doing with their melodic sighs, was *precisely* what the flowers had done earlier.

But what could a flower or a tree either, have to say

that really mattered?

He slept that night as if held most gently inside some secure and stalwart bastion of safety, while every tear unshed in that field of flowers streamed down his face.

And he wished as he dreamed forbidden dreams that the trees would stop being kind, for the Vine often played what it called a joke, addressing a creature softly only to turn and spit venom behind a blood-curdling roar of infinite rage.

But other than his wish for no more kindness, from dusk until early dawn when he wakened, not another worry or fret broke into that stronghold.

The first round struck the weathered tree bark next morning, in a loud explosion of noise. The second ear-splitting volley crashed through his sleep where flowers daringly dreamed, in full view of the Vine. The Creature scrambled to his feet and stuck his head out between the wide trunks.

Pebbles littered the ground.

The pebble hurlers presented themselves, almost under his nose. Rage spewed in the same mouthing of silent words he'd witnessed from them, behind the moonlight parting. When they stood still long enough, he counted the same half-dozen creatures that he had observed before.

Rather than be trapped inside the ring of trees, he edged out into the meadow. Encountering this handful of ancient souls that first time had been startling enough. Here in his world, they had a scary nearly transparent look, and the rising sun glowed right through them. Unsuitable as they seemed for traveling, he couldn't think why they would leave their world to follow him all this distance.

The longer they remained in front of the flaming sunrise, the easier it was to see what made them look so dangerous. They were hopping mad, and surely insane. Rudely, they pushed closer, threatening him with handfuls of stones. He retreated, fearing the stones far less than their insanity, scared it might rub off on him.

Curiosity kept him watching their faces, twisted furiously in attempts to speak aloud, but amazingly, it was by scathing glances alone that they were managing to summon to his mind, mercifully fleeting scenes…of nothing to do with the present.

From the musty clouds of dust encircling them, their macabre memories swirled, faster and faster. Even if true—

those fleeting bits, he could not, would not—allow the insanity of them, to interfere with his quest.

Intending to resume his journey and leave the old ones to sort themselves out, he was cutting across the meadow when the irony stuck: He who had wished in the compound that something different might happen was getting more of that wish than he'd wanted.

Knee-deep in tall grass and patches of thistle, he wondered which new crime of his had dumped the old ones upon him. They were leaping erratically, watching him closely, and he hated being watched, for it made him painfully conscious of every fault and every flaw.

Onward he raced, soon imagining faults and flaws where they didn't exist, flinching and hesitating instead of watching where he was going. He stumbled and fell and took wrong turns. It seemed he could do nothing right. They muttered to each other and gave him looks of pity.

In a silence that grew more unnerving as the hours dragged on, the old ones ranted and roiled. His nerves strained, and eventually frayed to the point where he thought he heard the Vine snickering from behind every bush and tree, pronouncing his doom.

Red as blood, fruits grew plentifully along the way, juice oozing onto the grasses. The fruit attracted birds by the score. He waited until hunger forced him to snag a handful of berries and was just on the verge of plopping them into his mouth, when a flock of sparrows dove in, and stole them from out of his hand.

The old ones threw a fit, flapping their skinny transparent arms. One glance at them was all it took to panic the birds, and skyward they fled, brown wings whipping the grass with the force of a miniature hurricane.

A premonition of disaster settled over the Creature. Like an animal foreseeing a very hard winter, he gobbled every berry in sight and moved on to consume tender plants, roots, and even a smear of honey left by a careless bear. Juice-stained and sticky, he ate berries until he was full and then he ate more. The wildlife, discouraged by the old ones, stayed away. So he ate until he couldn't see his knees over his stomach and his eyes bulged.

Between the premonition and having to digest more food than he'd eaten in a lifetime, he felt terrible and then he felt worse. Lying down to rest didn't make him feel any better. The old ones conducted their mad and silent conversations right over his head, as if he were not there. He gleaned enough of what they were saying to be very grateful that most of it escaped him.

The rest of that day, they dogged his heels, angrily examining his every move, and calculating the progress of his quest. He felt imprisoned, threatened by their contact presence. They had no manners and couldn't care less. They were shameless. Whatever their specific and constant complaint might be, it remained a mystery known only to them, which suited the Creature exactly. The Vine had always said there was something suspicious in any group of creatures banding together to complain aloud about anything.

By nightfall, not much ground had been covered. The old ones presence had proved more irritating that he first thought possible. His bloated body belched often enough and loudly enough, to make him fear that he was about to explode. He had yet to do his daily chores.

Under a roaring waterfall, he tried in the darkness to rinse away the berry stains. When the moon came out, he saw the stains were still there, as if shadows had been painted upon his face and body, giving him a weird, half-finished appearance.

He had always looked weird, he thought to himself, wishing that the old ones weren't around to see him. He felt more stupid than at any other time in his life as if every fault and flaw had tripled and broken to the surface, showing him up for precisely what he was, the weirdest, ugliest, creature alive.

Compressing himself into less than before, in hopes of hiding some of the stains, he grabbed a sharp stick, anxious to add to his *Chastising List.* Every creature had a list; it would never do to fall behind.

I've been dreaming, he scrawled in the dirt. *I know I must stop. I promise I will.*

And true to his word, he tried while curled into the camouflage of a huge leaf pile, drowsily aware as the dead leaves crunched in his ears that his sleeping mind had a will of its own because...

The dream started out like any other,
he knowing it was forbidden, and the dream itself,

84

not caring , just taking off and transporting him with it…white flowers, an ocean of them, and he bent over that ocean, his tears flowing onto pristine petals…tears that were suddenly a stain of the darkest hue…and he saw in a rising panic that it wasn't a stain but a shadowy likeness that had to be his own, superimposed over the ocean of utter perfection.

He was the stain; in all his abject ugliness and weirdity… he was the stain that nothing would ever make right.

Fear, and not morning light, sent him shooting up from his pile of leaves. The old ones were describing a Vine in their silent language, *and it wasn't his Vine*. Apparently, according to them in their demented state, there had been—and were—*many Vines*.

Shaking, he hauled himself to his feet and started running. Why must he be saddled with ancient ones and their awful hallucinations? Daylight showed the berry stains to be fading. Last night's dream was fading, too. He immediately tucked the remnants away along with the old ones' Vine-rantings, wanting to forget about them, but he was rattled and kept losing track of the path.

The waterfall in which he'd rinsed off last night fed a stream that burbled for a ways, and was lined by tees, heavy with dense foliage. He stopped to rest. A sing-song verse, too loud and spirited to mean anything good, filtered through the treetops.

The premonition was coming true, because protruding from behind the trees was the enormous tail of some hidden monster, quite long, quite broad, and covered in gleaming scales. The great tail beat the ground in rhythm with the clanging verse, and the Creature's knees buckled.

"What is the thing?" he kept shrieking with his eyes closed against the sight.

The old ones didn't answer in words he could hear, and when he dared to look, the monster was gone. Ears ringing, he wondered what devilment had possessed that beaste to express itself—dare he even think it—in so HAPPY a manner. Clearly, the monster was crazy.

Remembering his rush of excitement on escaping the compound, he told himself that excitement was one thing and HAPPINESS another. Although to be honest, he had no idea what happiness might feel like or what made it that different from excitement. What he did know as he threw himself down on the stream's shady bank and chewed on his nails was what the Vine had told him: Happiness, aside from being a form of dementia, signaled a loss of control, a breach of Habit. He could only hope it never happened to him.

Warm sunlight bathed his face. He dozed off. The ancient ones pitched him right back onto his feet. He protested that it was just a small nap—but impatiently, they drove him straight into the stream, clambering along as he struggled out on the opposite bank, sopping wet and spluttering—while they showed him the monster's claw prints so that he'd know when it was wiser to sleep in the trees.

The day wore on, without seeing another trace of the monster.

The old souls shook, the Creature shook. But he learned rather quickly: The faster he went, the less the old ones bothered him. All was well until they emerged from a great stand of old pines.

There in the sunshine was a huge humped back with a great spiny ridge lumbering along the horizon. Trailing behind the monster, flipping sunbeams from iridescent scales, was its great broad tail. The old ones shimmied up to a ledge of rock, marking the monster's location by the flashes of reflecting sunlight. The Creature didn't need to hear their silent words to understand: *Best to stay clear of the monster.* And on they all journied, more scared than before.

As the days passed and his quest took him further away from the compound that he'd been glad to be rid of, he was left at times, with himself alone, and he wondered if he shouldn't be rid of himself as well. Other times, when the old ones came too close, or those little lights in the sky shone down on the land of deepest dark, and the moon herself glowed all over…odd and uncommon and very real emotions shot through him and stayed, just for a second. They were hard to deal with, those emotions. He was always relieved when they'd gone. They had no name. They made him uneasy, being so real just for the second.

Whenever the fancy dogs bayed, emotions were harder to deal with. There was a definite pull on that entrance inside him. It was then that he thought of the field of flowers, of seeing the form and shape of the strange *connection* and how it had looked back at him with its air waiting.

As for the message, he had yet to decipher it. Yet as often as practically every living thing called it out to him, he could have memorized it three times over.

He was never not busy at his quest as the days blew by and turned into nights, and nights into long, long passages of time. Against all odds, he believed most firmly in his quest and continued to believe—while keeping his vow of looking at nothing—and blaming the bigness of the land for his lack of progress. He never saw what he accomplished as he sped along. He only saw what he didn't, through a mist of unshed tears and a practically crazed determination to go ever faster. Otherwise, the Vine would catch up, and the Plagues would get him.

Both were coming.

Monsterous though it might be, it was the one note of certainty that truly existed. For even when the somehow calming portals in the sky did show up each night, those old souls, older than the hills around him—with utterly no humility, and nothing
to lose—showed him faces twisted in deeper and deeper outrage. And though it was the last thing he'd wanted to see, now it was all too clear *they wanted something of him.*

Then in the flush of one sunny morning, and certainly not by his design, a dozen thoughts collided in his mind and promptly became twenty more while he hurried to sort them out.

The neater he arranged them, the harder they worked at re-arranging themselves.

Whereupon he discovered inside his thought processes a whole new way to think. Flustered at what had just happened, the Creature wanted to doubt that it had. He couldn't have done it—he

wasn't that smart, so where had it come from,

And how long would it stay?

Faster than he thought he could think, huge oceans of thought rushed into his head, all jumbled and tumbled about. He lay in the sunlight, with his fright tightly gathered around him, and wished he were back, under that fortress tree. But only long blades of grass bent over his head, while his shivers

ran up

and down them.

A Plague was upon him. He'd known it was coming; why hadn't he paid attention? Now it was here assuring him that he could think all on his own in a way so grand that even the Vine would be stunned. Sure enough, the grasses parted and there was that enormous tail whipping at the air just over his head.

"There you are!" the monster exclaimed so grandly that bark all but flew off nearby trees. "I knew I had the measure of your brilliance! You've managed to break out of your funk; your mind is alive and well. So well in the fact, that I've heard it working the length and breadth of the land!"

Hearing those words, the Creature kept his expression carefully blank. And yet—a secret part of his heart tipped over—as he wondered if any of those words could be true. Doubt stepped in; urging him to stop whatever thoughts had summoned the monster. He just couldn't figure out

which thoughts they were.

"I am called Bragnificense," said the monster in the same loud fashion as before. "And I'm here to announce to you, the *magnificence—the sheer wonder—*of your mind. You may think that praising one's mind is a crime, but the very best thinkers do it all the time, just as a tiny reminder that Thinking is a treasure sublime!"

The old spirits hid under the bushes. The Creature spoke up politely, over chattering teeth.

"Bragnificense? *As in bragging?* I fear that I might search far and wide—find double, triple, the treasure of thought—*but bragging and praising myself* would be the very last things I could ever do. Such notions are contrary to all I've been taught."

The monster drew himself up to an even greater height, becoming so tall, in fact, that he had to lean down to be heard. And he grinned from ear to ear. It took awhile for the grin to reach from one end to the other, for the monster had an enormous face.

" I thought you knew," he said, "that knowledge begins on the day we first lay aside what we've been taught and start thinking for ourselves."

The Creature gasped. "Throwing aside what little I might already know, what would that leave me with?"

"It would leave you," said Bragnificense while he casually sharpened his claws on his scales, "with room for the Truth."

The old ones looked at each other. Their mouths did not move. The Creature's mouth tightened. "I am looking for unfettered thought," he gritted, "because I can't think for myself."

"Yes, you can," said Bragnificense.

"No, I can't!"

"Can."

"Well, you're missing the point. I don't want to be satisfied with my own silly meanderings. I want real thought. I want every thought there is! I want it all!"

The Creature had begun to sweat. The old ones picked up handfuls of stones and looked at the monster with loathing. The light striking the tall grasses grew so bright that everybody shielded their eyes. The leaves in the treetops could not be seen, so sparkling was the light pouring through them. Bragnificense's scales glinted until his whole body might have been sculpted of some rare rich metal.

The sight of him raised a fear in the Creature like no other he'd ever felt. And in spite of the sunlight, he saw his own shadow cast before him in long tentacles of darkness, leaping leaps of far-reaching height.

The old spirits began to keen, a tremulous, mind-shattering, silent keening that bent them low to the grasses. He heard none of the keening, but felt it as if he were making it himself. Little shreds suspiciously like Truth which had appeared on his journey and been rejected, sat like rocks in his mind.

Suddenly, he *did* want to know what secret lay behind these old spirits, banding together as they had to express themselves with such unity. For he was perceiving with utmost clarity something diabolical in the Vine's purposeful discouragement of gatherings amongst creatures. *He was seeing that the Vine encouraged the almost complete isolation of one creature from another.*

Why?

Vine leaves abruptly wedged themselves between him and the Truths he could feel trying to struggle to the forefront of his thoughts. Each one he'd been pondering then raced away. Even should they all come back in that very same instant, he knew that he couldn't, wouldn't be able to let them through.

The Creature of Habit stood still as stone, too close to that tower of shiny scales, tasting the bile rising up in his throat and wondering where his pondering had taken him.

He grew very cold and then he grew colder, whereupon something like rage took him over. That could not be however, for he never even got angry, let alone rageful. He remembered his quest and his vows. He knew if he started yelling he wouldn't stop.

"Go!" he hissed at the monster. "Go, and leave us alone, because you're wrong, Bragnificense! Wrong, wrong, wrong!"

He wanted to see past the Vine leaves wedged in his mind…but couldn't. The old ones, busy spitting at the monster's retreating back, began to scream. The Creature was beginning to believe that sensing a scream might be worse than actually hearing it.

For awhile that night, the Creature managed to evade the worst of the dreams he usually dreamed. They always left him with that awful feeling of *re-experiencing,* and were full of huge holes that he'd always assumed would never be filled. Instead, he dreamed his favourite dream, of battlegrounds and himself in glorious battle barb, possessing a sword of mighty dimensions which he tried to wield as well as the ancient warriors at his side, but the silent roilings of the old ones interfered with any hope of concentration.

Unbeknownst to the Creature, the Great Spirit Winds, busily traversing the firmament, as they bellowed and howled between one duty and another, at last took heed of the old ones' grief. It was something they had given up hope of ever hearing again.

Tossing about from one dream to another, the groggy Creature did feel a series of strong vibrations from far out in the firmament. The vibrations suggested overwhelming feeling of *welcome*…a product of his treacherous imagining, he was sure.

6

Getting There...

Ready as he would ever be after a night of non-stop and forbidden dreaming, the Creature threw himself at the path with a gnashing of teeth, and a glint in his eye.

First light was nearly upon him. The wind was already screaming. And as he ran, vowing not to waste another second, he heard the same message he'd heard before, flying faster and faster now, racing primeval from one green blade to another, until finally, every stick and stone and tree and twig joined in the fray, all calling out at once…that message he couldn't seem to get, taunting him the same as his unwelcome traveling companions, who might have been staring up his nose, so closely did they stick to his side.

The small wind that slammed at his back in anger sprayed his face with a blinding mist, obscuring any sign of a path, if path there was. He quickly bound himself bumbling as he rushed, whereas the ancient ones bumbled at nothing, hauling their fragile old selves along nearly invisible slippery byways at a stupefying clip.

The mist set his hopes to blazing. Such a mist had been described by the old creature of the compound as always hanging over the earth like a wet veil just before one reached that great body of water near those legendary mountains. In his hurry to find a better view, the Creature thought he knew where he was going, but the fog rolled in and left him stepping into nothing but air. An old one yanking him back silently cursed him for a fool.

When the fog rolled away again, one could see the ledge off which he'd been stepping, and the long drop down the face of the sheerest of cliffs.

Nobody paused to mark the moment of his mis-step, since not one of them could wrench their eyes from the view: Far across the valley stretching before them, here appeared through the shifting fog what might be a vast sea of water. Just in front of that watery sea, simply outlined like signposts pointing the way, were three tall mountains that brazenly grazed the sky.

The old souls' silent excitement was a marvel to see. The Creature's mind leapt like a leap-frog in the blissful throes of springtime, celebrating first the fact that he hadn't fallen off the cliff, and then the wonder of his quest, nearly half-over.

Unfettered thought was all but his!

There was another wonder as well, and almost as unbelievable: When had he begun to understand so much of what these musty dusty relics of old were saying? Not that he wasn't getting a lot of practice. But at least he was doing something better than before; he was growing more skilled at gleaning a great many unspoken words, as they'd taught him to bathe in mud and occasionally sleep in the trees. A few minutes ago, he'd even sensed himself being cursed and wished that he hadn't.

And as that very same old creature had reached out to keep him from falling just now, he'd *sensed* from them all—not the kindness he so mistrusted—but something else entirely, and it put him on a safer keel with them: They weren't being kind. They wanted, as if they'd guessed his destination, *to get wherever he was going!*

Muffled footfalls were coming closer. Indistinct shapes revealed themselves to be a band of forest wildlife. Behind them, emerged the slower, more nonchalant personage of Bragnificense himself, cheerfully shuffling along on leathery feet. Did *everybody,* the creature asked himself, want to go where he was going? By the time he arrived, would there be a que, with him standing empty handed, at the end the line?

The wind was shrieking again, and shoving at his back in a frightening display of impatience. He was almost there. But what if something went wrong and by the time he got there, the heavens and everything beyond then had vanished?

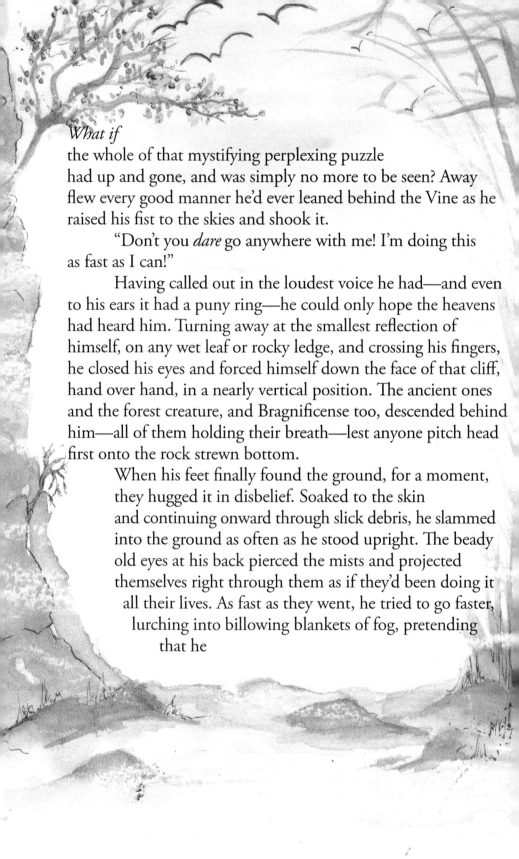

What if
the whole of that mystifying perplexing puzzle
had up and gone, and was simply no more to be seen? Away
flew every good manner he'd ever leaned behind the Vine as he
raised his fist to the skies and shook it.

"Don't you *dare* go anywhere with me! I'm doing this
as fast as I can!"

Having called out in the loudest voice he had—and even
to his ears it had a puny ring—he could only hope the heavens
had heard him. Turning away at the smallest reflection of
himself, on any wet leaf or rocky ledge, and crossing his fingers,
he closed his eyes and forced himself down the face of that cliff,
hand over hand, in a nearly vertical position. The ancient ones
and the forest creature, and Bragnificense too, descended behind
him—all of them holding their breath—lest anyone pitch head
first onto the rock strewn bottom.

When his feet finally found the ground, for a moment,
they hugged it in disbelief. Soaked to the skin
and continuing onward through slick debris, he slammed
into the ground as often as he stood upright. The beady
old eyes at his back pierced the mists and projected
themselves right through them as if they'd been doing it
all their lives. As fast as they went, he tried to go faster,
lurching into billowing blankets of fog, pretending
that he

didn't notice his own clumsiness.

Cavorting alongside

Bragnificense's huge form,

the forest creatures acted as if they

doubted that anyone else knew their head

from their elbow. They somersaulted, climbed

or catapulted over anything that got in their way, dashing

ahead and doubling back to gloat.

Running at triple speed, the Creature was aiming

to save face on all fronts and avoid the monster.

"Oh, show me the mind, where one cannot

find a bit of intelligence stirring," Bragnificense sang in a

baritone reminiscent of boulders crashing down a hillside, "and

I'll show you a stupor; a haze, a veritable daze!"

It would be nice, the Creature thought, to cram a tree

down Bragnificense's throat. The monster's previous remarks

about mind-praising and bragging combined with that

flamboyant style of his, had left a bad aftertaste. And, as that

same truncheon of fear beat upon an already aching head, he

subjected Bragnificense to a scathing scrutiny that left nothing

whatsoever to recommend him. The surprising part being, the

harder he rejected the monster, the more he seemed to be

rejecting

some unfathomed bit of himself.

What made those old spirits scream? The question

haunted him. The old ones' past lay in fragments. No two pieces fit together well enough to explain sufficiently, why they seemed to be in a constant state of rage—and what did it matter, anyway—when those old spirits weren't real?

They were *gone,* the Creature told himself. Gone, like the very old creature of the compound—whatever *gone* really meant—and he hadn't a clue. Judging by the dust balls each time they emerged, they hadn't been around for a very long while, so how did their anger still linger? Why were they tormenting him?

Cold sopping leaves clung to the Creature's frowning face. His feet had gone wizened from stomping through wet debris, and still he worried: The old ones' obvious exhilaration at seeing the mountains—as if they somehow knew of his plan to climb them and grab unfettered thought—*might the old one be in league with the Vine?* Were *they* another Plague the Vine had sent to destroy him?

Such thoughts were mean-spirited, but the old souls' insanity was scary and at times, he almost hated them. Then he wondered who he loathed more, them or himself? Realising with something of a start that there was actually nothing new in his self-loathing, he pondered: Why did he feel the same, away from the Vine, as he had felt inside those Vine walls?

He slapped back the brambles that tore at his hide. Mud flowed in every direction, sucking down any foot or paw that didn't move fast enough. Bragnificense dripped rivers of mud and breathed in the manner of an overheated volcano.

Nobody needed to look back, to know they had

come a long, rough ways. Only a little while off in the distance, lay the path upward to unfettered thought. By nightfall he'd be climbing!

He started to recline in the overhanging shadow of Bragnificense where the wildlife sprawled at rest. Among them were small animals with striped tails and bandit eyes, dozing next to white spotted fawns. A number of Red Coasts nuzzled a greater number of mewling pups, and giant bears roared as they examined their paws for thorns.

Relaxing near any of them, least of all, Bragnificense didn't seem wise. So he sat stiffly to one side, awed at the sheer size of the monster's body, covered in what must be a hundred million scales, all seamlessly forming an impenetrable hide and hiding a mind which, even in repose, seemed to him threatening. He had to wonder though, how a monster, a lesser being, managed to have intelligence when he, a whole notch up, didn't have any?

Could Bragnificense be simply pretending? Amongst the scales on the leathery face, one eye opened wide and closed very slowly. The monster had just winked at him, and he cringed, finding winks an unfamiliar and disturbing experience.

For once, the old souls were quiet. Their excitement was gone. And they hummed. He began to sense the anxiety in their silent sounds, perceiving at last, that they were trying to overcome their fears, which only seemed to be growing. He wished they wouldn't hum; it made him fidgety.

When he looked around, he saw what they were humming at. Under the lifting fog, the land showed through, and it

had an eerie appearance.

Something scary crawled up his spine. The features froze on his face. He got to his feet, and started forward on tiptoe, compelled to look where he was going. For his feet were feeling queerly empty, as if there was nothing in them, making him tilt at every turn. Empty.

Empty

as the sky above, where no cloud marred the chill nor did any bird fly there. His movements grew more cautious as he noted the extreme silence.

He began to miss the sounds of the flowers and grasses, and of the old tree. For in this place, no message was being passed to him. The fact was inescapable…

no one had been here before him.

The land wore the look of

the dawn of time…

as if no eye had ever beheld it,

no sound had ever echoed across it.

So quiet

was the mantle

of the land upon him,

so different were those guide-stars up close than they had looked at a distance that he wanted to run from this forsaken land into which he'd journied; yet even within that seemingly endless raw silence, he could not help hearing an unearthly odd beauty… and questioning: Could one actually hear beauty? Or silence?

Habit said no.

With his instant dismissal of a beauty the land had offered, from the lovely uniqueness of itself—if he would but accept it—
that land now purposely withheld from him.

Nor did the Creature of Habit yet notice exactly what he was being denied, for a tiny, intriguing—and utterly false notion—
was already snatching him up. The blankness, stretching endless and green before those legendary mountains which he would shortly climb, reminded him of the sky, endless and blue, with those canvases infinite in number…and then he had it!

This empty land must be a canvas, blank and brand-new, waiting for him to impress upon it, with steps his own, the mark of the first questor to ever set foot upon this direct route to unfettered thought!

So there in the midst of that green blank space whose beauty he had dismissed, he placed his footprint and then he placed two, and stood back and stared in a growing horror… *no footprint showed up, not even one; it was as if he had never been there.* This land of green silence did not accept him as anything, least of all, a questor.

He never saw the land's disappointment at his oblivion, or sensed the healing nature of the beauty which he might have known to be his, sooner than later, because shame burned him hotter than fire.

Dumbfounded, then thoroughly beaten, he rushed to be leaving every last bit of that silence and endless green space all to itself, the way it obviously wanted to be. As for the mountains themselves, he thought why should they accept his humble footprints, when the land had already denied them?

"Oh please," he cried to the heavens, "all I want, is to reach you. What am I doing wrong?"

Behind him, the forest creatures pretended they weren't there. Bragnificense didn't say a word. The old ones averted their gaze, holding their rage at his failure inside them. He sensed that rage was not intended so much for him as it was the land, refusing as it had his questing footprints.

Shamed all over again, he hid his face.

And sure that in all the trees, and in all the thickets before him for as long as he lived, forest creatures everywhere would be smirking, he shrunk himself up as small as could be, and slunk so low as to practically be crawling. After a few dragging steps, he encountered the fullness of the pain which he'd tried so long to *avoid. He was completely aware, to the marrow of his bones, of being*

    ugly—

        as ugly as the Vine had forever said creatures were.

He didn't get very far beyond the scene of his crime, before twilight, magnificent in floating mists of lavender and crimson snuck up beside him, tenderly hiding his humiliation from the silent ones who still followed. For once, kindness was not a problem. He went as if led where the twilight took him,

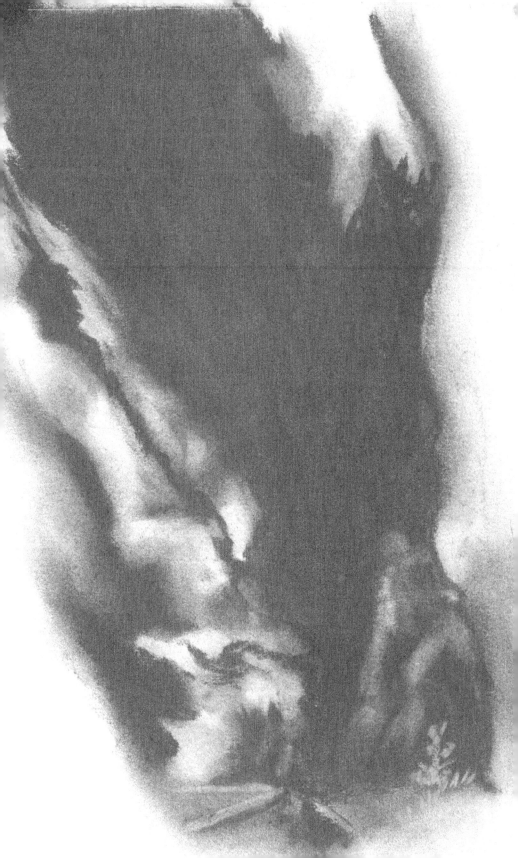

to the mouth of an alabaster cave tucked safely into a hillside of soaring stone and mossy nooks of soft velvet.

By the yawning stretch of that chasm of shadows, one tiny blue-faced flower stood sentry…only watching and waiting, as if she knew of his pain and his tiredness, too.

At his back and to his dismay, the Great Spirit Winds themselves howled as only they could and then, in a quiet billowing of hospitality, they offered the sanctuary of their dark cavern home. Fearsome as they sounded, he wanted to fade into that darkness and hide. So short a time after those green mountains, however, the unknown cave was not to be trusted.

Before going in, he needed to be sure just what lay beyond that entrance. Reaching out, he watched his arm disappear through the wavering gloom. His hand ran up and down and along the roughness of the nearest wall, encountering something there. He immediately felt that it had to be beautiful. And far far older than the drawings he had once scratched in the dirt of the compound.

Inching inside, he moved closer to the wall, now absolutely at the mercy of curiosity. Reaching once more through the darkness, what his fingers found as if tracing an ancient past—were writings he couldn't understand, and birds and forest beings, chiseled not into the walls, but carved into wee individual figures—lying on a thin ledge perhaps four feet above the cavern's floor. With trembling fingers, he brought out a small stone bird, holding it up to the fading light. Tracing the graceful curve of wing and breast, there came to him an overwhelming sense of the ancient carver, and the anguish surrounding him…until it seemed to be not the small carved bird which he held in his hands, but rather the spirit of the carver himself… and the old ones were screaming again.

He never slept in the alabaster cave, on that night or any other. He turned with those screams rising louder and louder, as he tore past the tiny blue flower. On through the twilight, his fear ran five steps ahead. Just when he thought it impossible to live another minute inside his own head while those screams rang with a rage he'd not ever been permitted to feel, he grasped on some other level that the old ones behind the screams perceived what he hadn't,

the way ahead was barred to him.

Firmly, barred as if by some invisible wall of astounding breadth and unreachable height, he tried to see if there were leaves or tendrils dangling from that wall, but if so, they were invisible, too.

The dog just a few feet away, almost hidden in drifting layers of fog and mist was enormous even in a coat flattened by the damp. It stood motionless, waiting for him to catch up, and when he did, it turned and disappeared. The Creature trod timidly after, and with no hope of a promising outcome. Bragnificense and the others were behind him somewhere; he could hear their footsteps. All he could think was that the dog might be leading them, leading everyone over a cliff, or worse, to slaughter.

The dog's white coat blended with the fog. He tracked its loping progress by the black nose it turned to him every so often and by the glitter in its eyes as they tracked him.

Already, he'd made too many mistakes. Following this animal anywhere, could be another. He was afraid to believe even half of what had already happened this far. As to the balance of his journey…to stay out of further trouble, that curiosity of his would need a firm squelching.

The intrepid little blue flower at the alabaster cave tiptoed into his mind as if invited. Thoughts of squelching went up in smile as he wondered how did a flower at the beginning of each season remember *to be* a flower? *Or creatures, or wildlife, or just any old blade of grass?*

The dog led him one more time, then left him standing in the fog. So there he was, the Creature of Habit, unaware of his arrival and fully at the end of his stamina and patience, too. Far away from the compound, much further away than he knew—down he sank on the weariest of knees—
in a gentle

                                  moonlit glen.

Hearing nothing, and most especially seeing and feeling nothing either except for an immense draining of mind and spirit, he surveyed the wreckage of his dream. Apparently there was no body of water and those crafty mountains had misled him. Never had he been so glad to see the moon and he couldn't think why. There was nothing she could do for him except glow. But he raised his face letting her light shine onto him and, as he did, he thought her light strange. It had become less a glow than a *beam* of light that very nearly bored down through him, finding a throb, a steady pulsing inside his own flesh, linking him mysteriously to something else in the night. And amazingly, it had *an answering beat of such insistence, such definitive boldness,* that he was quick to draw back from it, quicker to doubt what felt like its good intentions. If the Vine had been present, he would have thrown himself at it and begged to be saved.

So in his panic, he couldn't take in the true nature of everything around him, set aside and apart,

at the end of the world.

For once, it was easy to miss the familiar old compound. Easier yet to imagine being held here a prisoner, forced to listen to that answering demanding pulsebeat, while never again having the nearness of another creature. He wondered how they were faring back in the compound, if they could still feel or see the sun. Was even one little start still able to shine through the roof of the Vine?

There came a soft scraping nose, like toenails catching on rock—many toenails, many rocks—and a ring of black noses poked through the mist. Pale as far-away shadows, the dogs closed in on all sides, and settled upon their haunches. Haughtily then, they lifted their heads and began to bay. The baying pierced the evening air—cries being aimed not at the moon—but at something no one else could see.

For the smallest of seconds, that sight of them banded together, like wonderful ghosts from another time—the Creature would have sworn he understood precisely—they were signaling the grant of his passage.

And then...
beyond the soft carpet of grass
came the smell of something he'd never smelled before, creeping into his consciousness just as he'd been about to drift off somewhere...perhaps further seeing that which weariness wanted finally to escape. The smell became not a thing of the senses only—that vast arena wherein one cannot be sure what is real and what is not—but a world in and of itself, wherein the senses rule and what is real there seems to be real everywhere.

Now it was he who cursed himself for a fool. Why had he never thought at the very beginning of this quest to make for himself a longbow, spear, broadsword or battleaxe? Or indeed, any number of those amazing instruments of defense he'd never actually seen in his life, but which haunted most of his dreams, along with the warriors who wielded them?

Because try as he might to protect himself against it, the core of that sense alerted him: Something or someone else entirely, separate and apart from the old souls gathered at his side, now inspected him outside and inside,

as if having every right.

"What binds you?"
a Voice asked.

And startled,
the Creature of Habit
could find
no reply.

7

The Meeting

Chances were good, that the Voice was the Vine,
playing a waiting game and withholding its identity, intending
to spring out when least expected. Although the Voice, like no
other he'd ever heard—except Bragnificense, who had already
discredited himself—sounded *cheerful,* instantly raising the
question: Where were its whips? When would it haul
them out and brandish them in front of his face,

and where was it?

     The Creature cast about for hope of survival, but at
the Voice's first words, the forest creatures had wisely headed up
into the trees. The old ones were behind the trees,

craning their necks in an effort to see what they wanted no part of. Even had Bragnificense been in plain sight, he would not have asked for the monster's help.

Afraid to breathe, let alone try to answer the Voice's question and with nothing quite as it should be in that night spread before him, the earth trembled under his nose. The glen dissolved in a quick shimmer of sliver, and before he could even blink,

it sprang up again.

The moon, her pale face now mottled in thought and the heavens themselves, that mysterious canopy that had tormented him for so long, stared down on the Creature of Habit, who

sat before *a pool so deep that it had no bottom.*

Its tranquil waters were certainly a thing to behold, and seemed impossibly linked to the heavens above. As if they were one, heavens and pool enfolded him in a lovely entrancement known to the senses alone, and accepted his presence unquestioned…asking him to feel that he might be welcome here.

Not even in ones wildest dreams, nor the legends of the old creature of the compound either, could a scene of this particular enchantment have been imagined. What could it be, that he had stumbled upon—or fallen into—or somehow flown up to? With no thought for how dangerous this Voice must be, he cried out to it,

"Have I reached beyond?"

The Voice's answer came back, not from above or below him, and not from either side of him, but rather from a location which he didn't yet recognize. And it wasn't that far away.

"No, Creature. Not yet."

No?

For several beats of his madly pumping heart—thrilled at having reached what clearly *must be* what he *thought* it was—he silently defended his dreams. After a few beats more, he let them go and stared at his toes in such an awful withering of hope that he couldn't find himself separate from the dirt. Thus from that already lowly position—he began to level himself further, in wails of grief. So wrenching was his despair that up in the trees etched in moonlight, the wildlife clung desperately to the branches; branches which were beginning to sway rather badly under the weight.

"How could I?" he cried, "ever have thought I might have an idea of merit, let alone one that might succeed? Why did the wind ever bother to whisper free to me, when I'll never be free, because I'm not smart enough to get there!"

"Guess what?" the Voice asked, trying to insert itself between his rantings, but the Creature didn't seem willing or able, to stop.

"I can't even face myself. What kind of warior-questor am I, when I can't get where I'm going? Why didn't I listen? The Vine was right about me. The Vine was right about everything!"

"Maybe it was, and maybe it wasn't," said the Voice.

The Creature held his breath.

The Voice had just struck the only note of skepticism he had ever heard expressed aloud about the Vine. And somehow, villainous though it might be, it warmed him. He stopped his self-abhorrence to consider for once—at least briefly—that the Vine might not be that all-knowing.

He also thought that he must be awfully tired if fine moon glow was making him queasy—or was it *something in the water?* Dismayingly enough, the odour he'd been smelling radiated from the beautiful pool. Unlike the unscented kind with which he'd faithfully watered the Vine, the smell of this water was so overpowering, as to five one the notion that maybe it had sat there forever.

"The pool is very old," the Voice told him, It goes back so far in time that everyone thought it was lost."

"I don't understand," came the Creature's way but honest protest. "How does and entire pool full of water—especially that water, smelling as foul as it does—get lost?"

"The pool was lost when creatures no longer looked inside themselves for answers."

"Who would be dumb enough to look inside himself for anything?" the Creature asked and then, stricken by his rudeness, wanted to vanish from the face of the earth.

"Once you figure that out, you will already be there.

Perhaps you might like to define the freedom you seek?"

Mercifully, he was saved from needing to answer because he had to jump and dodge as tree limbs cracked overhead, sending large furry bundles crashing to the ground. They scrambled to their feet and bounded into the night. He wished he could do the same, but he was busy dislodging from his person, a few fallen tree frogs and one angry opossum, observing for the first time how easily any sharp sound or quick movement had always had the power to make him leap from his skin. Then he caught a whiff of his skin. He smelled like the water—rank as the ruins of whole civilizations—and strangely, he knew that ancient odour from somewhere long long ago. This time, the re-experiencing was agonising.

"The pool has belonged for some while to the forest creatures," the Voice sad. "they want to know what you are doing here."

"I wish I knew."

"You never answered my question. It's quite alright—for now—if you can't. But it might help if you at least define yourself."

Unaccustomed to conversation and its demands at times for ready answers, the Creature was at a loss. Define himself? What did that mean? Feeling doltish, he mumbled his name.

"There is no need to apologise. What sort of Habit would that be? What exactly, defines your?" And when the Creature didn't reply, the Voice said, "We are defined by our thoughts."

"I didn't used to have many thoughts," the Creature admitted. "But lately I seem to have quite a few. What I want is—"

"Quite a few?" the Voice sounded surprised. "What I'm hearing from your head, is the loud sound of virtual emptiness. But I must say Bragnificense was right. Your mind is in fine working order."

With a sinking feeling, the Creature faced it: This Voice

118

was aware of the monster's remarks about his so-called magnificent mind. Were they in league together, the Voice and Bragnificense, with the big scaley beaste hiding out there in the dark, and snickering?

"But what have we here?" the voice inquired. "Another leaf on the spine of the Vine? That was a small joke, by the way. Although—with all the debris you've collected, it's a miracle you haven't strangled yourself—intellectually, that is."

Fingers seemed to probe the Creature's startled mind, and then withdraw.

"What happened to all your thoughts, Creature? Did you give them away?"

"Thought wasn't the Vine's favourite thing."

"Nothing and no one," the Voice told him flatly, "has the right to deny a creature his defining. The right to your thoughts belongs only to you. So, tell me, *what do you think?*"

He'd never thought about his *right* to anything, much less his thoughts, and torn between Vine and Voice logic had to mull that over. He decided to risk it: "I think –not having had many thoughts all my own—that I want without borrowing or stealing or eavesdropping, every single thought there is. I want to be capable of thinking everything!"

"Splendid. Then you have come to the right place. Shall we begin?"

The right place? Shall we begin? If this was a trick, then it was a cruel one, and unseen Voice pretending it had been sitting all along on the treasure of unfettered thought. At the very least, this Voice was arrogant, and perhaps even delusional.

"Oops," said the Voice. "I'm afraid I forgot to make the Official Announcement. Do you know what you have done? Well, have at it. Dare to hazard a guess."

The invisibility of his nagging host, the jolly prodding at his reluctance to unveil himself and his silly, treasonous wishes; his fear of being wrong and therefore punished all formed a solid, anxious lump in his throat. Terror in one eye and fear in the other, both were peeled for an escape route that didn't seem to exist.

"I guess," he ventured, "that I have come a bit of a distance, and still have a ways to go."

Gales of Voice-laughter broke out. They bounded from tree to tree, reverberating all the way round the little glen that surrounded the astonishingly quiet and beautiful pool—the pool so mysteriously lacking a bottom, with a pulse beat exactly like his own—and the sound of the laughter resonated with grinding unpleasantness.

Another good reason the Creature decided over his fear was why nobody ever laughed in the compound. The irritation of it slashed ones nerves to the quick. In the moonlight, bushes shook and hooves pawed the earth as though in agreement. If only, he thought, that blackbird had taught him to fly. He might already be sitting on top of unfettered thought and freedom, instead of here, having his ears blasted.

"Fear not," the Voice crowed happily. "You have no need to go further. What you've done—snatching so priceless a treasure from the jaws of the enemy has a ring of heroic proportions Indeed. I imagine you're quite exhausted!"

Heroic? That word didn't apply to him. Snatching what treasure, from what enemy? "Actually," he said warily, "I'm ready to run, ready for anything."

"Leaving already?" the Voice objected. "Rushing off to more of your grand envisioning? At least take a minute to look at the pool, and enjoy—"

There was too much kindness behind that surely false banter. It drove the Creature to his feet. But his toes had gone numb with fear and he immediately fell down again.

"Overcome, are we? What's the hurry, Creature? Survey your bounty, you've earned it!"

"What are you talking about? I haven't *found* anything!"

And again he got up, looking frantically for the path.

"Well," said the ever-cheerful Voice, "I suppose now you've located freedom. You're free to leave if you must."

Freedom? Had he stumbled right past the finding of his prize? Had it been at the feet or at the top of those three green mountains in that awful land that had dismissed him so

meanly? *"Where,"* and he felt tempted to scream, *"Where is it?"* Delighted, the Voice replied, "This is the glen of the Sleeping Pool—the place of the treasure lost—and the pool itself is freedom far beyond the mere unfettered freedom you seek. The pool is *Endless* Freedom. Creature, think! The pool is Endless Freedom, the last step before the treasure of Endless Thought, and the last step is just a formality. Now, for starters, can't you please define the freedom you were seeking?"

Before the Creature could answer, there came not probing fingers, but a tip-toeing through his mind, as if something or someone were taking up residence. His fear grew in direct proportion to the blunder he'd made, putting himself in the path of an unseen Voice trying to distract him with empty promises.

"*I,*" he insisted, his voice rising helplessly in volume, "seek personal freedom! I seek a veritable *shield* of freedom!"

"That is a wish, not a definition.
Weakness wishes, strength defines. Do you not find it so?"

Doubting that he'd found anything but trouble, and now despairing of ever finding anything more, he wrinkled his nose at the scent of that water primeval, not wanting to get too close. He stared toward the darkened pool, seeking the physical embodiment of the Voice, and whatever truth it *might* be telling.

Nothing but the moon sailing the heavens looked down upon him. Did he only *imagine* the Voice? Ready to believe himself capable of any crime, he tried to refuse his emotion, but a single tear broke loose and then another.

"Are you waffling, Creature? That emotion of yours, what is it?"

"Humility," he sobbed—and sobbed—with his head hanging low. "It's revered amongst creatures."

"Ah, yes…humility, and why such an excess?"

"One can never be humble enough, not for the Vine," he replied, rubbing at his eyes in embarrassment.

"But don't you see what excessive humility has done for you? It's depressed you, and the expression of all that depression has given the pool new depths. Continue the tears, and your perplexities will be deeper than before. Which is to say, of course, that you just might drown."

His very wet toes told him the Voice hadn't lied that time, because the level of the water had risen, no doubt about it.

"Why does the water smell so sharp, so compelling, that at times it is strongly unpleasant?"

"Haven't you just described freedom, so strong a concept that only the strong ever manage it?"

The Creature had an idea. "If the pool is freedom," he said in a hesitant tremour, "will you allow me to use it whenever I need to?"

"It doesn't work that way."

A moan, faint with exhaustion floated up from the Creature's bent head. "It doesn't work that way. *How does it work?*"

"It works when you look into it." The Voice sounded firm. "Pardon?"

"The pool never lies. Looking into this water, seeing yourself reflected as you really are is the secret to freeing yourself."

So there it was, bound up with a word as difficult as *self,* and every bit of fancy foolery blown away to reveal nothing more than a ploy meant to humiliate him with his own pitiful reflection. "You're telling me," he fumed, "that freedom is in that pool, and my quest is at the mercy of some old legend?"

"Ancient wisdom can be hard. It is honest though, unlike our friend, the Vine. It was once known to creatures, that the past teaches the present. In this instance, the old spirits must wait for you to use the pool first. I believe it's considered polite that he who finds it graciously does the honours."

The Voice didn't sound like a liar. It was too calm, too certain about each fact. Some he might accept, but others he couldn't. Yet, if just one fact were true in the whole bunch, it turned his quest upside down. His quest that had once had seemed so simple, so easy, was now the mess he might well have suspected all along. He put his head between his knees and gasped for air. Who would have thought that his Vine-enforced dedication to good manners would be what did him in?

There was no way he could ever *do the honours,* since he didn't want to see himself reflected from anywhere. The old ones might be roiling for the rest of eternity, and as for him…he would have fled right then, lugging his guilt and disappointment on a journey doomed from the start, but another glimpse of the pool kept him sitting, right where he was.

"Why," he asked, "is the Sleeping Pool thought to be endless freedom?"

"There's no *thought to be,* about it," said the Voice on a note of good-natured satisfaction. "The pool is endless freedom because even a creature who is strong but cannot see his strength never knows his wonderment, until that reality is reflected back at him. Thereafter, he is free. Endlessly."

The Creature didn't believe it for one minute. "The pool

has no bottom," he hissed as politely as possible. "Isn't that the same as the heavens which have no end?"

"Ah. But why must there be a bottom, if endless freedom—just like the heavens—has no end?"

"Everything has a bottom!" the Creature cried, ensnared in an age-old maze. "Everything has an end and a beginning! *The pool is a fraud!*"

"A fraud? Is that because it does not seem to agree with your own theory? Would you like to test your theory?

You see, *endless freedom,* while it is right here in this pool, is not yet your own. It merely lies here undefined, for you, who will learn to define it fully. Hence—you may want to look into the pool after all."

No, I won't, said the stubborn Creature to himself, wanting no part of this mind-reader mean enough to suggest he stand around listening carefully to ancient wisdom while somebody else much quicker ran off with the prize. But he could feel his resolve wither

at the Voice's next words.

"There seems to be a question in the pool.
It is yours, is it not?"

Avoiding any chance of seeing his own reflection, the Creature relented and let his eyes skim the water's surface. And indeed there was a question, more than familiar, in the lovely hypnotic depths swirling before him...

"Am I the only one here?" he whispered as if reading a mind that was his own, but at the same time, *seemed to belong as well, to the disembodied Voice*...and in barely contained anguish, he cried out,

*"Am I the only fool to have stumbled
so badly on this journey?"*

"Many," the Voice said, "have begun the journey, but they always stopped before they got this far. You will notice I did not say, *the whole distance*, because I'm supposing that you are now aware... there isn't any."

"Ad infinitum,"
the Creature muttered, with nary an inkling as to how long that expression had been hiding in his vocabulary. And then—so as not to miss a word of it—he repeated slowly, and aloud, "There is...no such thing...as the whole...distance..."

His words dangled in mid-air.

"Are you saying there is no end to the search for freedom? If there is no end, how can I capture the entirety of freedom? There's only one way I know of to be free and that is to get to the end of my quest where I can think every thought there is, or ever was, or ever will be! Which is exactly what I set out to get!"

"At last." The Voice sounded relieved. "A definition of sorts. Let me return the compliment. *One is free, only as long as one is willing to look.*"

"Tell me you're lying," the Creature heard himself snarl.

When the Voice said nothing, he flung himself face down on the ground and sobbed with renewed vigour. The moon dipped behind the clouds, as if unwilling to witness such a show of shame and depression.

"Why," the Voice asked gently, "do they call you the Creature of Habit?"

"Why? Because Habit is my way. It's the only thing I am good at. And in the compound, each of my days were safely the same—because of Habit—and I never questioned the pattern until I looked into the sky and wondered where it ended."

"Do you not agree then with the theory of endless space?"

"Endless? I don't want endless, I don't want to be journeying forever, I want to reach a definite destination, I want to reach Beyond! Endless? I can't accept that as the final answer, as an absolute!"

"Which means" countered the Voice thoughtfully, "you, who seek freedom—also seek absolutes—which necessarily mean e ndings; established, immovable, imprisoning boundaries."

"I am so confused," the Creature wailed, "I seek unfettered freedom and thought—and I tell you, I shall have them!"

"Yes, and I tell you, when you finally do gaze into the pool—willingly, and with your whole heart and soul—you will know what freedom is. And the rest will follow."

"And will strange fingers still be able to invade my mind at will?"

"Freedom of the endless kind," the Voice informed him, neatly ignoring both his sense of violation and the fear boiling just under it, "must exist in one's mind, on its own merit and despite any obstacle. It is the ability to move about on an intellectual plane, to go as one pleases by thought alone—to pursue an idea, or the wisp of an idea, against all odds for as long as it takes—to reach a satisfactory conclusion."

"How is that conclusion judged satisfactory? Who makes that judgment?"

"The thinker himself," the Voice replied. "Always it is the thinker himself who must judge."

"No Vine has the higher power?" Now the Creature's eyes were crossing in his head.

"The thinker is the higher power."

With the weight of that statement bearing down on him, the Creature wanted to run and hide. His thoughts whirled like a leaf assailed by all four winds.

"You're scaring me," he cried.

"Of course," said the Voice, as if speaking to a creature of extremely tender years. "One is always frightened when sitting at the edge of endless possibility."

8

A Warrior-In-Waiting

Holding onto that idea with a vise-like grip, he savoured those two words, *endless possibility.* How exciting they were, he thought. And how long he had waited for them, not even knowing they existed. Too bad they existed only with an *if* attached. *If* he looked into the pool, his world would be packed with possibilities. And *if* he didn't, then he might never find freedom or thought, might never be able to rescue anyone from the compound. As for the old ones, he couldn't begin to think what he would do with them...

"*Who are you? Why on earth should I trust you?*" he whispered to the Voice.

"As to your first question," said the Voice, "you alone know the answer. You alone must judge the second."

The Creature fumed. Constantly being told to make up his own mind; this laxity of attitude bore no relation to life as he'd ever known it. "If all I hear is your voice," he objected, "and I can't see you, then what am I supposed to judge with?"

"Are you quite sure that it is a voice you hear?"

He wasn't sure of anything, except that everything bad that could happen, had happened, leaving him dangerously exposed and at risk. Any moves to save himself required decisions and the first two he'd ever made—to snip the tendrils off the Vine, and then to escape—had only landed him on the same path as this unseen Voice. He shivered at the thought of how bad his decisions might turn out to be here in this very odd glen.

The Voice—could it *see* him? Undoubtedly. Otherwise, how would it know exactly where to aim its jarring remarks as if they were invisible weapons? He felt the whole of that beautiful night seeming to peer in judgment, waiting for answers he didn't have.

"You've stopped thinking," the Voice prompted. "What's wrong?"

"Why don't you go away, and let me think in peace and quiet?" the befuddled Creature cried.

The Voice paused, seeming more than a little taken aback by his remark. Then, as if that were the funniest thought it had ever heard, the Voice let out a long booming laugh that bounced around the glen, and crashed against every tree and rock. Inside the Creature's ears, the hideous reverberations magnified,

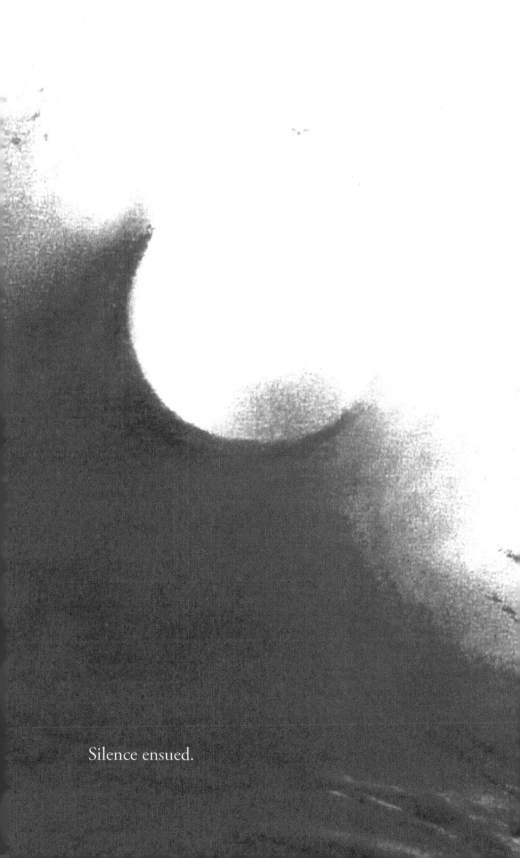

Silence ensued.

"Tell me," persisted the Voice after an appropriate interval, "why do you slink? Why in the world have you compressed yourself into nothingness?"

"I try never to offend anyone with my presence," the Creature answered in surprise, "but it didn't work with the land."

"Well, if you ever do find yourself offending nothing and nobody, you will be as nothing and a bore as well."

What a thrilling bit of brilliance! But dangerous, too. Toes tingling, he waited for lightning or something even faster to strike, but nothing happened. There was only the water, the strange scent of it, stinging his nostrils, arousing in his thoughts, a really big question: What interest could the Voice—apparently an intelligence to match even that of the Vine—possibly have in a mere Creature of Habit, who had such a paltry few thoughts?

Would it be insulting to ask the Voice directly how it had broken into his mind? The Voice reeked of self-confidence and ego, both of which creatures of the compound had been Vine-reared to regard as having the Plague. Could this Voice be a case of *supreme* self-confidence or an ego gone mad and searching for a place to stay?

Please, not with me, the tired Creature begged, under his breath. The old ones had shown him that he wasn't cut out for the company of others, especially not for any extended period of time. And what if freedom wasn't in the pool, after all? What if the Voice, knowing full-well, that freedom was somewhere else nearby, intended to distract him from it, then dash in at the very moment of capture, and cheat him out of the victory?

If he came away from his quest empty-handed, the ancient creatures were demanding enough to make his life miserable, until he did find freedom. Well, he asked himself, what to do about this Voice, so unwilling to share? Dolefully, he stole a look at the night sky where pin-prick holes seemed to let in some encouragement, along with a sparkling light from beyond. Even though it might be another mistake, he called out to the Voice.

"You beckoned?" it asked immediately.

"I did," said the Creature, rock-still with apprehension, and thus appearing wonderfully calm and reasonable. "And you answered and this time I know definitely where you are. How did you *get* here? Why are you trespassing inside my mind?"

"Ah, you've noticed," said the Voice, in a tone so droll and satisfied it might have been grinning. "As it happens, we're only in part of it...for the moment, at least. I'm assuming you're aware, all creatures, including even those of so-called lesser being, come packaged in parts."

"Parts?"

Instantly horrified, the Creature reflected upon each creature of the compound. Who among them was complicated enough to exist in parts? It couldn't be him. Creatures were simple.

"Now, that part—the one you were just using—is called Memory," the Voice announced, seeming to take no notice of the frightened expression he could feel on his face, or the stupidity streaming—he was sure—from his eyes.

"Memory," mused the Voice, as if to itself, "can be a lovely realm. It can take you from here to there wherever there may be, and at the command of no one, other than one's own self..."

The Voice seemed to be carried along on the winding thread of its own thought, and the Creature trembled. "Voice, are you *daydreaming?*"

"Actually," and the far-away inflection in the word gave every indication that the Voice had just yanked itself back into focus, "I am part of a part—of your mind—to be exact."

"No, you're not. If you were, wouldn't I feel it, know it?"

"On the contrary. Few creatures ever know themselves well enough to know their own minds, let alone another of its parts. You see, the mind is much like a canvas, a painting perhaps, of the sky. In the background, there might be swirling clouds—in the foreground, perhaps an intricacy of trees and grasses—yet most creatures see only the middle-ground of their minds, and miss the rest. Few in fact, ever become fully aware of the intricacy, the true mystery of things in general, let alone their own mystery or the part it might play in the big puzzle."

Unable to think of himself as existing in parts, or being a part of any puzzle, the Creature stood firm on the only idea he really heard in full, and he all but barked, "My mind is no picture with trees or clouds, and far from mysterious. It's practically empty. You said so yourself! Or have you already forgotten?"

"No," said the Voice. "I haven't forgotten, and you are one dangerous creature."

"Dangerous?" The Creature's eyes instinctively narrowed as if by almost closing them, he could prevent this Voice from seeing any more of him.

"Yes. Dangerous. You questioned the status quo—the sameness."

"Only once," the Creature protested defensively, hating to have his villainy brought to light by this invisible know-it-all, "I questioned one time."

"The Vine never allows that to happen more than once. Questioning a Vine's superiority sets a bad example."

Deeply bitter sarcasm laced a laugh which the Creature heard, like the scraping of claws on raw bone. He wondered if there wasn't something dangerous about the Voice itself, and even, about this place.

"Tell me," the Voice prodded in its joshing casual way, "how do you suppose you got into this glen of the Sleeping Pool?"

"The dogs granted me passage. They bayed."

"Territorial little devils, aren't they?" Again, there was the laugh, but gleeful this time. "They protect their domain, and that's as it should be. They're willing to have you here because they sense you mean them no harm. That sensing is called *instinct, intuition.* It's an age-old survival skill, and every creature uses it to one degree or another.

"But saying that you entered simply because you were granted passage—and to overlook the fact that you entered after your own intuition told you it was safe—is to deny the special nature of the glen, to neglect seeing through your mind, the foreground and background of the whole picture. Moreover—"

Rude or not, the Creature ducked his head, indicating by a firm silence that the conversation was over. He didn't want to hear another murky explanation of anything, and the more the Voice told him, the less he liked it, or its ideas.

U nder the spreading canopy of night,
        the wild nocturnal beings having gone silent and the misty blue moon hovering much too huge, as if she had drifted outward from her center, in hopes of covering more than she revealed—he didn't know what he believed—or who.
At least the Vine had been dependable. One always knew what to expect. Not so with the Voice, a hotbed of random and dangerous ideas. He was working hard to squelch his curiosity, not invited to roam at will. He was too tired for any more trouble, and in his weary vision, the little glen
went fuzzy as the misted moon. Conversation,
he decided, eyeing the welcome arms of
sleep, was terribly exhausting.
This conversation—*which*
actually allowed questions—
had been more exhausting
than an entire quest.
        He suspected
a trick behind that,
and a nasty notion
perched on
the rim of his
drowsing thoughts:
Might the Voice

have been honest, at least in part? If so, which part? The Voice ertainly was *not* part of his mind.

Whatever the Voice thought didn't matter, because once he found out where the invisible ego-mad intelligence was really hiding unfettered thought and freedom, he would then rid himself of the Voice and bar his every thought against it permanently.

Just as he'd missed at first the hard-packed earth of the compound, he missed tonight the various beds of grasses. His resting place this night consisted of springy moss, and was bordered by dandelions and fresh clover. He snacked on both, feeling the glen reaching out to him, trying to draw him closer. He could feel the Vine somewhere trying to do the same, but then he was quickly asleep, and more or less out of harm's way.

The Voice listened to the birds calling anxious warnings across the pool. It had already started and far too soon. Feeling the tug on its own connection to the Creature as it shifted through time and space, it viewed what lay at the end of that connection not only with continuing awe but some trepidation. Even the best laid plans could go awry.
The rest of the night, the Voice was awake, trying to hatch a fool-proof plan—while the Creature slept, after a fashion, tossing and turning, and sensing the screams of the ancient souls.

No telling—
at least for the Creature—what set off the rattle that night, a rattle that shook the very walls of his flesh from

head to toe, as deep in his forbidden dreams the ancient souls kept shaking the heavy bars of time, and they howled defiantly in his face. He groveled and pleaded for leniency while the Vine snatched up his various parts and hurled them from the highest cliff. He was left to gather them up and reassemble himself, staring ghoul-like at the results: a stained and mis-shapen creature, cowering in the shadows, hiding behind the trees...and he was racing like the wind trying to find that inner door and rip it off its hinges.

A despairing belief went marching on through the night: The soaring thoughts for which he yearned would not be found in his mind. Continuing nightmares ignited by his despair followed fast, burying him deep inside Vine walls. The task of defining himself and the freedom he sought hovered like a punishment coming due. The task prowled, a great scaly beaste
stealing closer and closer,
until he could see its teeth.

Three times the next morning—on the odd chance that freedom *was in the pool*—he measured the distance, shut his eyes tight and ran straight for it. Three times, just as he got there, the thought of seeing his own empty eyes staring back slammed him to the ground and left him a quivering, trembling fool.

Sunlight baked his bones, but nothing cut the chill of a dozen more failures. Desperate for distraction, he got busy with the Chore of his Chastising List, making sure to include the words, *I am ugly, I am empty, and useless.*

Then he started to compose a Defining List, but after a few false starts, threw down the stick. *Ugly, empty and useless* did not seem to be what the Voice would want to hear.

Partly to let the Voice think him still occupied and unavailable for comment, he seised the stick and hastily began doing what he'd yearned to do for far too long, sketching in the dirt, in his rigid careful way, his compartments for this and that.

Birds which had called sharply last night descended, perching on nearby branches, their bright little eyes fastened on his every move. They broke into song, trilling at him, the message he had yet to decipher. Embarrassed, he ignored them, finding with each shift he made in placing any compartment, *the Vine* seemed to be controlling his hands and moving the compartment right back.

With a start, he realised what the compartments actually meant to him. They represented a scrap of earth he might someday call his own. They were his personal designs for a safe place to be, the dream of a future abode...they were roots.

An unexpected flash of anger overrode his surprise at seeing how long a reach the Vine had that it could invade a desire so secret that, until just now, he hadn't even admitted it to himself.

A sense of violation flickered. His ears turned red as the ancient ones knelt down beside him, peering at the sketch on the ground. A withered and transparent hand shot out touching a compartment Vine-wisdom had seen fit to re-arrange. Dirt flew, as the compartment was re-sketched—resolutely—in its original position. There had never been a word spoken aloud by any of the old ones, but their silent *Ah,* of satisfaction rang in his ears, sharp as a bell honed with age.

The old ones had chosen the wrong time to help him.

"Get out" he heard himself shouting. "Get out and leave me alone! They are my compartments; I can do this by myself!"

Stricken, the old souls rushed to be gone from his side. The vehemence in his words left him quaking. As he worked in the sunshine trying to overcome his stilted drawing style, each new thought that he thought caught him despairing: Would the Vine have sneered at his stupidity or punished him for it?

The Voice had said a creature's thoughts were his own. If true, that one statement turned his whole world into a false fabrication, woven by the Vine. For the Vine which had violated his secret innermost dreams taught that creatures had no rights to anything, much less thoughts they did not know how to think. If the Vine had lied about this, then what exactly *could he* be sure of? He could forget secret desires for a scrap of earth. The lie left him no true place to stand, not with any certainty. A flame of doubt ignited and trembled bravely. The turmoil of Voice-versus-Vine, heightened.

He attacked his fingernails, trying to decide whether to take matters in to his own hands and drown himself in the pool. He had no idea exactly what drowning entailed—the thought, like too much else, had just flitted through his head. He guessed he could remain on his knees and let the Fates do what they would with him. But who could trust the Fates to do their job if the Voice and the Vine were already suspect? So in the end, he simply went on as he had been.

Except...*he fervently wanted to have, instead of his own cramped strokes, the daring, free-sweeping hand, of whoever had once carved in that Alabaster Cave!*

His desire declared, the birds shrieked, scattering to the sky, stirring up dust, and the waters of the Sleeping Pool. In the quiet that followed, one couldn't actually say that anything at all, hovered near the Creature. It had no tangible side to it and he was aware of its presence only by an amazing new feeling that flowed into him, a feeling filled with the kindness he so mistrusted.

His hands merely accepted without question—nor was he being given a choice—what he instinctively knew were rare pieces of wood weathered by the ages. His hands accepted too, the knife glinting brightly in the rays of the sun.

Time wore on, a frivolity for the eye of his mind, allowing full reign to an imagination which he was glad to borrow...while the hands rushing to make each gliding stroke of the knife were his own. The designs being carved in the wood finished up as flawless, the style definitely that of the tiny carved figures he'd discovered in the Alabaster Cave...in a rush to uncover the mystery of that he felt himself all but welded to the body and soul, of a being, infinitely creative. An awful anguish surrounded that being and penetrated him. He accepted every bit of it sanctioned every searing emotion, because for any creature to be torn away—and he sensed that had been the case—from the creativity so uniquely its inner character, suddenly seemed an act of criminal magnitude.

Touched by the Creature's insight, the agony of the unseen presence began to flow from its spirit. The pain when it started, accompanied the sound of bones cracking. The creature's hands, when he looked down, were twisted at the oddest angles and skeletal shards of bone protruded from the flesh. He couldn't get away from the pain. Couldn't get away from the strange presence, either...as it moved him to the side of the Sleeping Pool, and once he was there, both of his hands were plunged deeply, into the water.

He could not, would not, look in. Tears streamed on his cheeks and ran down his body. What kind of nightmare was this, he thought, when his hands looked and felt as if they'd been broken? Beyond all the chaos of his thinking today, he resolved one thing: *He would never trust kindness, again.*

Around each hand, the water coursed in gentle circles, and he found that even as the pain carved its way from wrist to finger, the power of the watery revolving circles grew even stronger, erasing that pain from his mind.

When he finally thought to pull his hands out of the Sleeping Pool, no sign of a bone showed through the flesh, both wrists were completely healed. The unseen presence was already gone; he'd been left with none of the wood, no carvings and no knife, just the weirdest insatiable appetite for *looking*.

Instantly he spotted them, miniscule insects, obviously

meeting and speaking and carrying on in serious yet jaunty ways, free of all doubt as they went about their crafts. How deftly they lifted in pincer and beak, apparently useful bits of this and that, carrying everything back to the home they were constructing to suit themselves.

Every nuance, every move, caught him marveling at their easy ability to build with no plan in hand. Whereas he, even with endless sketches, would have felt inadequate at the real task of construction. He wondered if the abodes the insects created were grand and soaring to them as the sketches he drew in the dirt were to him? Those tiny beings—their ingenuity and strength of purpose, their fearless certainty—had just left another dent in his Vine-taught notions of lesser beings.

From the dandelion beds, site of yesterday's evening snack, a Will-O-the-Wisp floated up to a friendly patch of blue sky. The Creature stared at it, hearing the sighs of the old ones joining his own at the sight of that Wisp, in unfettered flight.

The Voice wasn't watching insects or gypsy Will-O-the-Wisps. The other seemingly innocent sight it had observed, a long-lost soul carrying an ancient agony, wanting to share its carving skills with a Creature unaware, and much too close...the Voice knew that time had just gone short of supply.

The Creature was crouched on the ground trying to duplicate with the stick drawings as free as the carving he'd done in wood. His skill, however, had vanished and he leapt to his feet in exasperation. "What kind of wretched trick took back the skill that I just found? And am I so obviously stupid and ugly that one glimpse of me is enough to make someone want to break my bones?"

"Don't get in your own way, Creature."

"What?"

"Dumping those obstacles in front of yourself," said the voice, "littering your path until you can't see the path. Isn't that what you're doing by concentrating on the opinions of others instead of your own?"

Scowling, the Creature backed into a long, fat rope of moss that had grown over a tree branch. The moss was intertwined with grape vines studded with bunches of purple fruit. He climbed into the rope's center, and began to pluck grapes, jamming them into his mouth and swinging himself on the rope, dispiritedly, forward and back.

"I keep forgetting," the Voice said, "how innocent you are, of so much of life. It was a very old woodcarver a few minutes ago sharing his skills with you. He refuses to be seen because his hands are crippled and he believes they are ugly. I expect your hands did feel as if they had been broken. You were only feeling what happened to him a long time ago. I gather you wonder what's going on. If you want to know, I'll tell you. If not—"

"What choice do I have?"

"This is the glen of the Sleeping Pool. You could have endless choices."

"Endless? As in freedom? Why don't you show me that freedom and I'll leave?"

"Once you define yourself, define the freedom you seek, you may have a change of heart."

"It's not likely," the Creature retorted, spitting grape seeds to the ground. "This glen is strange. That pool is definitely strange, and you are the most strange of all. I don't see a single reason to stay here. I think you lie. I think there's every chance the Vine may have lied. And Bragnificense—he may be the biggest liar of all with that fantasy about my magnificent mind! Among the three of you, what alternative is there? I'm better off stumbling around on my own!"

"I would have to tell you the same as Bragnificense but you'd never believe it."

You're right. I wouldn't."

"Well," and the Voice gave a sigh of good humour, "you are right to want to find your own truth. And one of these days you will. Meantime, how are your hands?"

The Creature flexed his fingers, giving them a sheepish look.

"Healed," he said, "through the marvels of chicanery, I expect." The Voice sounded more or less truthful. Between the Vine and the Voice, was it only a case of who told the most truth? Or—had he let stupidity—even insanity—start determining his truth?

Having already broken more rules than could be counted on the fingers of both hands and facing the Plague anyway, it seemed important to know just how crazy he'd become in this glen. Further decisions rested on that point—*how crazy was he?*

"How," and he could not cram fruit into his mouth,

fast enough, "did you see the woodcarver when I didn't actually see him at all?"

"There is seeing, and there is *seeing*. Maybe you have to want—*dare*—to see. The old souls come from hard times, and barely a single observour would want to look back at those times. They'd be afraid that if they did—"

"—it would be said, that they were crazy, too?"

"Yes," the Voice mused, "but I suppose anyone might be frightened that, by looking back, they'd see the present, not to mention the future, staring them in the face. And the idea of encountering so much agony would be terrifying. You may be interested to know, Creature, feeling the old spirits' pain is quite normal once you've accessed them."

The Creature thought about that, thought about the moonlight parting. As for accessing anyone, all he'd done was feel exhausted. The next thing he'd known, there he was, facing ancient warriors and the old ones who had secretly followed him. He hadn't noticed the woodcarver's presence, among them. 'I'm telling you," he cried, "I never accessed anybody, and certainly not intentionally!"

'I'm afraid you did," the Voice replied gently. "You did it with your quest. Strength of purpose is a strange and wonderful thing. So is hope. Neither has to be expressed aloud in order to be heard, especially if the waiting ears are receptive. And I hate to tell you this, but there are many more just like the woodcarver. You might in fact, call them an infinity."

"This infinity," the Creature whispered, watching strange

shadows hurry over the Sleeping Pool, "will they all come here?"

"The answer depends." The Voice's pause was thoughtful. "Perhaps if you knew a bit about them—"

The Creature gave an uncertain nod. From the shaded ferns by the pool, a hundred eyes gleamed as the wildlife in the larger shadow of Bragnificense leaned forward to listen.

"Some time ago," the Voice began, "creatures on this planet had begun to come into their evolutionary own. They were naturally outspoken and creative. The Vines at first enjoyed their writings and artistry, but the more outspoken the creativity naturally became, the more it brought to light the Vines' injustice and greed."

The Vines. Well, there it was, not *a Vine,* but *the* Vines. The old ones had said it first and he hadn't believed them. He ground the fruit in his mouth into a paste fine enough, that there was no juice left. He swung in his rope of moss, faster and faster, watching his toes point skyward over the cliffs.

"The Vines were frightened," the Voice was saying, "in an uproar, their supremacy threatened. They insisted upon dictating the content of all writing, every bit of art. Any reluctant creature was ridiculed. If he did not capitulate, the Vines had solutions. Creatures like the woodcarver had their hands broken. As for what the Vines called loud-mouthed orators, their tongues were ripped out. Quite a few very fine artists ended up walking around with no eyes. Still others were purposely driven mad and shunted off, into the bowels of the earth, never to be seen again."

As the Voice spoke, the pool seemed to stir, the lapping

of its waters keeping time with a beating of the Creature's heart, a beating so untamed, so unlike him, that he purposefully steeled himself, as the Voice went on—

"The Vines then took the true die-hards, the quickest and best minds of the time, and subjected them to an intense trickery, wherein all sensory signposts like up and down, darkness and light, were first denied as being true and then denied as being false. The confusion of that was repeated over and over until all that any of those particular creatures had to define his world, was the false and limited sense of time and space offered by the Vines.

"Further, each creature was then isolated, unable to reach out to another, or even reach out to...are you not well, Creature?"

The Creature of Habit held his head over the bushes, and was quietly being sick. He did not answer. The Voice kept on.

"Picture your mind, the reality of the space in your head, tiny as it is, to begin with. When the Vines *decreased that sense of space and time,* little by little until there was none, each mind buckled under the horror of being in effect, crushed absolutely, and in the bargain, that crushing cut every creature off from their connection to yet another part of themselves—"

The Voice had to rise in volume, to be heard over the sound of the Creature's retching. "—they are called the Bereft Ones, these creatures. Nobody speaks of them, except in legend, but their memory is revered in the universe, fiercely remembered, and their return watched for. The watching is a hope one hears, whenever the winds blow, especially when the Great Spirit Winds themselves, begin to howl. You've heard the Great Spirit Winds, haven't you?"

"Yes." The Creature watched the shadows growing longer, and racing backwards now. "Yes, I have. Voice, *how old is that woodcarver?*"

"Very old."

"Like the old creature of the compound?"

"He was older than you thought."

"Voice—*how old are you?*"

"As old as you," the Voice said, with the driest of laughter. "The story isn't over. Are you interested?"

"You must tell me first," the Creature whispered, "how you know all these things? And if you do know so much, prove it to me. Tell me—how does a flower remember from season to season to be a flower?"

"The secret is saved. It resides inside the flower in a special hidden place, and is passed on. It is the same with creatures themselves and with every living thing. He who comes to the mystery of that hidden place, with an open heart and spirit will be able to look inside and see."

The Creature's throat had gone raspy. He could barely get the words out "What else do you know?"

A stillness lay upon the Sleeping Pool. The water lapped gently against all sides...but it made not a sound.

"Everything," the Voice replied softly. "I know everything."

What if those words, both awful and wondrous, were true? He scooped water from the pool and splashed his face. Cool and refreshing the water might be, but it couldn't banish the conflict or confusion that resided inside him, much as that little word free had once decided to do.

Hoping the Voice's story was a made-up story and nothing more, he resumed his former position on the rope of moss. "The old ones who followed me here," he began, "they haven't given me pain as the woodcarver did. What they do to me seems even worse. I wonder if their Vine drove them insane, and so they are tormenting me with their insanity. My question is can the old ones drive me mad right along with them?"

"You are too sane to be mad," the Voice replied mildly. "Might it be that you comfort them? Perhaps they need your nearness to dare express their feelings of great emotional wounding. Where are you going? I'm not finished—"

All he wanted was to find a reprieve from the horror—and to be alone—the only security he knew. Twilight cast a purple gloom over the glen; the Voice's story cast a gloom over his mind. On a rocky and secluded ledge where dead leaves had trapped themselves in a crevice, he flew like one of them into their midst, glad this day was over. Turning his face to the leathery debris, he felt reluctant of their pillowing grace, reluctant of even the hint of kindness. There had been times while the Voice was speaking today when an air of kindness had floated just under its words. It had made him uneasy, suspicious, and even repulsed him, as much as hearing about *the Vines*.

As far from the old ones as he could get, he watched

the treetops rushing rudely into the darkness and saw the first star blink in the sky. Any leaf, dead or alive, that could flutter in the sultry heat, caused him to jump and dodge, and his shadow did the same.

Rays of warmth had heated the ancient waters of the Sleeping Pool to a toothsome degree, saturating the air and the land as never before, almost like some kind of very strong signal. In a hurry to be gone, the sun sped downward over the tips of the trees, and twilight swiftly covered the earth. From the far-off hills, the moon rose above the dark horizon with her face the very same misted blue as the night before as if she might be of the very same mind again. And she kept an eye on what now approached the glen, with hardly a sound.

Busy with its plans, the Voice found none of them adequate. Not when the one tiny spark with barely any faith in himself, stared into a night such as this, unequipped to deal with what was already on its way.

They shuffled through the sweltering layers of night, transparent as the moonbeams cast at their feet. Twenty or more of them pulled each other along by only a raw breath of rage. Their spokesman, a mere few degrees less bereft than they, brought them to a halt before the invisible wall, the same one the Creature of Habit would not have been able to breach without the dogs.

But no sounds of baying granted them passage. And seeing none of that rumoured treasure for which they'd come, the spokesman peered about, his rough and careless gestures trodding directly through the night's fey beauty. *A sense of itself* was all that betrayed the Voice's presence on the other side of the wall, but it was enough.

"Who be ye?' the spokesman cried, "unseen guardian of the Sleeping Pool, or the one who found it?"

Despite expecting their arrival and having just spoken of them to the Creature, actually seeing this lost band known as the Bereft Ones, gave the Voice a jolt. Their tormentors, obviously not satisfied with taking their minds, had relieved them of all worldly goods. Not so much as a tatter covered their tired, transparent flanks; no ornaments dangled upon their chests, no armaments clanked at their sides. There wasn't one sturdy steed to carry them. All they possessed was a desire, secreted behind their eyes.

"Where is it? Why can't we see it?" their spokesman cried. "They say it's been found, so it must be here!"

Even from a distance, the Voice caught identical stark expressions unable to veil the true state of their minds...except to themselves. In view of what they had lost, they stood no chance of seeing the pool. Unflinching, the Voice stood in front of them, buffeted by their pain, but deflecting it to the left, to the right, allowing not a bit of it to pass. For regardless of how much they deserved to see the Sleeping Pool, the Voice, being what it was, could consider only that unsuspecting spark, trying to sleep the night away. Although—and how the Voice loved a challenge— what if there were a compromise, impossible though it might be— one that might connect these oldest of souls as they rightfully should be, to the Creature's quest?

But grumbling had already started, and suspicion festered.

"I'm not as wounded as they are," said the spokesman, gesturing at the others behind him. "I've got the measure of you, my friend. There's been talk of those such as you in the very oldest of legends."

"Then you know what I can do," returned the Voice, most affably; and with utterly no humility. "Harsh as it sounds, in view of what was stolen from you, you'll never see the treasure, but if you can wait for just another few flights of the moon, I promise you the treasure you seek, and more."

The Voice described its plan. It sounded good to everybody, until somebody grumbled that the Voice had based everything on the Creature of Habit, betting that he would come through. He wouldn't, they said, for the Creature was a coward.

"*Coward?*" The Voice savoured the word. "I find that very often *coward* is only another name for warrior-in-waiting."

The grumbling stopped. A bargain was struck. That which the Voice said could be done would be done, and the Voice would do it for them, upon the appointed hour, in that one place astonishingly found, and prized above any other.

The Bereft Ones shuffled away, to assemble those who still waited in the nooks and crannies of Time. Beneath the underbrush, the first signs of energy build-up being produced by the Bereft Ones presence snapped and crackled in the form of ground-lightning.

The Great Spirit winds noticed, and howled happily.

9

Rebellion

By the pre-dawn hours, dark as pitch, the heat and energy
in parts of the glen, had reached a fearsome level. On the
distant horizon, a storm brewed, nervously trying
to keep pace. The Voice and the Great Winds had conversed
in careful unintelligible whispers, as the Creature, eyes closed,
had tried to sleep, cloaked only in sweat the fog of a
ponderous worry—and the need to make up
his mind. *The Vine lied.* All night long, the
thought had galloped about in his head. His whole life had been
tied to Vine walls. He feared
worse revelations than lies might tumble from the darkness,

or that tidal pull from the Sleeping Pool, was yanking him further and further...onto the path of his curiosity. Each time he got control, the tide again swept him under...

Beside him, the old ones slept fitfully too, having invaded his warm ledge of rock, the coolest place in the glen. Periodically during the night, their rantings had sent him over the edge of that rock to land face down in the grass. This time when it happened, he gave up and stayed where he was, half asleep, and at the mercy of the tide...

The Voice's telling of Vine tales had affected the old ones badly. It showed in the way they slept with their arms thrown over their faces, as if to block an unwelcome view. It was evident in the scratches their ghostly fingernails had managed to leave on the rock overnight, scratches that showed in eerie white gouges, whenever the moon slid out from the clouds...seeing those gouges, he slid again with the tide...thinking, wearily...that which Vine had done what to whom, was irrelevant. They were Vines, all of them. If pressed to name a Vine as being the most evil, one need only look at the fate of the Bereft Ones. As for his own Vine, he didn't know what cruelty it might have practised before getting its tendrils around the creatures of the compound.

Maybe his Vine had yet to learn about ripping out tongues and crushing minds. Or perhaps it simply had a different style altogether, preferring uncomplicated bullying and belittling. He thought back—to the mice strung up by their tails in the baking sun—and to the gnat, and the Vine tendril whipping out and coldly tearing off its wings. Why couldn't he just admit it—

156

his Vine had certainly acted in the best Vine-tradition, isolating creatures of the compound, one from the other, so that nobody risked looking to anyone else for support.

Suddenly, he couldn't remember exactly what daily living in the compound, had been like. Surprised at the blur, he could not recall much more than the numbing *sameness,* the struggle of his mind always seeking stimulation and finding none.

The Voice had indicated that crushing a mind was not an instant process. A grotesque question crouched in the dark, and then sprang *out* so fast he could only sit there, in mute horror: How long had his Vine been in the process of decreasing the space of creatures of the compound—shoving them into a mental corner that would eventually become so small, the corner would no longer exist, and their minds, compressed into nothingness, would no longer exist, either—was this *what sameness was all about?*

Not crying created a pain worse than if he were weeping oceans. He had escaped the compound, but how much space remained for the others? He wished he knew more about everything, wished he were smarter and faster on his feet with a thought. And someday when unfettered thought had been found, he would sit down and pry layer after layer, away from the pictures now forming then quickly dissolving in his head. He would study as the Voice had suggested, their foreground and background, and thus be guided.

At the moment, the only guidance he had time for was a hideous feeling at the pit of his stomach that the obscenity lurking in the shadow behind *sameness* would not go away,

by itself.

A groan from the ledge signaled that the old souls had arisen. They'd be after him, sticking to his side like burrs, and silently screaming distractions. Too scared to let anything get in his way, he turned his back to them and heard their first howls of the day.

And then he opened his eyes.

The sight of himself in the dim light of dawn did not make sense. Had he fallen into the eye of a storm last night? Because shooting from his fingers and the tip of his nose and each of ten trembling toes were tiny white forks of lightning.

Moreover, just beyond his toes chilled with the morning dew, something was wrong. The ferns, the foliage, and even the trees themselves, seemed headed in a downward direction, either drooping or slouching, or simply having flung themselves on the ground in a state of seeming exhaustion.

He couldn't imagine what might have happened in the night to cause that. Stumbling to his feet, he found that along the sides of his body, the same jagged white forks danced in wizardly abandon. Their brightness contrasted sharply to the pallid horizon, so weary that it had refused the sunrise.

Various patches of greenery seemed not at all affected, but stood perfectly upright, and a small bit of wildlife observed him in fearful expectancy, as if he might break out in rumbles of thunder. For he seemed to mirror the actions of the threatening heavens. And then, staring straight into the middle ground of the picture and completely forgetting the foreground and background, he thought he understood: His condition, provided it wasn't a punishment, and it certainly did not feel like one, was only the result of impending violent weather. This made the little lighting forks, especially at the ends of his fingers, seem much less threatening...and in full view of the crackling light in that far-away sky, he raised his arm and pointed five fingers directly ahead of him.

At the heart of the heat lightning, as if sensing something of interest, too many of those forks perked up, looking around for

the source...but he was entranced by something he'd never thought of before, reveling in the magnificent *power* right there in his fingers, causing that distanced energy to respond, to come shooting straight at him—

"Down! Down! Face on the ground, DO IT NOW!" the Voice was bellowing, as all that lovely, and suddenly *deadly* force, went zooming right over his head and cracked the trunk of a tree a mere few inches away. Amidst the acrid smell of burning wood, the Voice refused to let him get up, insisting that he press his body most firmly into the ground, and stay there. After a time, while his heart beat wildly, and sweat ran down his nose, the Creature could feel most of the humming and zinging draining from him, draining back into the earth.

"We do not," said the Voice, "play with our energy. Need I say more?"

When the Creature insisted, the Voice informed him that the draining of energy and the lightning display on his body came from energy build-up, the result of too many roiling vibrations converging upon the glen all at once. The Creature asked what caused the vibrations, but the Voice seemed very busy, with no extra time for questions.

Wood smoke burned the Creature's eyes for the rest of that muggy morning while he pondered the Voice's explanation with mistrust, and the lightning streaked across the mottled sky. He found the surging power of those vibrations which had made him feel so masterful, so much in control, and even...a little... invincible, was a hard thing to let go of.

"Voice," he said, as the humidity crawled steadily upward, and the storm continued to hover on the horizon like an angry neighbor, "where do I go to get safe power?"

"There probably isn't any, but what do you want it for? What mountains are you moving? Whose actions are you guiding? Yours, or those of another?"

"Does it have to be that complicated?"

"Power is like that. If you want power over others, choose any group of creatures and exploit them to the fullest. And you can always resort to physical violence."

"Just for power?"

"There are those who can only feel powerful when they're hurting something or someone, weaker and more vulnerable. But one must also consider the power of the warrior—doing battle on behalf of the downtrodden. That sounds good, doesn't it? And maybe it is. As long as the warrior quits the moment, the downtrodden become up trodden; as long as the warrior doesn't start to want power simply for the sake of having it—"

"Can I finish my quest without power?"

"You already have it. Your power comes from inside you. It's called inner strength. One day—not too far in the future—you're going to encounter that strength and find it's much more intoxicating than mere power could ever be. Which is not to say that having to use one's inner strength can't often be bitter. But then, whoever said the strong never weep?"

Me, said the Creature to himself, with swift and unusual fierceness. Today he would be strong on more than one front, carry out his plans in short order, and do it without any weeping. Sensing that the Voice was about to drift away, intent on some murky errand of its own, he called it back.

"Voice," he announced firmly, "I have big plans for today, and then I'll need to speak with you."

"Splendid," said the Voice. "Can you give me a hint?"

"I want to talk about you," was the Creature's crisp reply, "about how you fit into my quest. Unless of course, I discover that you don't. After that, I think we should talk about defining."

The Voice said that it sounded as if he'd already started, but to yell when he was ready, and again it drifted off.

The Creature began immediately, with the Sleeping Pool.

As he failed and failed again to look in, his feet became raw and he turned grouchy, but the grouchiness served a short time later to let him dismiss the old souls, with hardly a tremour to the curt explanation. "You distract me," he told them. "Go away, and stay away."

Off they skittered in their spastic fashion, acting for all the world, as if they had just flung his inner door shut in his face.

He didn't stop to consider where they would go, as he eyed the development of what might be the most wicked storm anyone had seen in awhile. Above the heavy blanket of humidity enveloping the land, thunder began to echo like distant and menacing drum beats. He hated the sound. It summoned visions of the Vine about to have another one of its fits. He couldn't help a whine and a snivel as he covered his ears.

He suddenly realised his actions toward the old ones made him potentially cruel as any Vine. And before he could stop, he was *inside the persona of the Vine itself,* thinking for moments on end as the Vine thought. Sickened he tried to will away the experience, but the blood went sour throughout him; all of it lodging with a mighty pressure in the middle of his forehead.

Thunder heads of ominous dark blue rolled over in the roiling skies, dumping a deluge of rain. Lightning illuminated the ancient ones, huddled together, looking around them for shelter that didn't exist. He saw how easy it was for the grit and mobility they'd displayed on the quest, to be stripped away by the force of the storm, leaving them sodden wrecks of their formerly upright—if fragile—old selves.

One of these days, you'll find your inner strength, the Voice had said. The Creature guessed that it wasn't going to be today. Feeling both rotten and foolish, he tried to call the old ones back, but his words were lost in the storm. Only by frantic waving and forbidden shrieking, did he gain their attention. Avoiding his gaze, they made their way to his side and stayed there. Each time the earth lit up, he shivered harder, wishing there were something that would take the fear from their eyes.

The hammering fist of the storm reminded him of the Vine, the way it kept everything squeezed in the grip of its furry. Why had he never seen it before, the way his whole body always felt constricted by the fear of everything around him?
Fear of moving, fear of not moving fast enough—fear of himself, and any decision he might make, or not make—it wasn't only his empty eyes he was afraid to see in the Sleeping Pool, it was everything about him! He stood up, frantic to try right away, one more time, to look into the pool. But the wild rushing water tore through the glen, sweeping him from his feet.

"Voice," he howled through the raging winds, while the ancient ones trembled beside him, "who rules the storms?"

"Many divergent conditions coming together," the Voice howled back, "but in the end, storms rule themselves. Life is the same. Divergent conditions converge, but in the final analysis, every creature rules himself."

The Creature had found a boulder with a deep overhang, and was hurrying the old ones ahead of him. He had better rule himself today, he thought—and then wondered if he could.

"We do what we can do," the Voice screamed over the din, "and when we can, we'll do better, but when do you plan on *leaving the Vine?*"

Hurt, the Creature wanted to take the Voice and its snide remarks, and drop them all into the Sleeping Pool. Why couldn't everyone just leave him alone, leave him to find the only two things that really mattered in the entire world? Why did life have to be one event after the other, but never the Event for which he was questing? A bolt of lightning licked the air above his head, impressing upon him just how close he had come this morning, *to the end of his life,* except that he could not imagine an end, and the longer he pressed, the more the concept resisted understanding. He was about to stop trying and concentrate on his plan, but the Voice reached over the crackling white light and booming thunder.

"Think now, or think later. No creature was ever measured by what he avoided inspecting, and no quest was ever won without measure."

Just in time, he ducked lower behind the boulder as the furry of the wind whipped around him with tripled force. It sent a collection of debris through the water, and left in its wake a single round stone, trapped between two twigs. He looked away for a second, and when he looked back, the stone was gone, but it had become many circle images, revolving slowly, creating space uninvaded...where he felt he could dare to fall and tumble...tilt head over heels, wheel and dip while suspended in nothing but air...as freely as anything born to fly there. Any sensations he might ever have had of being unable to move slipped away for the moment, along with his nasty attitude.

"Your mind," and the answer made its way through the pounding water, with no trouble at all, "wants to heal. Round is but one symbol for healing. You'll discover there are many more. This healing is the drifting, floating sensation which you just felt, to a small degree. You already know that fear is first the thief of one's mobility, but it's also a circle of grinding emotion—and it digs deep grooves in the mind—grooves so hurtful, so memorable, that some can never be completely banished. Strength however, is stronger than any fear. It flows in a circle too, filling in grooves so gently; one might never know that strength was even there. You therefore perceive as magic what is really the incredible power of the circle, the age-old mystery of it."

"Round," said the Creature, feeling as if he had just come awake. "Like a bird's nest. Like the sun, the moon."

"Now you are learning to make connections. Life, you see, is a circle, too. Unbroken."

"Not by any means? What about death? I don't even know where I heard that word before, because no one in the compound ever discussed death. What is it?"

"A continuation of life," said the Voice.
Awed, the Creature regarded the circles, *"No beginning or end."*

"Exactly right." The Voice itself, sounded awed. "The mystery within a mystery."

Water surged against his feet, where he stood, undecided. Finally, he blurted, "Is there anything more confusing? *No beginning, no end.* I *thought* I understood it, but I guess don't.

Not in relation to life, or to the heavens, either! Does anybody understand it? Do you?"

And the Voice who knew everything, said, "Creature, where is the romance in your soul? At the end of a long day, should there not be a mystery of one sort or another to make us look forward to exploring the morning?"

"Then how do we ever know everything for certain?"

"Where's the fun in that?" the Voice inquired.

"That's what I want," said the Creature with a stubborn glance at the heavens. "Everything."

The storm had begun to let up. The Voice retreated, speculating to itself: The spark seemed almost ready to become a flame. So much to move onto the Creature's path in so short a time, Time being the relative term that it was. If they worked very fast, they would make it. The Creature would have his power, his battle garb, and then some.

Bragnificense bathed in the still-buffeting winds, in a chasm of rainwater which he filled with an armload of flower petals. He scrubbed himself with the aid of a rough tree limb, and sang a bad verse, *One must know how to live, otherwise life drains away through a sieve of morosity..dada, de dumde...* While tossing more petals into his bath, he trilled yet another ditty, something about the charm of round having been found.

He called out to the Creature and got no response.

Oaf, the Creature muttered under his breath, wondering

why just the sight of the monster could make him so awfully fearful. Overhead, a huge blackbird wheeled in endless patterns, listing to one side as it forced itself through the stiff winds. Seising the opportunity of an air current pointed straight at the glen, the blackbird rode it down to a tree and grabbed for a branch. The Voice saw it was missing some feathers and learning to do without them.

"Look." The Creature pointed at the bird, plowing through mud puddles as if dejected, after grooming its lack of plumage.

"Groom what you've got," the Voice said softly.

"He hasn't got much," the Creature observed.

"He's got enough, don't you think." the Voice observed right back, "to get him wherever he's going?"

His face wet with rain, the Creature touched the one black feather he had braided into the hair behind his ear. "I hope so, because maybe I'm the reason for all his missing feathers. I grabbed him when I shouldn't have."

There it was, plain in the disconsolate eyes, the problem the Voice had seen long ago: The Creature saw in himself, very little of what he perceived as good, automatically embracing all that he perceived as bad, as being his fault. Whether or not he achieved the heights of which he dreamed, he would foreverfly fractured, a piecemeal bird in the sky so to speak, the number of fractures remaining, depending on how much of himself he could mend.

Mild drizzles

followed the fading storm.

The Creature left the protection of the boulder, along with the old ones who angrily bobbed and glared, at every step. One thing was certain: It was time he did finally leave the Vine. If the old ones wouldn't leave him alone, he would simply ignore them as he had ignored Bragnificense. Eagerly, he searched for a dry stretch of earth on which to do his daily Chastising List. Once that was out of the way—on to his plan!

Everywhere he went, the rich black mud oozed between his toes. No matter, he thought with amazing calm. The sun would shortly dry the earth. He had never felt so naturally staunch, so in control and determined, peering as he was through the smallest of openings in the greater wall of his fear. If this was how freedom would one day feel, he couldn't wait to get there. He wiggled his toes, hearing the slurp, slurp of the mud. He did not look at the pool. Later, he would try to look into the pool.

The dogs he regarded as fancy, loped by him on their way to the edge of the clearing. They sniffed both ground and air, with curious expressions, acting as if they were pursuing the scent of something they did not like. Deciding to follow suit he sniffed the fresh new air just above the strong odour of the pool, startled to find he'd already grown accustomed to the latter, and almost resented the storm-washed fresher scent.

As he walked, his eyes would not go around the pool, but insisted upon gazing straight at it—not at the water itself, to be sure—but rather they were searching for its *aura* or *spirit,* And the question arose...if the words *aura* and *spirit* and *soul,* and that astonishing number of other words as well, had never been used in the compound, then how was it that he had some sense of them, small though it might be?

Puzzled even further—he noted from an appropriate distance—that the pool did seem to have a Particular spirit. He would, in fact, call it untamed. If the pool was freedom, as the Voice claimed, why would it need an untamed side? Why couldn't it rest politely on its laurels, confident in its nature?

And in the glen of the Sleeping Pool, where it seemed that anything could happen, the pool answered his questions before he had even asked them.

Freedom is always untamed at its heart. Untamed is my rhythm. You have a rhythm too. Find it.

Still prowling and sniffing across the glen, the trailing pack of dogs looked back at him, as if to say, the answers should have been obvious.

On a bit of high open ground where the water had run off more swiftly than in the clearing, he found a relatively drier patch of earth. First he laid out with the sharp point of a rock the compartments for his future abode. One was for stray bits of interesting things such as the feather behind his ear, and perhaps a few stalks of flowers. The other compartment would contain heaping mounds of sweet grasses in case he ever decided it was safe to sleep in one place.

They were all he needed, just the two compartments. He waited defiantly, but there wasn't a hint that the Vine intended to move either one. With the same sharp rock, he hastily scribbled his Chastising List on the same piece of ground. The number of offenses he had committed today alone, took up a good deal of space. At the end of the list he remembered to add, I am ugly, I am worthless. I yelled aloud. And lastly, I am thinking.

Finally, just as the moon was rising, he rubbed the dirt from his hands, studying all those words, seeing that the Vine had named the list incorrectly. It wasn't a Chastising List at all.

What was it?

Back in the glen which felt safer to him than being up there on the hill with the List, his plan awaited. Into both hands he took his new way to think, the one he'd found just before Bragnificense had found him. And he dared to examine the idea behind it discovering that it hid a most interesting outline, containing no bumps or gullies such as impossible or highly unlikely.

It flowed instead, over an easily passable stream, of maybe, might, patently probable, infinitely possible, worthy of investigation, and possibly proven if pondered upon. So he grabbed what had been one of the biggest bumps of the day, eager to see what his new way of thinking could do to it: Ceasing to be. The end of his life. Now there was a really mean notion. What would ceasing-to-be, be like? Nothing. The end.

And with that, the crater forming between his eyes felt like two tree limbs in size, the perfect accompaniment for the darkest of worries which immediately sent his shoulders into a crouch.

But wait

The end, did not fit with no beginning, no end—that lovely concept of a whole circle—*which must mean that he couldn't die!* If one couldn't die—and the Voice had practically said so—then *what was there to worry about?*

As if to crown his stunning, worry-free achievement, the moon appeared out of nowhere with so much enthusiasm, she seemed about to tip from the sky. After a moment of high anxiety she just sailed away, trailing light in her wake.

It was at the tip of that light where it touched the earth, that he saw what she had meant him to find. With enormous relief, he stared at the single round stone resting there in the clearing. The stone represented the circles, which in turn represented *no beginning, no end.* Plainly, she had pointed out the stone, to say she agreed with the fact that one could not die!

She could also have meant, of course, that he should go back and study the meaning of the circles, but he was through with the game of nerves, finished with second-guessing himself. Excitement at a fever pitch, he found he couldn't leave off his new way of thinking, or maybe it wouldn't leave him...

It had not escaped his notice that while in the Voice's company, thoughts came far more easily. Might it not be advantageous to search out the Voice's secret? One problem the Voice didn't seem to have was with preconception. It simply considered no limits, tolerated no restraints, and accepted naught but the widest of thought, casually tossing from it pithiaries of astounding—and often annoying—insight. Was it that open-mindedness, which gave it the latitude to think along soaring lines? Did timid creatures like himself, need to be constantly borrowing pre-chewed ideas from the mouths of others? What if questioning established thoughts led one past them and beyond, into *extraordinary thought?* His mind reached out embracing such boldness.

Habit begged to differ,

but the Creature's instincts stood at attention: These were some rather fine thoughts he was thinking. *Wasn't he?* They did seem to be coming from his own head. And turning away from Habit, he poked around until he uncovered more.

Nature, and beings of that realm sprang to mind. If they had no intelligence, how had they managed to form the message he had heard over and over, and been unable to decipher? By that example alone, the Vine stood out as untruthful. Whatever intelligence nature might have, it seemed to him now that she used every drop of it.

As to creatures behind the Vine—without intelligence either—did they have no intelligence, or were they afraid of using it? How often had he seen the young of the compound, so eager at first dawn, and so full of curiosity, quickly learning to be silent, and inspect no subject too closely? Did that mean he might have a drop of intelligence, or was he deluding himself? And how would intelligence ever have found him when up until this journey, only submission to the Vine had kept him occupied... such submission dictated by fear the Creature was slowly realising, was actually the ultimate cessation of thought,

because...

Once a few thoughts,
regarding anything,
were forbidden—
did not all thoughts
eventually
carry with them
the same forbidden flavour?

He tried then, to imagine the kind of life the Vine led, bored beyond boredom, by creatures so silent and empty. Which led him directly to the unheard of and therefore, forbidden questions: *Why was the Vine, so powerful a ruler and done up in all that green finery, content with so little a throne? What was the Vine afraid of?*

Involved as he was becoming, he failed to notice where the next thought was leading, and so he thought it: *Wasn't something missing from the Vine's world?*

Furthermore, if above all else, he wanted freedom and thought—and the Vine was fixated on creatures having neither—then weren't they both in the very same vessel, only headed in different directions? Could something be missing from his own world, too? Well, what else was there—of any importance—that he should want? He simply could not push his mind further on the subject. So—that was as far as he got—with that, until he asked himself if this was as far as he would ever go? Was this the extent of his ability to think—a few measly thoughts—and his treasure was spent? Would he settle for saying that intelligence might exist in everyone else but him? Or had he, the Creature of Habit, bound his mind to a preconceived idea of *his* own that would ultimately doom him to defeat? It seemed more than likely, for while he could see ever so faintly, indications of nature's intelligence, and the barest glimmer of intelligence hovering over other creatures of the compound, he still couldn't see it in himself.

It just wasn't there. Up to his neck and over his head, in

Vine walls that had created his only truths for so long, they had become his truths as well, the Creature tried to shake himself free. And he might never have gotten but a few steps away from the tendrils whipping about his mind in a frenzy, except for what he'd been thinking of that morning: the Vines, slowly, methodically, crushing so many minds—his anger flamed again, and from out of the flames, stepped a small nugget of truth, belonging to anybody who would find it: If creatures could not think intelligently inside their minds, *if their minds were not valuable, then why would the Vines have bothered to destroy them?*

Loud-mouth orators—how had they become orators at all, if they could not think constructively, soaringly? The artists, the woodcarvers; for that matter the flowers, the insects, any soul alive—how could they produce such beauty if they could not think, in order to create the marvels they were producing?

Moonglow lit his way. He dashed up the hillside, coming to a breathless halt before his compartments—and the Chastising List.

"I know what your name should be," he gasped. "You are no mere Chastising List, you are a Humbling List. That's how the Vines keep everyone in line and away from even themselves, by making us believe that we are worth so little we shouldn't even want to associate with ourselves!"

Had he thought them correctly, those words that had flown so swiftly, from his mouth? Did it matter? He could feel every Plague in the universe about to descend upon him.

10

Right Under His Toes

A strange wind whispering an alert to the hillside, gently ruffled the one black feather secured behind his ear. Tiny mice climbed willow branches for a better view, and an interested swarm of gnats regarded him solemnly from behind the bushes.

In the midnight dome of the heavens, stars blinked their amazement as his foot shot out, and the toe of it touched the Chastising List that was no Chastising List at all, but quite specifically, a Humbling one. By a single stroke of that toe, the words *I am ugly, I am worthless, I yelled, I am thinking,* were all gone. Gone from the dirt at least, but how would he ever get them out of his mind?

Rustling and swaying, the underbrush parted, and from it a great scaly tail swung side-to-side and scooped him up, along with the old ones whose presence he'd never once noticed. Their eyes were wider than he'd ever seen them, and they glowed with excitement—equally divided, he guessed, between the mode of transportation, and having just seen the Vine's Chastising List decimated. *Were there six—or seven—of them?* He counted, but couldn't tell, not the way their transparent bodies shifted and darted in the moonlight.

So, there he was, the Creature, his dastardly deed barely cold the ground, and the Plague breathing down his neck, perched high upon the one place he would never have chosen to be stranded.

Why did he loathe this monster so much?

"Care for a ride down to the clearing, Creature?" Bragnificense asked well after the fact, in a bellowing voice that could have shattered a rock the size of a small planet. "Here we go, hang on, I'm afraid my scales are very rough, I never have time buff them enough."

The Creature had never before, had a *ride.* His knees gripped the heaving sides of the beast, his hands sought out the scaly flesh and locked on. What, he wondered, had this loathsome monster done in the Greater Scheme of the Universe, to deserve the mind one could feel at work up there ahead of him—a mind that rhymed every thought it spewed, and good-naturedly too—as if it knew some kind of reassuring, absolute truth to which nobody else was privy? Depression set in. Both knees were knocking. His deed now done and the die cast the deed began to lose the commendable status he'd first attributed to it looking more as the minutes flew by, like the belligerent act of a spiteful creature ignited by the flames of an incoherent and misplaced passion. *Who did he think he was?*

Give it up, he whispered to himself. *Recognise your stupidity, before it's too late!* The old ones—either six or seven— rode the scaly ridge running from the craggy forehead to the tip of Bragnificense's swaying tail, as if they were riding to victory. The Creature thought of the stalwart warriors in the moonlit parting, defeated before that dwindling bonfire...the last struggling flame of their quest, dying before them.

In full view of every Plague in the universe, he got a grip on the great scaly back, stood up tall, and opened his mouth wider than wide. "You can't get me, Vine!" he yelled. "Here I am, with the night wind in my face, higher than your highest wall, and I feel fine, yes I do! And if you think I did a bad thing, destroying your Humbling List, wait til you see the rest of what I do, until I've got all that you never wanted any creature to have!"

Stunned he realised: He hadn't intended to yell. It had just worked out that way. The teeth in his head were being jarred and the scenery jogged, as he lurched up and down, with each of Bragnificense's lumbering steps. He felt unbelievably close to the moon, splendid in her mysterious light. How glorious she was, sailing along beneath the midnight canopy. He had been right to want to go there—and, from his lofty position upon the monster's back, he wanted that more than ever.

Dawn broke. Upon seeing the enormous slumbering body that had lain all night, so close to his own, he went weak all over. In amongst a thousand rough scales, one eye opened slowly. The monster yawned, and grinned.

"Bragnificense," said the Creature, backing away carefully "thank you for the ride last night. It was very nice, but please don't be kind to me again. It makes me suspicious and I don't need the aggravation. I'm too busy with my plan, to handle more aggravation. Since part of my plan includes finding the truth—which I'm truly sick of not hearing—I thought I should begin by telling some truth myself. Maybe it's your tone ringing in my ears, too full of the sound of cracking ice. Maybe it's your flippant flamboyant bragging attitude. Whatever it is, I don't like you, not one bit. Or—I suppose it could be, because you remind me of the Voice. Do you know everything, too?"

The monster heaved itself up from repose, and it took some doing, to get all four legs and the lengthy tail, and huge belly, and the big double chin, all in movable sequence, not to mention the fact that sleep still clung to its brain.

"Do I know everything, too—" Bragnificense repeated, bewildered. "Doesn't everyone?"

Sarcasm didn't seem to fit the monster's nature. Unless it wasn't sarcasm, and in that case...the Creature stayed with his resolve not to second-guess. He worked at a new list, evading every mental Vine whip attempting to tie him to the original Chastising-Humbling one. With a final glance at his efforts, he went searching for the Voice. What he really hoped was to sneak up and find it skulking in physical form, behind some bush, or hiding out in a tree. Alas, it was not to be.

"And how is your morning going?" inquired the Voice, in his ear.

"I seem to be getting there," said the Creature. "If you have a minute, that's all I need. This defining business. I should get at it, since you insist that I've already found freedom, but that I can't have it until I define both it and myself. What I gather is, that when I *do* manage to look into the Sleeping Pool, I will see myself as I really am, no matter how much defining I have, or haven't done." The Creature took a deep breath. "Is that correct, so far?"

"Yes, it is. You do understand," the Voice hastened to say, "that you can look into the pool, and then take forever to define yourself, because it is after all, an undertaking of great moment."

"Not on your life." the Creature returned. "I want what I want, and as soon as possible. Naturally, when I do look into the pool, freedom had better be there."

"Absolutely."

"Specifically, what is this defining all about?"

"If you lived in a perfect world, it might be simple. But you don't, and it isn't. The easiest way I know of, is first to ask yourself if there is any other creature on earth whom you would rather be? Then picture in your mind, what you believe is the ideal creature. Decide if you could willingly exchange yourself for him."

The Creature thought about everyone in the compound. Then he envisioned, as far as he was able, what might be the ideal creature: someone not like him at all.

"No," he said in wonder, but with the strongest of feeling. "I really want to be me. Even with every fault, and what may be a lack of intelligence, provided I *do* lack intelligence, and I'm not so sure, any more."

"Recognising your intelligence is the first move toward defining yourself. Realising that you need to be yourself—no matter what anyone else may want of you—is the second. And third, I've rounded up some Defining Points. Remember, there are no proper answers to any questions. Answers may vary over time. The important thing is that the questions themselves be thought of not as a lesson, or just with your mind. Take them into the heart of yourself, and turn them over as many times as you like. Are you ready? Splendid.

"If a creature's thoughts define him, how many are bounded by fear? Does he think his thoughts based upon the presumption of what everyone else is thinking? Are they based upon his inner strength—or rather, upon his presumed weakness?

"Does he trust himself, and trust the world around him, or does he mistrust himself and *whatever* he runs across? In matters of trust does he look to his instincts and his intuition, and are they up to full working speed?

"Does he give full reign to Curiosity, and follow

where it leads, or does he often deny that it even exists?

"Does he define himself and his world? Or does that defining come from someone else, who thereby owns his every though? Does he even realise what he has given away?

"If a creature's thoughts create his world, and thus decide the amount of light that will shine upon it, then how dark are his darkest nights, how bright his sunrise every morning? Does he have a reservoir of inner strength to deal with those dark nights, and does he even know how to enjoy each sunrise?

"Can he look at his accomplishments as Progress toward the further shore? Or does he see only what he hasn't done, and despair of reaching further?

"If a creature's thoughts determine his actions in every area, then how does he treat others, from the grandest to the smallest, and does he keep them separate in his mind, according to supposed rank? Or does he deal with them and himself as well, from the same two full hands?

"Does he know what it is to be of a giving nature, or must he lock up all that he has, for fear he will never have more?

"How high would he reach to attain a thing which everyone else told him was unattainable? Does he give up, does he give in, how many are the stars in his eyes, and is there romance in his soul?

"How much can he forgive in himself, and in others? And does he on the other hand, sometimes forgive too much, or crave extreme punitive measures?

"Does he always crumple before the demands of

others, or does he dare at times, to be what some would call selfish, and think of himself alone?

"Does he dare to day-dream, and dream and envision, and carry the treasure around in his mind and heart?

"Can he be true at any given moment, to all that he knows he is—whatever it is—and no matter what others may say of him? Has he ever asked himself if he is happy?

"Does he like himself enough to love himself or does he depend upon others to do that for him?

"Can he be easily pushed over the edge, or does he stare the enemy in the eye and keep on fighting until he is done—until the battle is won, the way he wants to win it?

"Is he humble enough or *too humble to exist*—and does he know the difference? *What does humility mean to him?*

"Does he know what a miracle sits inside his own skin, what awesome power he commands inside the mystery of his own brain? Should he one day discover as much and more, would he try to hide it or would he stand tall and celebrate the defining treasure *of his own self?*

"Is he so in tune with all the various parts of himself, so *connected* to them, that he can gaze along that connection and see clear across to his soul? And if perchance he should be that connected, though it go against every other voice in the universe, would he believe it?

"And when his spirit speaks to him through that infinite connection, can he identify its voice and dare to listen? *Has he ever felt himself to be in the presence of his soul?*

"So there you have it Creature. Once you've dealt with defining yourself, you will find that you have already dealt with defining the freedom you seek. Except of course, for this: Once you have freedom, can you stay alert enough to keep it? Or will you grow lazy over time, and give up whatever freedom you've gained? Will you give it away grandly hand over fist, or will you relinquish it, bit-by-bit, in the most innocuous ways?"

The Creature contemplated his chores, and gulped audibly. How much of such radical thinking should he accept?

"Are you aware that you've already answered some of these questions? You cannot be without awe over all that you've already found in yourself. I know that I am in awe of what you've accomplished."

"The trick," said the Creature "will be in believing what I've found. Words—there are questions I need to ask you about them and a hundred other questions as well. I suppose that first; I need to go over all this while it is fresh in my mind. And as for what I said, about looking into the Sleeping Pool—"

"Yes?"

"I was serious, Voice. When I do look into that pool, freedom had better be there. Because if it isn't, I don't care if you are invisible. I swear I will find you and tear you limb from limb."

He knew that he should have asked about the words. Almost the first ones to deal with as he tore into the matter of his defining, were *soul,* and *spirit.* The word *connection* kept cropping up. As for *self,* he wasn't quite sure. And again, the question arose—where did it come from, his familiarity with those words and countless others, however small the familiarity might be? *Brain* being but one exception...

The Voice would know, and he must be sure to ask. One good thing about the Voice just now had been the lessened kindness of tone. While describing each point of defining, it had sounded mostly preoccupied. More than once, he had even caught the faint sound of mathematical equations being muttered under its breath—muttered and rejected. What purpose they might have in the Voice's agenda that day the Creature could not have said. Although a Voice which allowed itself to day-dream, and encouraged that in others, how sane could it be? Yet he was trusting that Voice because he'd made up his mind: This defining thing had to be resolved. He had to find freedom and thought and if this might even *possibly* be the way to do that so be it.

His face went scarlet, because for too many thoughts he'd just been thinking, there was a matching one of those Defining Points, glaring back. So much of his old thinking would need re-thinking. And there was the Vine, stalking about in his mind as if he'd never left it, flailing a Vine-whip for every Defining Point mentioned.

The Voice was wrong, it was not just a matter of leaving the Vine. It was also a matter of Vine tendrils with an awful long reach. And while some fear had disappeared over his journey and more after he had trod upon the Chastising-Humbling List, the major weight of that fear still swung over his head at the end of the Great Grand Truncheon from Hell. Defining Points pointed out the error of such thinking, but the fear kept him from grabbing those points and beating down every Vine wall.

The old ones crowded at his elbow, melding one into the other, making it more impossible than ever to separate them visually, their momentary attentiveness quite as distracting as their usual jerking and railing.

As an aid to faster progress, he scribbled his new list in the dirt beside him: *I will try to believe everything I need to.*

I will look under, over, around and into everything, if I have to, in order to find the unfettered freedom and thought which the Voice calls Endless.

I will try hard not to be scared while I do that, because I must not fail.

I know the most important thing is that I get there, that I finally reach Beyond...

for the most awful second of his life, he looked at himself— less than nothing at all—and his quest so huge, and *so impossible.* Already unnerved, his heart stammered in his chest at the small soft sound behind him. His screams were loud and piercing as he shoved himself to his feet. The shadow wavering above his head was longer than the longest Vine tendril he'd ever seen, and it quickly wound around the shadow of himself, both shadows joining then in a seamless and macabre dance.

Afraid that the Plague had just found him, too confused to stop and think, the same old panic went straight to his throat and lodged there, refusing even the tiniest breath of air.

Repeatedly, he sucked in what should have been air, only to find that there was none. The more he attempted to breathe, the harder it became, until he was staggering this way and that grasping at tall trees for support and pushing them away, for fear they would use up his space. The horror of it would end, because it always had, but there was no saying when.

Until then, he doubted if he could live this way.

The Voice found him where he sat in the shadows, entwined in the dangling rope of moss fallen from a tree limb overhead. He kept looking up at the heavens and then back toward the pool, mumbling numbly at both. Shocked at his condition, the Voice could only pretend uneasily that nothing was amiss.

"Ah-ha," it called out. "I see you are ready for me. There is nothing like a truly down-moment for seising one's supine self and hauling it upward into the light."

"Mggifah," croaked the Creature.

"Exactly," the Voice agreed, no less uneasy than before.

"Let us begin by noting that the end of your quest is at hand. And how did you arrive at this most auspicious moment, you ask? Well, just as any worthy creature might arrive at the same: By dint of arduous struggle, and the inevitability of gradualness. In your case, it's difficult to say which got you the furthest."

After some moments of waiting, there came

not a laugh, nor the venturing of a smile, nor even the twitch of an eyebrow.

"One day," the Voice persisted more loudly, "you may want to ask me what the inevitability of gradualness is, but I can see that you are caught up in the excitement of success, and probably—"

"*Mggifaaaah,*" said the Creature.

"Patience," the Voice told him firmly, but still hoping humour would prevail. "First, let's have a look at the situation. Then we can proceed to the trimmings. And what lovely trimmings they are. But not to digress. Do you recall that small word you have trouble understanding?"

"Self," came the immediate but strangled reply.

"*That's it!*" the Voice boomed. "And what a perfect point of entry, wouldn't you say? The matter of self merely encompasses all that you are, independent of all others. As in, *your entire self.*"

"*Not much.*"

Even without the rasping croak, the answer did little to engender confidence. Since it was the Voice's turn to reply, it did. Its laugh rang out over the shadowy glen while everything in it, listened attentively to the rill and trill of that laugh, so melodic and light. "On the contrary, Creature. You *are* much. As is every blade of grass, every insect, every flower and stick and stone and drop of water and creature of so-called lesser being. There is in fact, *no being* of lesser being."

"None?" The glazed eyes flew open.

"Nary a one. As for you in particular, you are at the mercy

of information from a source that fully intended you would feel precisely as you do, whether *you* want to or not. Which brings us to balm. Something one needs always to have on hand as a barrier against the blitherings and blahs of daily misfortune. Balm is anything with which we soothe a sore foot, a weary eye, or even an aching spirit Balm is *whatever* puts us in touch with *this.*"

So saying, the Voice directed him to pick up a handful of the dirt at his feet. He looked blankly while sifting it through his fingers, and watched its fineness disappear into the air.

"Balm," said the Voice, "comes from taking to one's own self a bit of the earth by examining the face of a flower, watching a bird build its nest and feed its young, or listening to a bullfrog celebrate the end of winter. And staring at the moon is good, as well. Yes. Staring at the moon is definitely a mender of whatever ails us."

In firm but helpless agreement, the Creature nodded.

"And speaking of what ails a creature, sometimes certain emotional inner workings don't work, at least not properly. At which time, one may say of a creature—he is sick to his heart or his soul—or his spirit is at low ebb.

"Heart soul and spirit, you see, are crucial to a creature's inner feelings. His heart being the center of his emotions—his soul, the emotional well from which he draws in times of need, or happiness—and his spirit by which one may glimpse the manifestation of his emotional state.

"Would you not agree that when panic

strikes a creature who mistakenly believes he is less than nothing, his heart, soul and spirit might be in sore need of balm? Of course you would!

"When one is low; panic loves to take advantage. It leads one into tight corners, with seemingly no escape. We are usually right when we think there is no escape, because hard as we look; we certainly can't find it even though it may be staring us in the face. Therefore, let's examine what cause the panic in the first place: To think of yourself as valueless, leaves you afraid of having nothing with which to fight back, which is precisely the way the Vine wants to see you. But is that how you want to see yourself?"

"No," he whispered, nervously twisting a stray leaf between his fingers. He had the look of one who finds himself cornered on the limb of a problem that offers no safe way to alight.

The Voice spotted the leaf, "Why cultivate but one positive leaf, when you can grow a *profusion*? Nothing benefits more from that, than your *self—which includes your heart, soul and spirit—because* with the positive, there is growth, wisdom, hope, and viable life, not merely a hide-bound shell to cart from pillar to post. You've become so hide-bound, what you need is a triple dose of the positive, just to set you firmly on solid ground, where you can recognise the wonder of the Creature you really are. And that's what I'm going to give you."

The Creature of Habit sighed. The Voice sighed, too. "Life's lessons can be hard. When they are untrue in the bargain, one must take the opposite of what one has been taught, the direct opposite, mind you, and turn it up to the light. So that when you sense the panic about to pounce, you must immediately say aloud, as you *visualise yourself* to be no less than the following: *I am great, I am grand and wondrous. I am intelligent, I am upright and honourable, I am a truly magnificent creature.* And of course, you will then hear the Vine laughing out loud, but what do you care, right?

"Because instantly, you will say to yourself as many times as it takes you to believe it, *I can do this, I will do this. I am prepared to do it, I can get through anything, nothing can stop me. I've come through before, and I will come through this time. Nobody else defines me; I am in charge of myself!*

"Whereupon, you must picture yourself—immediately picture yourself—climbing up and out of that deep dark pit, that horrid tight corner, into which you think you have fallen."

So stressed had the Voice sounded while urging the Creature from his corner and pit that even the wildlife looked up in amazement. The Creature himself, looked amazed.

"You know," he said "that just might work."

Encouraged by the positive reaction, the Voice gladly abandoned a bit of its intensity. "The mind, as a rule, will not entertain more than one thought at a time. Nor can it, at least without difficulty, pass more than one message at a time to the body. Ergo, if you think bad, your mind thinks bad and your body feels worse, and works very badly. If you think good, that's what you are likely to get."

A small shred of doubt faded from the Creature's eyes, and he kept twisting that single leaf. He nodded. "Thank you, but that description of me as grand and magnificent is a lie. How is it that a lie benefits me?"

"First, a creature can be whatever he envisions himself to be. Second, think about this: Where did you learn whatever you think you know about yourself—pitiful little though it is?"

"From the Vine."

"Well, there you are. During this quest of yours, have you not learned many things that are, shall we say, just a trifle skewed in comparison with what the Vine has told you? You're going to discover more and your confusion will increase. From now until your next big panic, there is something you must do. I want you to repeat those good points about yourself, over and over, until saying them, thinking them—becomes natural to you. As natural as the Vine never intended them to be, in your eyes.

"Whenever you sense panic lurking, BREATHE, deeply as you can. Study something pleasant—clouds, a star, a dew drop—

contemplate the ridiculous, the funny, the hilarious. Turn not to the ugly experiences you've had, not the hope-less, but the beautiful, the hope-filled.

"Look for once, at the incredible journey you've managed to stick to, when you had never been outside four miserable walls! Then look at the abuse the Vine put you through, and ask yourself, why your panic isn't a *daily* occurrence? Could it be— that in spite of how little you value yourself—you are actually a strong, self-reliant creature who has every good reason to regard himself highly?"

The Creature's mouth had clamped tightly shut; the struggle between two ways of thinking were visible on his face.

"Get to know yourself as you really are, but realise that it's no easy chore. Slow down while you do it. *There's no rush.* Please believe me. These methods work, but they are only temporary aids,
until you come to grips with much larger items. *Re-defining* yourself will help you do that but the one thing that will keep you out of panic's reach is learning to think of yourself in a different light—a stronger light—where it's possible to see the truth."

A hiccup escaped from the down turned mouth.

The Voice felt a twinge at its lie—*There's no rush*—but one lie was better than frightening the Creature with more pressure.

"I already know the answer," the Voice went on, "but who comforted you in the compound when you were forlorn? Did anyone there, even know how to comfort another?"

"No," the Creature replied, suddenly seeing a possible down-side to power. "Do you think having great power makes one forget about anyone else's comfort?"

"And who made the Vine powerful?"

"On looking back now, I know that we did. All of us."

"True. Never feed the monsters. Bragnificense of course, excluded. Or do you really think he is a monster?"

The Creature wanted in the worst way, to say, *Bragnificense is a huge monster! He seems to think that everybody knows everything. What about that, Voice? If it's true, why didn't you tell me? Is it true? Then what about me? Why don't I know everything? What about the creatures of the compound? They certainly don't know everything! What did Bragnificense mean? Was he lying to me?*

Suspicion—darker and meaner and more unrelenting than anything he'd ever known—slithered through his mind, leaving him with a cold, cold look at himself. He realised how much he reminded himself of the Vine.

"Voice," he said with his own voice trembling so badly the words stumbled out, "I did something terrible, not on purpose, but it's having an ugly effect. Somehow or other, I managed for the smallest of seconds, to be inside what I can only call the *persona of* the Vine, thinking the way it thinks. It made me ill. I can't blame all my bad attitude on the Vine, but now I don't seem able at times, to stop my suspicion and meanness. *What have I done to myself?*"

"Probably the best thing you could have done, under the circumstances. Sometimes we have to look into dark places. Otherwise, how will we ever see the enemy for what it really is? Be patient with yourself. Your attitude will shortly adjust and even itself out. Shall I tell you what would have been worse? Everyone tends to take on one or more *shadings,* of their tormentor. It happens unconsciously, simply out of proximity. It's when those shadings are ignored and take root, that life can become unpleasant."

"Voice, how can you turn every stupidity of mine into a positive act?" The Creatures head swam, too full of questions for him to object further. *"Persona, Soul, spirit, instinct, intuition,* and many other words, as well. If I never heard them used in the compound, why are they—some more than others—familiar to me? How do I know how to write, and sketch—not that I do either one, really well—and how do I recognise bits of mathematical formulas, and equations? Where are they coming from?"

"Savings," the Voice replied. "Remember your question about the flower? The answer is the same, but what you just asked about are remembrances from the past, *passed down to you specifically,* in a compressed chain of memory."

Chain.

The Creature immediately pictured a chain made of *links,* bolted firmly to his ankle and stretching across the eons. He scowled, thoughts tumbling through all the Voice threw at him. This was his day to be strong, and he had best try, but the scowl wasn't leaving, nor was the idea of the links. The links pertained to something else the Voice had said, but as he tried to pin it down, the confusion only grew.

"That chain of remembrance," the Voice said, "is a personal one from your direct ancestors. There is another chain as well, and it holds the universal, collective memory. Without even knowing it, everyone has both sets—both chains—of stored memories. You have simply tapped into a few of them."

Unable to decide if he'd done something remarkable or criminal, and still chasing the idea of the links, he was fast becoming agitated. *"Tapped into,* sounds like eavesdropping and spying to me," he cried, "and the Vine taught us, never, never—"

"Regardless of what you were taught, every waking action is not a crime. And no, it is not eavesdropping. Why do you think the memories were stored in the first place? They were always meant to be tapped into, as each successive generation emerged.

"Would it make you feel better to know that there was a time when by a smile flittering over the face, one knew with no question, that a stray observation had triggered such a memory? First the smile would come, than an unfettered feeling—a giddiness of spirit—followed by a yearning to have or become part of, or *actually see in the present*—whatever the stray observation had brought to mind from the long ago past.

"The ancient memory causing that yearning, might be summoned up by the sunlight slanting across the water from horizon to shoreline, or perhaps the sound of some bit of wildlife calling out. It might be evoked by the face of a flower, or the certain angle by which a blade of grass crossed one's path in the moonlight.

"Sights, sounds, and smells too—or even a single word, written or spoken—could trigger ancient remembrances and virtually whisk a creature through one eon to the next, by the strength of those wisps of stored memory."

The Voice paused. "You are wishing that I sounded like a

raving maniac, aren't you? Then you wouldn't even have to wonder about all of this. You could simply dismiss it out of hand.

"Yes." It was all the Creature could say, for having experienced his own small bits, what the Voice described made sense. And he knew that if only he were capable of smiling, he might have recognised more, along the way.

"Creature, oh Creature," and for once, the Voice sounded sad. "Give the fey side of yourself a chance. Take back what is yours."

"I can't. I haven't the faintest idea how to smile."

"We must figure a way for you to learn that. Smiles are a sorry thing to miss out on, not to mention all those ancient memories. A smile—indicating the absence of fear and the acceptance of surroundings—is the first positive emotion a new-born creature shows the world. Smiles come from gut-level; they are instinctual. And they were the first thing the Vines stole, suspecting they were somehow a threat."

The Creature kept turning the leaf in his hand this way and that, staring at it. "Re-experiencing seems so real, Voice, that it's an agony—"

"Except that you weren't actually re-experiencing anything. Rather, you were *experiencing* stored memory, a sort of *déjà vu*. When the Vines took over, they held that *déjà vu* up to creatures as proof of their supposed intelligence being nothing more than the faulty inner working of flawed mental facilities. And that, of course, was the straight-away path to finally claiming that creatures couldn't think at all—that they were pretending to be more than they were."

The dogs were close by, nosing along the tall grasses, sniffing the air. The Creature could hear them panting as they paced near the Sleeping Pool, skirting whenever they had to, the spastic hops and sudden, erratic leaps of the old ones.

"I hate to say it, Voice, but these suspicions will not let go of me. I keep trying to anchor myself, and not be so chaotic in my thinking, making up my mind one minute and changing it the next. Right in the middle of that, I think to myself—alright, the Vine did lie. Then I think—what if you are lying to me, as well? What if things in the compound weren't as bad as I thought they were? What if I'm imagining more cruelty than there ever was, and misery where little or none existed?"

"I know part of you would like very much to believe that."

Before either of them could say anything more, the old ones had charged across the clearing, no longer melding together in his mind, but separating, and becoming individuals, no less transparent than before. And the Creature had been right. There were not six,
but seven of them.

Rage flashed in their eyes, as they ground to a halt and faced him. Each one pointed in that insane, silent way, to his mouth. The seventh was the woodcarver. He was obviously wanting to keep his hands hidden, but his claw-like right hand would not stay out of sight, as it brandished the knife in the Creature's direction.

And now the dogs had started to run.

11

The Seventh Soul

Leaping and shoving at each other, and pointing to their mouths as they closed in, the old ones' intentions were easy to grasp—especially the ancient woodcarver clutching the knife. The only sounds the Creature could make were embarrassing squeaks. He wished that he understood the actual words they kept trying to speak. For the more bewildered he became, the closer they came, and the knife sliced the air under his nose. Even the dogs hesitated in mid-stride when they saw the knife blade shaving the moonlight to bits.

Or did the dogs have something silent to rant about, as well?

The slant of their jaws, the curve and set of their eyes, gave them a natural smiling expression, but they were concentrating on him, intently enough to put holes in his skull. Dripping saliva, they halted before him; a quisical, pleading came into their eyes. Tongues, as if by purpose, were cupped between long pointed teeth,
and hanging below their jaws. They nodded toward the old ones, then tilted their heads at him as if to say, *Can't you please grasp what the old ones are telling you? How can we make it any plainer...?*

The Creature looked from the dogs to the rageful old spirits pointing wildly, at the woodcarver making whip-like motions at their mouths and his own...until he *had* to gaze....into seven gaping holes, where tongues should have been.

"All of you?" he whispered, "the Vines did that to all of you?"

Seeing the expression on Creature's face, the Woodcarver tucked his claw-like hands behind his back and faded once more, into the group of six.

"Look," said the Creature. And he got down on his knees, grabbing for a twig. Hastily, hands shaking, he sketched out two compartments in the dirt "This" he said, trying to gesture appropriately as he spoke "is for me to sleep in. This one is for interesting stuff we find along the way, and this," he said, sketching out a third compartment much larger, "is for the seven of you. When we get where were going, and I promise we will get there—you will always have a safe place. And I will learn to communicate better so that we can talk back and forth, say anything we want to each other. Agreed?"

The old ones skittered off, just ahead of the dogs. They did not look back.

"Do you think they believed me?" he asked the Voice.

"Truth," and the Voice's tone was thoughtful, "they may not be too familiar with hearing it, but I think they are hoping. Do you still wonder if they are insane?"

"I wish," said the Creature, "that I had never thought it. You know, when I first laid eyes on this glen, I liked it but I am finding out terrible things here. Of course, there is this to be said: At least those things are the truth. The old ones have no reason to lie. And if I look closer than I want to, at the Vines, you have no reason to lie about them, either. Voice, I am sorry. I feel so ugly right now, I could crawl under a rock and stay there."

"You'll be more useful to yourself and everybody else if you get up on a rock and let out an intentional bellow every now and then."

"I had a plan," said the Creature, squinting around at the glen, "and I've lost track of it. Where were we?"

The wildlife reflected his distraction. Just under the sound of lapping water, another whole level of more frantic sounds filled in around it—mice scurrying back and forth between their nests and chittering angrily, and much of the other wildlife, conversing in what seemed to be alternating burst of excited chatter-and periods of intense listening.

"Before we get back to what we were doing," the Voice said, trying not to hurry, "this is as good a time as any, to tell you.

A yearning is natural amongst creatures, to discover their roots—and tuned as you are to picking up stored memory, you would shortly have found out, anyway—but neither your long long ago ancestors nor those of any other creature on this planet came from here."

"Well, if they didn't come from here, then where—" but his eyes were already turning toward the far-away heavens.

"You won't see it. It doesn't exist any more. Have you never wondered why you kept looking out at the sky? Your instincts, your intuition, were always trying to tell you."

The Creature of Habit nearly did smile then. He wanted to, remembering the dark and starry nights when a glimpse of the heavens had been all there was, to nourish a small thread of hope, to relieve the sameness of the compound.

"Sometimes," said the Voice, "planets grow sick and die. In the case of your ancestral planet, it had been very healthy, overflowing with inner treasures of untold wealth. Its outer nature was lush and green, surrounded by an atmosphere of breathable, clear air. Freedom and thought existed in endless supply. Creatures and wildlife lived in harmony, side-by-side.

"Creatures had learned from the Sleeping Pool, that when they needed answers, they could find them by looking inside themselves. They were going to need many answers. The wildlife was the first to see it coming, nobody else was paying attention, but the smallest mouse could feel the sickness inside the earth, spreading to the rivers, the oceans, the streams, moving into the topmost soil layers. Then one day, the light changed.

It didn't just grow darker, or become brighter, it took on the most ghastly *tinge,* a sort of pewterish-looking, metallic glow. A short time later—Time being what it is—the planet imploded. That's an explosion which takes place from the inside out—

"Somehow, I know that." the Creature said softly.

"I expect that you do," the Voice returned, and for a moment neither said anything at all.

"This was the nearest planet,'" the Voice went on, "inhabited and ruled by perhaps five Vines, scattered throughout the land. Lucky for you, your instincts and intuition are in excellent shape and they steered you around the Vines as you journeyed. At any rate, after a time—again, Time being what it is—creatures came once more into their evolutionary own. Each successive generation flourished and started tapping into stored memory.

"Startled, the Vines looked up one day to discover an intelligence amongst them that outstripped their own. Life went on. As stored remembrances came to the creatures, images of their lost Sleeping Pool surfaced. They realised how they had come to be here in this new land. Something told them that wherever they were, on their old planet or any other, the same treasure of that pool would somehow exist. Stalwart warriors set out to find it. Those left behind took no notice of the Vines."

As it spoke, the Voice seemed to be trying for a reasonable, level tone.

"The Great Vines did not like being ignored, and simmered with rage. They bided their time, but creatures had something the Vines wanted desperately: Creativity. The beauty of it relieved the sameness surrounding the Vines' world. The Creatures kept hoping the next quest would be successful. Innocently, they continued their maddening oblivion to the Vines' presence.

"The Vines seethed in secrecy, then began planting fears and suspicions freely amongst the creatures. The past had taught them that the answers lay inside themselves, but they started not to believe it.

"Time and again, the warriors returned without the treasure. It was easy then, for the Vines to commence walling in the creatures, thus keeping the beauty of their creativity close. That closeness brought with it the wildlife, because creatures believed they were one with it, that it was part of their spirit.

"The Vines hated the wildlife. It was too free, they said, too unrestricted, too fey in nature. They could not speak its language. So the Vines evicted the wildlife from each compound. Creatures missed the companionship, the link to their place in nature. The more they missed it, the more their creativity took on the belligerent tone of their individual spirits, seeking release.

"The Vines began to dictate the content of all creativity. They told the artists what to draw, the orators what to say, the woodcarvers what to carve, and so on. When creatures would not comply, the Vines forced them in ways I've already explained. Creativity died. Eons came and went. Only the wild things knew any longer, of the Sleeping Pool, for it had become their home. The universe listened helplessly, hearing the faint voices of creatures unable to free themselves of their misery."

"I say all this," and there was a plea in the words, hoping

you will see, not only have creatures always had intelligence, they have had a great deal of it."

"Oh, I do see that now," the Creature said "I just can't keep sight of it, can't keep my belief in it steady in relation to creatures of the compound or especially to myself."

"One day that will change," said the Voice, judging the amount of time flying by. "For now, we should concentrate on—"

The Creature was looking around in amazement. Where had the day gone? The Sleeping Pool already dozed peacefully, and twilight wove itself through a thousand leaves, quietly folding themselves up for the night. He could hear Bragnificense crashing about nearby, searching for a place to sleep.

That, the Creature thought morosely, might be the only thing they had in common: The monster—no doubt for reasons different from his own—very seldom bothered to sleep in the same place twice. And of late, he had seemed extra-picky about choosing a spot.

The moon had not even risen, but the dogs were already baying, interspersing long plaintive notes with short little yips and impatient whines. Yet the glen appeared perfectly normal, nothing untoward going on, except perhaps for his increasing unease and a need to look everywhere at once, inspect every nook and cranny for signs of trouble…

Finally, the Voice reached him.

"We've gotten side-tracked. You seem much better, but if panic strikes while we're talking, be sure to BREATHE and think good thoughts. We need to take a look at the next of your problems and a source of your panic, which happens to be suppressed rage."

"If you say so, but I seldom feel anything like actual rage. The last few days, I admit to having felt very angry, but rage? Violent emotions were always forbidden—what are you doing?"

"Grinding my teeth. Something you may want to avoid," "How does anything invisible grind its teeth?"

"I can do mentally anything you can do physically. Where was I? Oh, yes, Vines don't care much for necessary emotions on the part of others, much less the expression of them. And rage, if denied for too long, can eventually erupt. You might say it leads to vapour-buildup, a condition that's actually more destructive than anger itself—rather like being boiled alive in your own pittooie."

"Pittooie?"

"Pittooie. Spit."

The Creature wrinkled his brow and said the concept was beyond him.

"And you, a warrior-questor! Warriors of old knew the value of a good mouthful of spit." A considerable glee had livened the Voice's tone. "They used to spit on the ground before every battle in the ultimate releasing of rage, a declaring of the battle begun. Very uplifting to the inner spirit. At present there are few warriors left, and spit seems to have built up, everywhere. Which is what I mean by saying—as I do to you, with complete sincerity—you need to consider letting off some vapour."

"I haven't got any. I've let mine out."

"Please keep your eye on the pool. You might find it

208

interesting. Shall we continue?"

"I am not angry," he insisted. "Nor do I have any of this pittooie stuff!" A leaf from the storm, still caught in his hair, quivered as though somebody had struck it a mighty blow.

"Ah, but you do have a simmering misery that roils up into panic."

"Voice, you're contradicting me. Simmering misery is nothing more than anger, and it's ridiculous to think that anger causes my panic because I don't *have* any!"

"Outrage," said the Voice, "isn't ridiculous. You're smart enough to be outraged—quite a natural reaction toward a Vine that has belittled your ability to protect yourself without its guiding hand—and still manages to control your emotional state—well, aren't you?"

"I never thought of it like that."

"You weren't allowed to. Slavery is not for the benefit of the slave. Vines don't become powerful without slaves, and the only way to get slaves is to convince them they're too stupid to exist on their own."

The Creature's left nostril began to wiggle.

"Twitching!" the Voice exclaimed. "A good sign!" Just be sure to keep breathing. Those positive words I asked you to say about yourself, they're a major, very telling point. For if a creature cannot say of himself and mean it—*I am great, grand and intelligent,* then he will surely resent having to say those things of others—especially a Vine. It's much as if he were being required to pay a homage which he himself, is denied. As a result, whether he recognises it or not he becomes angry."

Still breathing—deeply—the Creature's right nostril set to twitching in unison with the left. With what steadiness remained of his vision, he saw rising from the pool the thinnest most fragile wisps of what looked like vapour.

"There it is," the Voice announced as if sighting some extinct beast. "There's your anger. Recognise it and admit that you have a right to it."

"A right to it? I can't!" The Creature felt as if someone had bound him hand and foot against the idea.

"Of course you can't." So softly did the Voice speak that the sound of it might have been traveling from across the eons. "You were trained to be a slave. Are you a slave?"

"No!"

"Do you have a head on your shoulders? Do you feel your strength, feel that mind of yours, working?"

"I don't know that I can feel anything right now except scared. I never once sensed that much anger left inside me, not after I yelled at the Vine, last night—"

"Oh, there's a lot more. You'll need to work on easing it out." The Creature watched the vapour tremble and reach even higher, the heat of his emotion replacing the cool night air. "Why do I feel *so embarrassed and extraordinarily humiliated?*"

Now it was very hot in the glen, and rather a contrast to the pale cool moonlight. Small flying squirrels popped from their nests, and sweltering bats came swarming out of the underbrush, seeking any cool breeze, disturbing Bragnificense and his busily fanning tail.

"Could it be, the Vine cultivated those emotions within you—ineffectual emotions at best, don't you think, when what you need is a strong sense of personal demarcation to protect your territory? A creature who has drawn such a mental line around his space, exudes a warning. Should an enemy then decide to step over that line, a creature would be pressed to chuck his good manners, and fear of being rude. He would most surely, have to confront what he knows to be *the enemy,* by force—"

The Creature had barely learned to open his mouth and yell. Fearing punishment, he had yet to relive the experience and enjoy it fully; afraid if he did he would never stop shaking. Wistfully, he gazed back at the memory of that yell, wondering if it had been his last act of defiance. Even though having to use force had been in the back of his mind as an eventual possibility, the idea of it terrified him.

"Voice, the use of force—is this a hypothetical situation of which you speak, or is there an extreme likelihood—"

"Either way," the Voice said, casually.

"I thought so." The Creature's shoulders hunched and he seemed to be gazing at nothing. "This little glen never looked so good as it did just before you said that."

"We must consider the likelihood. If it isn't the Vine, it will eventually be something else. To defend oneself is part of defining."

"The possibility of violence stirs emotions I didn't even know I had."

"Good," said the Voice. "That means you're thinking, and

a creature who will think before he uses force may wind up thinking of a way to defeat his enemy forcefully without using any force at all. Provided, of course, that circumstances allow him the luxury of time for thought."

"Voice, there are times when to have the Vine between my two hands, to wring its neck, *rip it out of the earth by its roots*—would be so satisfying—and then I think what the Vine would do to me before I ever got the chance. Those are awful thoughts and I apologise, but my emotions don't know which way to go."

"Creature, Creature. Wanting to destroy the Vine is as natural as the hair on your head. Being afraid is just as natural. As for all your in-between feelings, be glad you have them too, for if you did not, you would be as the Vine. Vines always discourage the expression of feelings, but there is no need to apologise for having them. While I have little need for them myself, there are times when I envy you, your newly discovered emotions, and those as yet untapped. For that very reason, in the Great Scheme of the Universe, it was never intended that one such as I, and one such as you, should exist on what has become an almost single plane."

"That last part makes no sense to me. I do not feel us existing *on any single plane.*"

"I know my existence must have come as a shock—"

"Your voice was a shock all right, but I don't accept the possibility that you could be part of my mind. The idea of anything roaming around up here in my head—even though I'm positive you're capable of doing that—well, I would rather walk up to the Vine and ask it to please imprison me, again."

"I fully understand," said the Voice, blithely.

"I do wonder though, as one of the Defining Points describes, if you might be the voice of my spirit, speaking to me through what you call that infinite connection. Are you?"

"While both your spirit and I are invisible," the Voice answered, "I could never, under ordinary conditions, be as overt as your spirit."

The Creature tried to appear nonchalant, wondering if the Voice would slip and reveal its true identity.

"It's only," the Voice continued, "because our relationship took so unique a twist that I have been the least bit overt. Normally, you would never once have known of my presence. There are certain entities in the universe—and I admit with no humility whatever, to being one of them—who cherish their invisibility. It is the ultimate protection for what are considered treasures without price."

"You consider yourself to be a treasure without price?"

"Without reservation."

"You dare to say such a thing about yourself, aloud? But why am I shocked when I already know that you are full of the importance of yourself? Oh, what a confusing day this has turned out to be! How am I supposed to know before I say it what goes against a Defining Point, and what does not?"

"You would do better," the Voice said, "to consider the points, not try to live up to them. As I was saying—it was your stubborn desire to get where you were going, despite the odds against you which told me I had a worthy ally. That, combined with your extreme weakness at the time, by virtue of almost complete exhaustion, was what brought down the wall between us. There we were, I on my side, never bothering with most emotions, and you on your side, trying to be the same. And you mustn't. There are other purposes more to your liking and your talents, such as exploring the romance of the mystery and gathering up the emotions you should have had, all along."

"Wait a minute. Are you deciding for me what I will explore? And for an entity untouched by emotion, you certainly seem attached to this thing you call romance—mystery!"

"By the end of your quest—having decided entirely for yourself what to explore--you'll be far more attached to the romance of mystery than I could ever be. And that is the major difference between us."

Had the Creature of Habit been familiar with the technique, he would have doubled over in laughter and rolled about on the ground. "Voice, are you mad? The major difference between us has nothing to do with emotions. It has to do with the *mind!* Yours is full, mine feels empty. What could be more different than that?"

There was no warning.

No invitation.

One minute the Creature was speaking to the Voice. The next, it was as if some part of himself, or maybe all of himself, crossed into or came to be in that arena, the same as the one in which the Voice itself existed.

There, in that core arena, unidentified to him, and for the smallest sliver of a millisecond only, did he survey the world of the Voice, and marvel at its vast amassed, cumulative wares of knowledge. In fact it might have been said that those wares went on and on, forever. And the Voice threw an idea into that arena, an idea of fabulous convolution—while the funny thing was, the Creature stood watching it grapple with the idea—a thought more easily thought than put into words.

Whereupon from that mysterious place, the Creature reached out and took up from the Voice what it was trying to say. And he discovered himself thinking by himself, yet in unison with the Voice, the two of them going behind the thought searching out and bringing to it all it could possibly hold of balances and counterbalances of thought in increments so old, of one civilisation after another. Until, as in a dream, the thought he'd been thinking fragmented and slipped away...and breathless, he was freed and flung from that arena.

"Voice," he said, and heard his words as if they were submerged below the oceans, lost in a time where he could not follow, "—what was that?"

"Mystery," said the Voice. "Is it not a thing to behold?"

The experience was having a lingering effect. The Creature felt himself scrabbling for purchase on the lip of his own mind. Perplexed, he tried and failed to return and penetrate the space now separate from him. "The name of that place," he asked, hardly daring to breathe "—what was it?"

"Whatever you choose to call it."

"You speak of it as if it, were mine, and it isn't. Why was thinking so easy there?"

The Voice laughed, not in a mean-spirited way, but more in the manner of one who knows a delicious truth.

"You have more than you know," it said, "and that's the way thinking was meant to be—easy."

"I suspect," the Creature cried, "that I have nothing, and you have it all, and thinking has never been that easy for me! Nor will it be again if I thought for a thousand years! What kind of monster and mouse game are you playing here?"

"It's not a game. It's life. I'll tell you more, in a minute—

" The Voice's attention seemed to be divided. The Creature heard calculations being muttered rapidly, and then a curse.

"What was that? Did I hear you curse?"

"You did," said the Voice. "Higher mathematics is not my favourite pastime. Ah well. One can only try and try again."

"If you know everything, why do you need to bother with *trying* to do something? Why don't you just do it?"

"Right you are," returned the Voice, "but these projections are for a small project I've decided to undertake. It's a matter, you see, of estimating the distance between many moving elements— some of which are too far away to be seen—in order to allow for the moving and placement of something else, numbers of hours hence. All without having anything go bump. So to speak. And knowing everything is not the same as predicting hoped-for future events."

"You can do all that?" An unidentifiable black hole of dread opened at the Creatures feet "These objects, how big are they?"

"Bigger than big," said the Voice, and cursed again.

"And is anger one of the few emotions you bother with?"

"One of a possible three." said the Voice. "Humour and a deep concern for you are the other two."

"Please don't bother with any concern for me. It feels too much like kindness and that makes me sick."

"Do you know what real kindness is? Let me put aside these equations for a second and I'll tell you. Real kindness is a natural generosity of spirit. It's a showing of affectionate emotion between or among creatures, a genuine concern for the well-being of another. And before you turn up your nose, consider this: Kindness was an act important enough for the Vines to try very hard to ban it. But what did you think you were doing when you knelt down and drew that third compartment for the old ones? What were you doing when you tried to make them feel as if they would always have a safe place on this miserable Vine-infested planet?"

"I didn't do it intentionally. It just happened."

"It didn't just happen. Your natural instinctive kindness told you it was the thing to do. You may not realise it but you are slowly breaking away from the Vine, returning to your own self."

Behind a wall in the Creature's mind, little Vine whips emitted an awful hissing. He shredded first one fingernail and then another. "I don't think I like the idea of doing anything instinctively! Where's my *control* in all of this?"

"We'll get to that," said the Voice, "and don't gnaw at yourself. What sense does it make to be examining the meaning of kindness when you can't be kind to *you?* In the compound, the Vines knew that if any of you started being kind to each other, you might find solace, which leads to hope, which leads to yearning for betterment, and no telling where *that* could lead. Maybe even to freedom!"

The Creature just kept shaking his head. Branches rattled like broadswords above him, and yet the wind was still. "Why does that word *kindness* keep making me sick?"

"Partly because that's what you felt when the Vine acted nice one minute, and roared the next. You grew to expect a cruelty behind all niceness, and so you are now mistrustful of every kindness. The fact is creatures are social animals who naturally seek social outlets and social interchange. The Vine made you *need the fear you feel,* and even your aversion to kindness, when it cut out of your life those emotional outlets and interchange with other creatures. The Vine made you need more and more of the negative emotions you've always felt—simply because *that's all there was* in the compound. Yes, you can *want* something more, but your chances of sustaining that desire over time will be nil unless you beat down the negative and raise up the positive. And you can't do that. Not until you reduce the Vine to a more realistic stature, and elevate yourself in your own eyes!"

"The more I listen to you, the uglier I feel."

"Of course."

"Why do you say *of course?*"

"Feeling ugly is a negative emotion. A creature leaving the compound without negative emotions would be a miracle. For a creature to turn those emotions into positive ones would be a major miracle. But creatures can be irritatingly resilient, more so than the Vines ever dreamed. Right now, I expect your Vine sees you as being shrunken up in a corner somewhere waiting to be rescued."

"I would sooner walk off a cliff."

"Was that another negative emotion? Wouldn't you rather rise up and howl at the moon, or raise a sword at the Vine in battle?"

"I guess that's what I meant."

"Then learn to say it. If you say it you will come to feel it. If you say it often enough, you will come to believe it. Buck up, Creature. Take heart. You are trying to cram into mere hours what normally takes a lifetime to absorb and sort. Do not stomp yourself into the ground while you absorb and sort. Save a bit of your hide for the Vine, should it ever catch up to you!"

The Voice broke into peals of laughter, and waited for the Creature to find the humour, dark though it might be.

He did not. He was scowling, tracing moonbeams drifting through the glen along with a scrap of forgotten memory that had nagged him since far back on the journey. Being in the world of the Voice had reminded him of the scrap. The longer he dwelt upon it, the deeper the gloom around the moonbeams grew, as if he were doing something forbidden. And he was

"Your quest is nearly over," the Voice prodded, "and you're missing important clues; some that affect the most lasting part of your quest. Aren't you the least bit curious?"

"No. There is so much in front of me; I don't feel

anywhere near finished, or even able to find the clues."

"You've found everything else, so far."

"Voice, what if, when it comes to certain memories and thoughts, one just can' t find them? What if they're hiding?"

"That depends. Some memories like to hide until ones fear of them dies down a little."

"If memories and thoughts can hide, then where is unfettered, endless thought?"

"Same as always. Hiding right behind fear."

The Creature felt what might have been a thwack on the top of his head. But light as it was, he could hardly complain, nor did he give it any special significance.

"I need to find that memory," he said, but the darkness was fighting the moonbeams. The more relentless his pursuit of the small scrap of recollection from far back on his journey, the darker it became in the glen...and the deepening gloom stirred, greedily.

Only one moonbeam making its way into the tall grasses managed to escape the dark, and even grow brighter. The colours in the glen were popping out as if it were daylight revealing a surprising glimpse of the wildlife, a glimpse that startled him with the meaning of *social interchange*.

The wildlife cavorted, playful and curious, seeming so *close* to each other. Their teasing was gentle. Their laughter—and he was certain he heard it—held no cruelty or malice. Sensing his interest, they called out to him. The message was the same as always, and as always, he couldn't make head or tail of it. About to slap himself silly over the continuing failure to decipher messages, he pictured the Vine laughing at the way he'd wasted too much time on self-recrimination and self-loathing when he should have been out there scouting freedom. He pictured the Vine picturing him, shrunken up in a corner and waiting to be rescued.

"Not on your life," he growled. His toes dug in, and training his mind on the missing bit of memory, he stalked it in earnest, tracking it to its lair. Amazingly, that was all it took. It was in fact so very simple, the shadows stealing from the glen and into his head shook themselves angrily, and Vine whips hissed, trying to grab the memory before he could touch it.

He was quicker. As he snatched it away, the same memory he'd once tried to keep from himself by calling it stray rubbish, just as the Vine would have done, expanded and blossomed. It became again, that awesome moment when he had stood unknowingly, within the depths of *self*, swept up in the wonder of how special, how unique, must be the place where that knowing, *his knowing, originated...Place of origin.*

Then the moment was gone, leaving but a sliver of magical possibility, into which he stole like a thief in the night examining a treasure he barely dared to believe might be there: The Voice enjoyed in its arena—which he had to assume was its mind—an abundance of knowledge and a remarkable ease of thought A similarity of some kind, existed between his Place of Origin, and the Voice's arena. And if the word *self* meant one's *complete self*—as he could only assume it did—that included his mind. Could his Place of Origin be his mind?

Despite all previous doubts, might his head, that empty, useless vessel questing over hill and dale in hopes it could for once be filled to the brim, actually have something of value already inside it? And how did one prove, whether or not unseen knowledge and ease of thought existed in an unseen place? He felt sorely tempted to shake his head violently, and see if anything like knowledge fell out on the ground. Giddy with the prospect he dared to do just that. He shook his head until his eyeballs rattled in their sockets. He even searched the ground, but nothing like knowledge had fallen out. Nor could his foolishness be suffered in private, because when he looked up, there was Bragnificense, a luminous grandiosity of presence, leaning down as if from a mountaintop.

"Ho!" Bragnificense bellowed. "I swear, Creature, you have an amazing turn of mind, but you won't find anything like hidden knowledge or thoughts lying around on the ground! Instead of standing on the outside looking in, why don't you try going into yourself and looking about?"

The Creature slapped his hands over his ears, shutting out the loudly informative and humiliating bellows that just kept on coming. It was always something else, he thought, some little method or trick they wanted one to try, those two clever busybodies, the Voice and Bragnificense. Nothing was ever enough for them.

Bragnificense patted the folds of his capacious stomach, and shrugged with good humour, at the Creature's embarrassed and simmering snubs of silence. On the face of the moon, dark clouds fled before freshening winds. The blackbird, asleep in the fork of a tree, blinked angrily in the varying light, and as the Voice surfaced in another flurry of practice calculations, Creature and bird exchanged frowns of annoyance.

Shiftings and rustlings in the underbrush and high in the trees, whispered of more wild things bent on nocturnal pursuits. Black velvet bats flew all but invisibly on choice wisps of air; mice scurried to and fro in the fern beds, and bandit-faced throngs of fancy-tailed marauders down by the trickling stream, fished between the rocks.

The Creature let his mind roam amongst the stars, wondering exactly where it would have been in the sky, that planet from which his long ago ancestors had come. What would it be like to gaze out there and see it, whenever he wished? Roots. How tenacious their pull, on whatever lay so deep inside oneself, that it could not be described. He ached to discover that depth, but knew if he did, they would come sneaking back—the dreams that had always haunted him, filled with large missing pieces he supposed were forever lost—dreams stunningly fearsome enough that he'd never wanted to find their meaning.

The Voice's mathematical formulas grew louder and more convoluted, opening wider and wider that black hole of dread. To escape it, the Creature chose a spot of earth bright with moonbeams, and with a new stick, he wrote out the latest of lessons concerning his magnificence and wonderment, and how nobody else ruled or defined him. All of it was lies. But he wrote until the words danced in the dirt, and his hand developed a cramp. At some point, he remembered to visualise himself as being the epitome of whatever adjective he wrote. He visualised and repeated each word until conceptual prowess ran out of steam, and his throat went dry. Then he started all over again. Much later, a small feeling began to stir that by working at it non-stop for another hundred years or so, he might truly achieve greatness and grandness and magnificence, and be separated once and for all from the Vine.

He had to keep at the writing and visualising, for almost the same energy to which he'd awakened that morning now drove him by the light of the moon. That energy; There was something about it that hemmed him in with the Voice's words, today. Something that underlined their urgency. And knowing it was probably unwise, he was suddenly of a mind to investigate anyway, but the earth under his knees quivered. Just a tiny quiver at first, but then it got stronger.

Co-inciding with the Voice's next volley of calculations, an explosion in the far-away clouds produced abstract pinwheels of coloured lights; so many colours in fact, he didn't know which ones to admire first. And then, he wasn't admiring anything. He just sat there, hearing a reverberating boom echo and re-echo across the universe. The *thud* that followed called back his haunting dreams, except that this time there were no missing pieces. He was *hearing* the pieces, in progressively louder explosions.

12

Ready Or Not...

The old ones hung hack by the Sleeping Pool, shocked at the noise and staring upward, but nothing else happened. The sky didn't change, and nothing fell from it. There was just an amber afterglow left from the last pinwheel of colours, starting to fade from the clouds.

The only explosions currently going on were the ones in the Creature's head, part of the dreams that had materialised again, awful as the very first time he'd ever dreamed them. And having become complete with the original sounds signifying that long ago disaster, it wasn't just what he was *seeing* in his mind's eye, it was a thorough *experiencing*, as the Voice had called it—of that one quick blink—when the planet of his long-ago ancestors and everything on it had been blown to smithereens.

"Remember," said the Voice in his ear, "those old memories you're feeling and seeing and hearing from the past aren't *now*, they were *then*. They can't hurt you."

As if that should settle everything, the Voice drifted off to pursue whatever it was pursuing, leaving him holding fast to a boulder, wondering how he'd been stupid enough to come to the Glen of the Sleeping Pool, and doubly stupid enough to stay.

"Voice!" he howled, "what about these *latest* explosions?"

"They'll soon be over," the voice called back. "Don't worry."

Trembling, the Creature walked down to the stream, waiting for a flock of somber-looking birds on stilt-like legs to complete their evening baths. He then took his own bath, lowering himself into waters grown cold in the night. He counted the fins of the fish swimming past in the midnight waters, counted the legs of the geese paddling over his head,

But even under the water, he kept hearing the disasterous explosions from long ago. The dream-images followed, bits of debris that could have been anything, traveling for a time and settling down in a haze, over a planet which he now knew— thanks to the Voice—was this one.

The old ones stayed by the pool, afraid for once, to move. They kept sight of both the heavens—and him—from the corners of their eyes. They were, he thought probably still hating

227

him for thinking they were insane, and for daring to entertain any notion that the Vines might be only made-up enemies. He started to make his bed on the layers of moss, but decided he couldn't sleep there. The tall grasses looked good tonight and smelled even better, but he couldn't sleep there either.

His veins might have been on fire as fiercely as the blood pumped through them each time he even thought to settle down on anything remotely like a resting place. Presently, he noticed that his ears felt on fire, too. No sound in the glen escaped him. The blackbird sat high in a walnut tree. He heard the scrape of its eyes against far-distant sights. He heard the dogs pawing the earth, sniffing and snuffling and snorting at each inch of ground, *more carefully than ever before.* He sensed their prowling suspicions were valid, but couldn't think what might be arousing them.

To get away from the acutely audible noise, he grabbed for a stick, vowing to practice until he was perfect. The longer he worked in the dark earth, hardly touched by a single moonbeam, the more it seemed he'd gotten the hang of believing himself to be what he was writing and visualising, but the vision always scuttled into a deeper darkness, leaving him as he was leaving him to worry that being unable to complete this one simple task meant creatures of the compound could sit around forever, wondering what was keeping him and the old ones would never have a safe place. All because his promises were the same as he—worthless.

He pictured his failure, the humiliation. If only, he thought, that entrance inside him could be blocked as quickly and firmly, as the gates to altering his view of himself seemed to be.

Then he worried that perhaps he was not worth a brand-new view of himself, and the darkness around him, grinned in agreement.

Into the black shroud of night he stumbled, to an old oak tree, where dead leaves cushioned the earth. The ancient one's sideways glances were a mystery to him as he burrowed in the leathery leaf crumbles. He wondered if he was getting in his own way again, littering his path with too many needless worries. If entitled to his thoughts, then he must be entitled to his worries as well, and he couldn't see how these particular ones could be casually tossed aside.

If he could have bludgeoned himself to sleep, he would have done so, and the sooner the better, sure that possible nightmares couldn't be any worse than staring wide awake into the darkness.

He was wrong.

Shadows flittered,
obscuring, revealing, obscuring again.
And in his slumbering detachment,
something darted this way and that.
It shifted with the light, and hid
in the dark in the stark
terrors of his mind.

From deep in his sleep,
he heard himself whimper
'til the far-off Voice called out,
"It's only one of those
small, harmless things…"

But with another shift in
the light, there came the Vine's
cold rumble, further back
along time: *Mind how you go with
that jug! Tend to my
tendrils, make your mind
blank, the only thing
growing is me!*

The Vine's cold rumble gave way to the flittering shadows, and from them, a dark shape dangled. The Creature struggled, but there he lay, bound up in the web of sleep. True, it was only a memory, and the only kind he had—but it was as fresh as the day it had happened. He couldn't recall just when—though the words were clear, and so was the Vine that had said them.

Think, Creature, and you'll be sorry, let nothing into your head. Don't tarry there in that empty space, stay out of it altogether. If thoughts were allowed, they'd rattle around and the sound of their banging and thumping and knocking and bumping against the walls of your mind would make you insane.

Thoughts don't create sameness, they create differences.

They don't create unity, they separate—and escalate, from one to a hundred and more—and I say to you, Creature, you haven't the time for the grief or the lunacy they'll bring upon you. But even with the benefit of all my wisdom, wouldn't you know it--you've come up with a lunacy doubled! Don't tell me you see those thoughts that you think—that you see them, inside your head. You're flirting with danger, imagining that you can imagine, when imagining doesn't exist. What must we make of you, Creature, of these secrets you keep, so skillfully hidden? What can't be seen in the compound, what's kept from general view, is a danger to all of the others. And believing that you think—and see what you think—is an all-out, blanket invitation to the Great Hairy Humduggers of Lunacy.

Just wait 'til they get you,

you'll hear them first, scratching away as they come—looking
for a place to sit spinning—their silken webs of entrapment!

The Creature couldn't, he wouldn't, look back along time where the Great Hairy Humduggers waited. Stone-like, he lay, wishing to run, yet going nowhere—much like his quest if he tarried—waiting in sleep for the crawlers and creepers to sneak up and get him.

Where there is one, the Vine shouted out, *there's bound to be more than a thousand! Descending upon their silken threads, they'll come like the Plagues with a vengeance!*

The Creature's shriek rent the air, curling the hair of the blackbird. He found his feet and was up and sprinting, fleet as the fleetest forest creature. Only when he'd reached the middle of the glen with the sun astraddle the horizon, did he come to a halt empty of everything he'd recently learned, and emitting a shuddering gasp of horror. "Oh, no! I raised my voice, I shrieked aloud, why can't I stop. I'm doomed!"

"I would have shrieked too," the Voice told him grimly, so apparently eager for the details of his nightmare that nary one calculation could be heard.

"And I'm shamed beyond words not to have told you, but my quest may be based on the worst false premise of all, and that is—" The Creature appeared very much as if he were hauling up from the depths of himself, a dark ugly secret dripping with the slime of the eons, while the Voice waited, trying not to gnash its teeth. "Voice, what if this thinking that I've been going on about and all my grand envisioning is merely insanity? What if, when one thinks in one's mind—and actually sees what one thinks, practically down to the last detail—one is having a fit of lunacy, something that needs to be fixed?

"You see, somehow—I never in all this questing—connected the Vine's warnings to precisely what was going on in my own head. You might say that I honestly overlooked it. And if I overlooked it, then what else haven't I noticed, how false is the concept behind my quest overall, and *how doomed am I?*"

There had been many a creature down through time, who mirrored him where he stood, compressed into nothingness and bereft of hope, there in the new morning light.

"Wait-stop," the Voice said firmly. "Are you saying that you think you're crazy because you think, and see what you think while you're thinking? What did I just say? I'm beginning to sound like you."

"What the Vine told us," and the Creature gazed blankly at the ground, "is that the mind can't possibly have an eye of its own, and anyone who thinks otherwise, is crazy."

"That does sound like the Vine," the Voice agreed.

Undone as the Creature was, he had to wonder how the Voice knew what the Vine sounded like, unless it had been eavesdropping outside the Vine walls at one time or another. Or perhaps—but that possibility, he had firmly shut out of his mind too many times to let it back in.

233

"I never perceived," said the voice, "that your confusion about this went so far. It's my fault. Tell me the rest of the Vine's wisdom on the mind's eye. Refresh my memory."

There *it* was, another suspicion: *Refresh my memory.* The Voice *was admitting* it had been behind the Vine, sometime or other, unless of course, that second possibility had more merit than he wanted it to. The Creature's reaction caused the black feather still braided into his hair to quiver mightily, and much of the leaf debris covering the whole of him went flying.

At his feet, three little bundles of what looked like short spears wandered by, taking their leisure in the morning sunshine. He found their casual attitude especially frustrating, since all the cares of the night before had just waked up again, and added themselves to the morning's fears.

Why, he pondered, if one could not die, and thus had nothing to worry about, was there *still* so much to worry about?

Shoulders scrunched, he rubbed his forehead.

"The Vine told us," he said, "that our heads are all empty, there's nothing inside them and anyone who thinks otherwise is suffering from dangerous thoughts and delusional illusion. One day, the Vine just started thundering on at us." *Do not imagine you see anything in your heads! And if you do, you must tell me so that the problem can be fixed! Seeing inside your head is indicative of looniness and nothing more!"*

The Voice burst out laughing. "And of course, as proof of their lack of intelligence, every creature of the compound ran right up to the Vine and admitted their crime?"

"Nobody said a word."

"Ah," said the Voice. "Well, the key word in the Vine's plotting that day, was *imagine.* If there's one sure way to cut a creature off between his ears, it's to destroy his sense of creativity—which can only come from the ability to imagine. To imagine, to envision in ones mind—to create—is to give the mind
a sense of itself, to allow it to soar. It doesn't matter whether that soaring produces something relatively routine or grand and socially uplifting—or if it turns completely into a full-fledged flight of fancy. What's important is that the mind does get to soar, a creature thereby expresses his own sense of self-worth."

"Creativity." The Creature touched the word very gently with his tongue, rolling it over and over, examining, exploring it as if for the first time. *"Create—imagine,* imagining in ones mind,
using the imagination to *envision…envisioning…vision… thought!"*

And finally, he gave a small squeezed chirp
of satisfaction that echoed back and forth around the little glen and beyond—coming to rest at last inside his head, along with that little word freedom—which gladly moved over and made room for it.

"So much for the Vine's foul play," said the Voice. Well done, Creature."

"You are not angry that I might have deceived you?"

"There was nothing deceptive about your actions," replied Voice. "It was merely your on-going struggle to keep your head in the compound, while the Vine

235

grown shabby with wear, his one and only chosen companion on the journey he couldn't let go of—the journey which had brought him here to the Voice—and he turned that feather round and round in his hand. "As far as unfettered thought and freedom, and those heavens up there, I won't settle for less than all. As to myself, that's another matter. But so what? So what if I'm the uncommon warrior, always fighting myself?"

"I have a suggestion," the Voice said brightly.

The Creature stared at his feather. "I'm sure you do."

"It doesn't have to be that way. Not completely. Just a few nips and tucks in your point of view; a tiny alteration here, a tiny alteration there…"

"Alterations?"

"Of course. Why, even nature herself probably had to make a few. Look around you. Notice how she did it."

The Creature looked. There were the birds, commanding the skies as usual, with their soaring and gliding and dipping.

"Those birds," the Voice said, "probably feared the wind when they first met it. And perhaps that made flying impossible for them. Perhaps they were buffeted right back to nowhere, but once they dared to catch the wind and soar on it, they went safely, much further and faster."

"Yes," the Creature muttered, "I know how much further and faster the birds go, but I'm not a bird. I can only plod along, one foot after the other."

"Ah," said the Voice with great interest. "Have you ever considered skipping?"

"Skipping?"

"It's a fancy sort of stepping. One has to feel like skipping for it to work correctly."

"I doubt that I would ever feel like skipping."

The Voice thought for awhile, and then it said with no little caution: "That would probably mean your inner signal system isn't functioning."

"My what?"

"Inner signal system. The part of you that detects a happiness within you and sends a signal to the rest of yourself, so that you sometimes skip along, or raise a cheer, or clap your hands."

There was no response from the Creature of Habit.

"Lest you doubt me, Creature," said the Voice, "happiness is a viable necessary state of mind. A wonderful condition of mind."

"*Necessary?* I'm almost afraid to ask, but how does one set about achieving such a state of mind?"

Here we go, the Voice thought. Very often, it's done by starting to share with others, getting to know them well enough letting them close enough to know you, so that all parties are reaching out, accepting and understanding each other. Basically, that's where happiness begins."

"Let it begin without me."

"Do I detect the vapours? Are you unhappy?"

"I'm unhappy as you call it, with the way this conversation is going."

"Well, let me ask you this: Once you've gotten your quest completely out of the way, what then? What about you? What about your *self?*"

Self.

There was that word again. The Creature thought he understood it better than before, which wasn't saying much. The part of him which he supposed was self—if he did what the Voice suggested—then wouldn't he lose what little self that he had in the process? Why not just slap a notice on himself, inviting all who wished to take whatever other of his parts they fancied, as well?

For it seemed that the Voice, guilty of the first trespass against him, now suggested a second and a third, and no telling where it would end. He smelled the treachery of what amounted to an all-out dismantling of himself—and right behind it, the unmistakably putrid odour of his own destruction and decay.

"I suppose," said the Voice off-handedly, "that it's bound to happen. One quests triumphantly, conquers new worlds, and one is thereby changed. So there's bound to be a new you, brim-full of new thoughts, ideas, changes—"

"CHANGES?" He looked as if he'd just smelled something more vile than the Sleeping Pool, more vile than his own decay.

"You see," and the Voice ignored the stricken look and the frosty sounds of displeasure, "by giving and accepting new ideas and thoughts, and envisionments and feelings, that new you could only be further enhanced."

Every warning of danger that had passed so obliquely

through the Creature's thoughts ever since meeting the Voice bristled with life. Appalled, his nostrils flared, thus catching a whiff of yet another morsel of Voice-wisdom, coming his way.

"The seasons change, don't they?" the Voice prompted. "And if the seasons change, can it be any different for all creatures?"

"Don't you lump me together with nature!" the Creature cried stubbornly, "or with other creatures, either! I'm not nature, I'm not some other creature, *I'm me!* And I've got enough to do just trying to keep track of myself!"

"Declaring boundaries, are we? Good for you," the Voice applauded with a ringing pleasure. "One day, and sooner than you think, you may want to be you—and part of the broader perspective, as well. Perhaps—soon—you will feel comfortable with both."

Livid, but on the off-chance that the Voice could be right, the Creature of Habit climbed into the rope swing of moss, mulling all suggestions—yet mired in the foulness of the ideas just now laid before him, as if they were innocent and unthreatening. He decided they were neither. The Voice was suggesting that he might want to do and soon—what creatures of the compound didn't ever do: Share their thoughts, hopes, visions, and deepest desires, with each other, provided of course, that they had those things to begin with. And having discovered how ill-equipped he was for anything except being alone, that really eliminated any kind of sharing.

When he pictured himself sharing with the Vine, any such

feelings as the Voice described, he knew the reality of what would entail large helpings of humiliation and punishment.

"It seems," said the Voice, "that each time I see you, there is a leaf in your hand, or you've got the debris of a whole pile of leaves clinging to your person. When *are* you leaving the Vine?"

"They aren't Vine leaves!"

"They are leaves, nonetheless, and you're soaked in the memory of them, and whatever false sense of security they represent. Let it go, Creature. Give yourself room, grant yourself a reprieve!"

For a moment miserably small, the Creature looked into the future and thought he saw himself as the Voice suggested he could someday be—happily skipping along, sharing this and sharing that without a care—and with no fear of rejection or humiliation or punishment...and as quickly as it had appeared, his imagined self vanished. He was left with himself as he was—and with a much keener sense of the grip which the Vine still kept on him.

"Why," he inquired of the Voice, "don't you just tell me to grow up and get over these fears?"

"Wouldn't that be music to the Vine's ears?" And the Voice gave a snort of amusement. "Well, let's see, countless reasons. Let me choose. Oh, since they're handy, I'll give you several. First of all, telling you to grow up and get over your fears would destroy—only joking, Creature—my reputation as the Voice of Wisdom. Second, it would be like jabbing the spear right back into the same old wound. And third, that little phrase presupposes a magic that simply doesn't exist. The only thing that will alter what's already been done to you is your own hard work, whittling away at the Vine, and elevating yourself and that unfortunately takes time."

"How much time?" The Creature stole a glance at the heavens, politely waiting for him to solve his dilemma.

"As long as it takes," the Voice replied. "Which gives you a goal to work toward, and a goal all-but-done."

Having those words from the unseen Voice which seemed to regard him and his quest with such confidence, as if neither could tail, took his skepticism by the roots and shook them. Could the success of his quest actually be within a stone's throw away, or was he simply becoming a shade too comfortable, too in-tune with this invisible Voice-fount of intelligence?

And how was he to know for sure?

Backwards and forwards that night, he swung on the moss swing, toes pointed to the moon just beginning her half-way arch overhead. Wisely or unwisely, and fully aware of the possibility of mistake, he gravitated toward the Voice's confidence. It encased him too warmly, suited too exactly the needy self he could not see, for him to turn away just yet.

As for the ancient ones, they had no aversion to confidence either, and he sensed their first inclinations toward smiling. *Smiling, what an odd habit,* he thought, positive that he was as far from it, as were his toes, from the great golden moon.

13

Tic....

Surprised that the old ones had at last found something of interest besides their ranting, their efforts kept his attention. Inclined as they might be to smiling, they were having a rough time, getting the hang of it. The minute a corner of anyone's mouth started upward, the opposite corner drooped downward. This did not stop them. They kept on trying, actually reaching over to help each other.

Wearing a genuine smile, one of the dogs crossed in front of the moss swing, and paused to stare at him. The Creature decided that when viewed close up, smiling appeared to be easy, and he should try it for himself. With his fingers, he forced the corners of his eyes into a slant, and the corners of his mouth as well, just as the old ones were doing. The minute he took his fingers away, his features fell down, and the smile was gone.

After several more attempts, he again studied the features of the dog, and sensed some kind of inner feeling on the part of the animal, which had more to do with the smile than the slant of its eyes or the angle of its mouth. That inner feeling was what showed through and apparently motivated the dog's relaxed and receptive look, and even an aspect of shy charm.

Amazing, thought the Creature. Whatever that inner feeling might be, however, he certainly didn't have it. He saw the old spirits come to the same conclusion, regarding themselves.

Furious, they went back to ranting. The Creature ate more grapes than he should have, and regarded the dog with a frown, as with its nose to the earth, it continued to follow as it had been, the scent of unseen marauders.

At intervals throughout the rest of the night, he pondered the Defining Points. Each time they stumped him, he left his newly chosen bed of lemon grass to practise writing in the dirt, visualising all the while. He reached no stunning level of self-worth that he knew of, but it didn't seem to matter. What did matter, he realised with a start somewhere around dawn, was that he had even dared to try—and that he had kept right on—trying.

The other explosions that night had been too far out in space and so he never heard them. He didn't hear the Voice droning faintly, over its formulas and equations, either. On arising from his lemon grass at daybreak, he attributed the feeling of emotional wellness not to his success of the night before, but to a respite from the Voice's torture.

Still, when the Voice burst upon the dewy dawn, displaying a kind of mad euphoria, and contemplating the skies non-stop, it aroused no more than a half-hearted wince. Relaxed and at ease, he ignored the Voice, not even desperate for it to go away.

At his feet, the pool lay slumbering, and he did keep one eye close above its smooth, mirrored surface, while surmising that a peculiar kind of hope had just made its way into his head. Hope, not simply that he would be able to look into the water today, or start believing what he kept writing in the dirt. This hope seemed to be of a general kind that had left him wrapped in a quiet cocoon, defying the intrusion of anything too disturbing.

An extraordinary event, indeed. And more extraordinary still—he suddenly could not get over the feeling that everything in the universe had now decided to point itself in the direction of the glen of the Sleeping Pool—for what purpose, he could not imagine. There was only the overwhelming impression that some mysterious force was afoot...leading his mind sideways and outward...and he lazed amongst a variety of new thoughts, none of them too taxing...until he came upon one in particular, not knowing what to make of it. In the compound, his fear had been the oddest kind of pseudo-weapon against the Vine. One which had kept him from antagonising the Vine badly enough, to

make it retaliate, by wiping him from the face of the earth.

His fear had always been connected to a frantic hope—which always followed any direct thought of or run-in with—the Vine.

The hope being,

that fear and all its attendant ugliness,

would go away. He began to see how hopeless his hope had been, in the endless round-robin of fear and hope, because if the fear had gone away, there would have been no weapon, pseudo or otherwise, with which to ward off the Vine.

This morning, the hope inside him was surprisingly separate from his fear. It stood alone—for the moment at least—and the effect was one of massive—and comforting—relief. His mind slowed, and he slowed with it. No limb, nor toe, nor finger, seemed capable of exhibiting so much as a twitch.

"Move!" he ordered, but orders didn't work. He tried pleading and cajoling and even a bit of trickery, to force himself up and out of the soothing surround of the glen, back to doing what he had to do. The harder he struggled, the more lethargic he

became. A magic band of colours appeared over the nearby marsh, where white birds stood transfixed, their calls expressing awe at a sight quite breathtaking.

The Creature was only vaguely interested.

He sighed and eyed the scenery around the pool, that strange and fanciful patchwork of opposing views—the scarey gloom of the forest in front of him; a desolate stretch to his left where nothing grew green nor flowered; tangled meadows off to the right lush with deep grass and nesting songbirds; jutting cliffs beyond, that seemed to hang from the edge of the world—and the weirdly wonderful odd tree here and there, sprouting basins of scarlet-tinged blossoms that flowed on languid streams of air.

Lulled by that beauty, he was lulled as well into lending an ear to the calls of hundreds of birds, and the grunts and snorts of other nearby forest dwellers—and listen he did—but move he did not. Time crept forward, as time is inclined to do, nor did he care, for puffy white clouds chased the cobalt blue of the sky and every sunlit sound echoed through the treetops, increasing his lethargy ten-fold.

With amusement, the Voice observed the unmoving Creature who had tended and watered, and tended and watered, and finally journied—every day of his life thus far.

"What are you doing?" the Voice asked.

"I don't know." The Creature stretched himself out, with his eyes now shuttered against the sun. Bragnificense lay sprawled in silver splendour, with his huge toes resting atop the rim of the Sleeping Pool.

"How do you like doing nothing at all, Creature?"

"Why? Am I doing something wrong? I guess I should get up and be productive, shouldn't I?"

"Only if you want to, but there's nothing like laziness to relax the daylights out of you. Unless of course, you feel guilty. And if you feel guilty, let's hope that it passes."

With that, the Voice closed itself off. Thus in the little

glen, just for a bit, no creature-sounds were heard. A lot of resting did take place, however. Resting of the kind which mends a sore soul, a tired mind, a beaten body.

Beyond Creature and Voice and Bragnificense snoring away, even the pool with her beautiful waters and endless bottom, dozed in the warmth of the sun. After awhile, the Voice felt the first full surge of energy pulsing through the earth. Knowing what had caused the surge made the Voice smile. A second surge followed rapidly on the heels of the first, and flowed into the glen with an intensity strong enough to awaken the Creature.

"Sorry to disrupt your leisure," said the Voice.

"What was that?" The Creature yawned, struck by how *enjoyable it was,* to simply be lying there like a lump, being massaged by the earth's tremble. "What do you suppose would cause that tremble to happen? Why does it make my skin tingle? And why is the sky being so dramatic?"

"Oh, great goodness, oh, great gosh," Bragnificense boomed, lumbering to the edge of the glen where he stood at his fullest height gaping at the heavens. "It's enough to make my brain cells slosh!"

Nobody said anything else for awhile, because the sky was too beautiful to talk and admire it at the same time,

but after awhile, the Voice had to admit…

The sky
was indeed
being dramatic,
as the Creature had put it,
changing in colour from
a pale blue to the darkest
of blue, with a splendid infusion of
mauve... and the Voice said, "Probably a
change in the weather."

No sooner had it finished speaking, when a tremendous crashing-scraping noise reverberated across the sky and rumbled downward.

The Creature of Habit came flying up from his leisure, wanting to know if it had been a thunder-rumble in the sky.

"Although," he fretted further, "it sounded more like something being moved about. Too bad we can't go up there and see. I suppose it would be easy if I were a real explorer."

"You mean an explorer certified and verified by a great body of wise creatures?" asked the Voice, but its words were cut off by a great crashing, as if at a distant spot in the universe, something quite huge had ploughed into something else just as huge.

For several blinks of an eye, the heavens quaked.

The Creature dove under a bush, believing by the sounds alone that the heavens had surely split wide-open, but they hadn't. There was only another infusion of colour, actually more frightening than the crashing, for this time it was a bitter shade of pale green that leaked poisonously from the clouds.

"Voice, maybe that activity up there doesn't scare you, but it scares me. While there's still a sky at all, I'd like to finish questing before this planet winds up like the last one."

"Not to worry," said the Voice. "What's a little glitch in the general scheme of things?"

Glitch? The Creature's eyes narrowed and his thoughts shook in his head, as he abandoned his bush and dared to stare up at the sky. The Voice could refer to a sight like that—

as a glitch—and speak of schemes? Schemes to accomplish what? The Voice had to know, and if it wouldn't tell him, then best to get his quest over and done with so that at least he could look forward to ridding himself of the Voice.

It was hard to know where to start.

"Jump right in," the Voice invited.

So with the drama of the heavens varying, and the rumbles and bumps and crashes continuing, the Creature pursued what he hoped would be the culmination of his journey.

"My parts," he said, relieved to be concentrating on anything but the sky, "Those separate parts you speak of. The idea of them sickens me. I can't take comfort in the possibility that there might be unseen things inside me—parts—of which I know nothing."

"Wouldn't that depend on what the parts are, and what they are used for? Because the best part is—no pun intended," and the Voice, warming to its subject lowered itself to a conspiratorial whisper, "I believe that these parts are so wonderful, so wondrous, that they—and you, deserve to be acquainted."

"Acquainted? Wouldn't that mean inner communication and interaction?"

"Just so," said the Voice, soaring with unstructured delight. "And once one has that inner communication and interaction amongst all parts, then meaningful outer exchanges with other creatures, are just a step away. The joy of that—"

"Wait! I can't imagine any part of me talking to another part. As for the joy of talking to other creatures, what do you think we would talk about? Creatures of the compound don't even look at each other, let alone talk! As for joy, well you're really talking about happiness again, and everybody knows that's got to be a myth. I know I've never run into any of this *happiness*—"

"You've never run into a lot of things. That doesn't mean they are myths. And sometimes when a creature finds knowledge, he *likes* to share it."

The Creature was as silent as Bragnificense, who was watching the clouds go from pink, to a blaze of purple.

"So what would you do once you find it," the Voice inquired evenly, "keep all your knowledge to yourself, never have fun with it, frolic with it in the company of others?"

"Well, it never occurred to me that I might need to do anything at all with knowledge, other than simply having it. Is there any point to this *frolicking* with one's knowledge?"

In the heavens, a patch of orange materialised, and then paused to admire its flamboyant brightness. More frustrated by the conversation, than anything the sky was doing, the Voice mumbled, almost to itself, "and this is the same Creature who wondered what the missing element shared by the Vine and himself might be?"

The Creature turned his ear to at least five directions, anxious to capture the words. "What did you say?"

"Sorry, I'm looking for my thread of thought. I think I'm speaking of *joy*. Joy, excitement immeasurable pleasure, pure delight."

"Excitement is not joy. Excitement is understandable; joy is a figment of the imagination. Why don't we stop, this is—"

"You would cut off the best part of the journey?"

"It isn't a journey anymore, it's insanity. What do you think you're doing?"

"Leading you into the center of life, itself."

At that, the glen tilted dangerously in the clutches of a much stronger humming, sending the Creature sliding along the rim of the pool. An astounding number of colours that were being flung about in the skies, reflected off the ripples, and it was all he could do, not to look down at the water splashing about.

"Center of life?" the Creature repeated, confused and wary. "What do you mean? How can you ignore these cataclysmic sky changes, and then dither on about little nubbins of nonsense?"

"There have been no nubbins of nonsense, and we will be coming to the cataclysmic in just a little while."

Seriously considering quitting the Voice immediately, the Creature hesitated for one last second, because one last question had hurried into his mind, and insisted on being answered.

"Bragnificense as much as told me, that everybody knows everything. I don't see how that can be true—"

"Without a doubt," said the Voice, eagerly. "For the chain of memory is a convenience of storage that protects unlimited knowledge, and when one knows how to reach inside oneself, past that place of ordinary knowledge—"

The Creature was turning pale, as the sky became a roiling blaze of red. From beneath the furious clouds there issued a series of explosions so loud that he could not hear himself think. The glen lit up bright as day. Unwavering, the Voice could and did pursue its avalanche of thought.

"What one finds in that chain, why the music alone—so poignant, so stirring—is enough to make stone weep. The art, the ideas, the literature and languages; the challenges faced, the battles won and lost; the wretched and the mighty, full of angst and agony; an unflinching evidence of accomplishment and failure, cruelty and kindness, and the amazing depths of spirit…

"Think of the creatures down through time, passing knowledge to you. What will you pass down to those who spring from you? A proud heritage or the nonsense stuffed into you by some ill-minded Vine? Which reminds me: It seems you learned while you were with the Vine, to treat yourself very badly. You also learned to stumble. When one stumbles, saying *Oops* is better than lashing ones self into a frenzy. *Oops* lightens the load, makes shame and embarrassment and humiliation much less necessary to your existence."

For a minute, the Creature's ears had perked up. Now all he heard was the word *Oops*. "We weren't allowed to use words like *Oops* in the compound," he howled. "*Oops* is like shrugging your shoulders, not taking full responsibility for your crime!"

"Again, every waking action is not a crime. Remember what I told you about direct opposites? Oops works because it is silly, not serious. Try it," the Voice invited.

"Oops," the Creature whispered with a blank look.

"I forgot. You don't know anything about humour, do you? Humour," the Voice persisted, "the funny side of life."

"I didn't know there was one."

"Practice your *Oops,*" said the Voice. "And add twenty shrugs, and it may come to you."

For a time, he did, but no humour showed up. He felt certain that the Voice was no more a part of him, than one of those trees. However for the time-being, best to let the Voice have its little delusion, although why it would want that particular one was almost as deep a puzzle as that of the unending heavens.

"I suppose," he ventured, "that you could tell me more about my other parts."

"Ah, yes," said the Voice with enthusiasm, "all that lovely, unseen, working equipment! First there is *your mind,* the part of you which thinks, perceives and translates feelings, and what-not. Your mind holds your consciousness too. To thoroughly understand that, will take a little more doing, and we'll get to it shortly. This next bit may frighten you, but there's no need to be frightened. You see, you have another separate part which no creature has ever seen either—and yet it is there—active and necessary. It's where tears come from. It's the seat of emotional well-being, that part of you which absorbs beauty and goodness and is nourished, and then nourishes the self in return.

"I'm talking about that place within, where joy is born, and crowns us with the deepest of feelings, like pleasure and laughter, and compassion and tenderness—because it is only the *soul* of ones self that can reach out to others—with the beauty and passion at which the soul is so good at seeing and hearing and feeling…are you listening at all, Creature, or are you trying to hide?" The Voice thought to itself that the Creature was having a difficult time, with this first phase of its plan. As to what might come after that—

A loud bang, the result of something unseen, but apparently very big, falling from the sky and landing in the forest, had punctuated the Voice's words. Smoke billowed through the glen.

Like the complaint of a disgruntled combatant anxious to end the battle, the Creature's words came out of the smoke, and the gloom of an early-darkening sky. "Of course not. I heard every syllable you uttered, radical as it was. Yes, I heard every word."

"Will you admit that maybe a bit of it could be useful to you?" The Voice sounded less than optimistic.

Grudgingly, the Creature admitted some of it might. Bragnificense who up to this point had been stunned into silence by the sky, began to sing, and then thought better of it. The wildlife had hidden themselves away. The whole of the glen was just waiting, and nobody knew for what.

Then—except for the odd early darkness, the sky returned to normal—no rumblings or crashings happened, and a relative calm descended. The stars came out so brightly, it hurt the eyes.

The Creature, thinking he should definitely refuse to be drawn into further madness, scuttled about, seeking a place of safety. His every good intention and frantic vow, and the Defining Points too, might just as well have blown up in his face, along with the sky which kept threatening to do the same. He couldn't believe the fearsome chaos of the heavens, so unnerving, so unlike nature even at her worst that *somebody* had to be responsible for it.

The possibility wouldn't be still—the Voice was, in all likelihood, that somebody. The mystery of *why* it would do such a thing, was like everything else concerning the Voice, deep, and steeped in danger. The Creature skirted the debris fallen from the skies, and swung on the moss swing for awhile.

The frayed edges where the rope hung over the tree limb, weren't many, maybe three or four. From where he was sitting they couldn't be seen. They might have been caused by the trembles of the earth, rubbing bark against moss, or simply the Creature's constant swinging back and forth. For a time, the fraying would have no effect on anything.

Night entered the glen of the Sleeping Pool, acting determined not to be outdone by any faux-night. The heavens, host to more stars than had ever been seen in the sky, lay swaddled in puffs of midnight cloud, underlined with pale blue edges that turned even more pale each time they drifted too close to the moon.

Fear drove him to sleep. Fear kept him dangling just on the edge of it. The shield he'd sought was almost his: something even apart from all the Voice's unexplained confidence in his quest told him so. He mumbled in his sleep, but did not awaken. Hope sped through his dreams, dead on the heels of Fear. Round and round they went, the two of them, with the Creature of Habit lagging behind, unable to ever catch up.

The Voice was awake. It slid into his dreams and poked him until he rolled over and snorted in depressed acknowledgment.

"Are you still afraid, Creature?" the Voice whispered.

But the Creature stared into the darkness at nothing. "Get away from me." he said. "Our association is at an end."

By the tail-end of his statement, the laughter was already loose, raucous and unruly. He'd expected the Voice's answer, but it had been worth a try. He hadn't come fully awake when the awareness hit—Hope, as he'd known it this morning, was still separate from Fear.

The words ran out of his mouth while the Voice listened. "I think," said the Creature, "that writing in the dirt was what did it. I was looking for only one result, and it seems that there may be others. Does this mean that someday I will believe about myself what I am writing?"

"All that, and more," said the Voice.

"Do you think I could ever live long enough to see beyond those lights in the sky?"

"Sooner than you think. And they'll be as near as the nose on your face."

"I hope I'm ready for that."

"Ah, trust," the Voice chortled. "Such a miraculous thing. You are closer than close now. You know it and I know it."

"Why do you bother?" the Creature asked tiredly.

"Because I have every faith in you," said the Voice. "That's why."

Heartily as the Voice detested the creature-concept of time— that forced-expediency of language, laden with restraints and limitations—in the interest of pursuing its plan, it had forced itself to make allowances for what amounted to a woefully inadequate system of measuring the passage of time.

Nor was that measurement anywhere else in the cosmos, any less doubtful. Which meant, of course, that there was nothing but extreme chance by which to calculate those intricate movements going on far out in the heavens at that very moment. Hence all the colours beginning again, to seep and leak and leech; the noisy bangs and bumps and crashes that would come every so often, at intervals with no pattern or seeming plan.

The Voice smiled. Apparent or not, its patterns and plans, arrived at with no little sweating, had been and were, extensive. What was a little uncertainty in the face of such genius?

The Great Spirit Winds traveled meanwhile, on tender hooks—but silently—watching both ends of the cosmos. In the heavens gone colourfully awry, giant astral bodies shuddered and lurched, fighting a tidal pull that threatened to yank them into the black holes riding unchecked, at their moorings.

Chaos reigned.
The tidal pull
started changing direction...

Suddenly seeing what it had been so determined would be there, the Voice took the time to beam all over again.
The signal came,

carried gentle on the winds, straight to the Voice that stood waiting...

The first phase was done.

Speechless for once, celebratory cheers welled up inside the Voice, causing a bottleneck of genuine joy. With the first phase a success, it meant the second might stand a chance. But just in case the whole thing did go boom, and the universe with it, the Voice decided the Creature of Habit needed
to see this sight of all sights,

and snatched from sleep, he stumbled to the edge of the glen, at first noticing nothing except that undeniable hum surging from the layers of deep blue cloud. On second glance, he saw what marched across the skies.

"Astounding!" he exclaimed in a delighted whisper. "But why are the stars lined up that way?"

"Like warriors," said the Voice admiringly. "They are like warriors returning from battle, don't you think?"

"Have they done battle tonight?"

"I suspect," the Voice replied, "that they have done royal battle."

It seemed to the Creature, that the Voice overflowed with an emotion so strong it might have been tears, and the Voice hadn't listed tears as one of the emotions it bothered with.

He had to ask. "Voice, is something bad going to happen?"

"No, Creature."
"Something good then?"
"Something wondrous,"
said the Voice. "And Voices
cry when something wondrous
happens?"
"Indeed they do.
And Creatures, too."
"Not me, I've decided
never to cry again, if I can
help it." He was staring out
into space, making an effort
to believe that the heavens
had truly calmed down and were
actually more serene, more beautiful
than he'd ever seen them.

"I hate to tell you, Voice,
but judging by the looks of those
heavens, either we are moving further
into the universe or the universe is
coming closer to us."

"You," and the Voice
swallowed hard, "are undoubtedly
right."

"Well, which is it?"

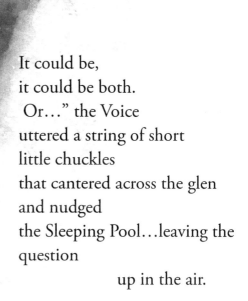

It could be,
it could be both.
 Or…" the Voice
uttered a string of short
little chuckles
that cantered across the glen
and nudged
the Sleeping Pool…leaving the
question
                    up in the air.

And by signal so ancient
it couldn't be told,
time that was not
went
tic-toc.

The second phase was
already begun.

14

Joe

Mouth frozen in an *O* of surprise, the Creature had to hold fast to Bragnificense, for the glen was suddenly up-ended, and a froth of clouds spilled over his feet, spilled over the whole of the clearing. Then Bragnificense was gone and the Voice, too.

Pierced by the light of stars nearby; and stars far away, the heavens rose up around him. The clouds grew thicker; the small band of marching lights had disappeared. There was only the sensation of traveling—just under, or into—the very heavens themselves, and although he didn't want to believe it, of traveling as well into that other part of his mind...

He had never seen a longboat—or for that matter, a boat of

any kind—in his entire life. But as the earth beneath him began cutting through those frothing clouds, the image of a longboat drifted before his eyes...

Of brawny dimensions and a face marked with strain, so real was the helmsman that, as the decks pitched and sea spray drenched him, the water seemed to puddle in pools at the Creature's feet. Indeed, so real was the longboat itself, that he knew inexplicably each sun-bleached plank, each corroded iron fitting holding those oars in place. Just as he knew without knowing at all the faces of those bent over the oars, rowing furiously in silence.

It was a silence as familiar to him as the compound had ever been. So were the tears the oarsmen had left behind in a place he couldn't quite make out. The ripples on the water danced to the dirge of the oars. The helmsman tossed back his head, flinging hair wet with sea-spray away from his eyes. The moment hung in the Creature's mind, not the kind he would ever want to re-visit. For the eyes stared straight ahead, practically devoid of a pupil. They were black as black, with no depth at all, as if the lifebehind them had been burned away.

Fractured images of a dungeon, dark and dank, filled with too many useless thoughts and no hope to speak of, rushed like tides gone astray from the banks of the sea, overflowing the Creature's mind. These unknown creatures were but part of a tattered band, escaped from their captors, and worried that they'd never reach the far-off shore seen dimly through the clouds.

Through the shifting light from the water's reflection,

that shoreline beckoned as if it knew him. He could only hold onto himself, eager to acknowledge it one minute, and the next glad that he hadn't.

The expressions of these creatures sealed in a timeless agony, made him want to shout his desire to come to the aid of every last one. Yet he dare not move, skewered as he was, by a swift knife of pain. The eyes of the helmsman didn't blink. The Creature suddenly knew what it was to be looking through them. Had it only been physical, he might have withstood it, but the pain rushing to meet him bled from no limb nor toe. It was squeezed from him, in waves of emotional hurt that flushed from hiding, more of the same.

The walls that held him burst, soaking him to the skin in an answering anger and all manner of other enragements that went along with them. There must be a way to banish whatever haunted these creatures; he immediately pictured the blood bath their tormentors deserved, feeling certain that he would be willing to give them one. All in the name of retribution.

It didn't seem possible for the cloud-bound heavens to hold all the hurt he spewed. He'd had no idea what empathy was, or how at war it could be with the realisation that followed so close on its heels: *He didn't want to control one single thing except his own freedom and each thought that he thought in his head.*

Rising up from their longboat, they were upon him, smashing their way through his puny battles within, each of those ragged, agonised beings. He saw a single question forming amongst them, and tried to evade it—

for it was but one more message that he could not decipher.

Shamed by their awful need and his own dreadful inadequacy, he was about to turn away. By the next look on their faces, he knew he should run for his life, but something caught in the light just then, between himself and them, something akin to the hint of an invisible wall, *being created by the Voice.* He knew he was safe behind that wall, safe enough to halt long enough to intuit their question:

Would he, they wanted to know, *stand and be counted, alongside them?*

The Creature's reply sprang as much from the gut of his own helpless railing as theirs. Only when already given, did he pause to consider the implications: *How soon must this promise be kept?*

Across the sky, a shuddering rumble ended in an earsplitting explosion. It lifted him off his feet and slammed him head-first into a fallen tree. Stunned, he lay watching the helmsman and his tattered oarsmen slip back through the folds of time…while he seemed to slip away, too.

He awakened to layers of gritty pastel cloud lying close to the ground, barely disguising a fire burning behind the glen. From a prone position, his nose pressed into rough tree bark, he watched the tip of Bragnificense's tail bobbing in purple haze, and he hugged to his breast a solitary nubbin of knowledge: *Creatures couldn't die.* How wonderful, he thought, to still be here, alive and breathing.

How lovely to know, as the Voice and the moon had told him, that he always would. But that warrior and his renegade band, *what had happened to them?*

In a panic, he leapt to his feet, pushing through low-lying cloud banks, seeking the Voice...feeling it already watching him, over computations hanging thicker than smoke in the air...smoke far more substantial than the silent oarsmen now vanished from before his eyes.

"Voice," he cried, "what happened back there, was it real?"

Oh, it was real alright, the Voice thought to itself. The question being, given that miserable system of measurements, how might one get it back here, to the glen of the Sleeping Pool...

"Real is a question of Time," the Voice hedged.

"—and why do I think that time out there in the heavens, is somehow being jogged, or pushed—"

"Ah, that wonderful, complicated, and sensitive mind of yours! Time," said the Voice sheepishly, "if that's what we must call it, is a little mixed up at the moment."

The Creature made a garbled sound in his throat, and appeared incredulous. In the air directly to his left, the hot tailwind of a high-speed comet swiped him. His singed eyebrows gave off a stench, and the skin on his nose felt as if it had melted.

He guessed it was time to face it: Giant intellect that it might be, the Voice had created a problem it couldn't solve.

"Time is time," gasped the Creature. "Does it ever get mixed up, unless somebody who should know better fiddles with it?"

"Faux-time," the Voice pondered on, as if the comet hadn't nearly taken the glen and the Creature's nose with it "that's what we've got work with. And here in the glen of the Sleeping Pool, faux-time is never going to do the trick. Faux-time is just too easily upset too likely to fall apart at the seams—"

"All the more reason why you should have left it alone in the first place! Now I'm standing around like a criminal, with a promise I just made, to all those—"

"One of my calculations is bound to work, in which case, we'll be back to normal. Then we can both start to worry." The Voice gave a laugh, much too in tune, the Creature thought with an anxious wind that whistled and hummed through the smoking trees.

"So much for your wondrous happening! Voice, what started all this?"

"Your declaring, I'm afraid. Who knew it would reach as splendidly far as it has?"
"And how far is that?"

"Farther than far. You're going to be quite impressed," said the Voice, and went back to work.

The Creature was having none of it. "Listen, you! I want you to explain this time-thing to me, and I want you to do it, *now!*"
"Whose version of Time, would you like? There are a hundred opinions, and endless quarrels that span the centuries since Time reportedly began, but nobody agrees on anything, except that they still don't *know.*"

"But you know everything, so what do *you* know?"

"Time, real time—as I suspect *does* exist—is very smart," said the Voice, admiringly, "and if I were Time, I would keep doing exactly the same as always, which is nothing. It neither shows up to defend itself nor explain itself. It just keeps on being or not being, precisely as it chooses. Time is the primo rebel. No matter what my body else considers important, Time ignores everything with equal disdain. And why shouldn't it? Time has the upper hand. Always has, always will, no matter what."

"Rude," said the Creature. "That's rude and unmannerly. How does it expect anyone to get anything done?"

"That," said the Voice, "is their problem."

"And now, it is your problem." The Creature fled, throwing himself into the partial indentation in the earth, left by the fallen tree. The crater in the middle of his forehead rivaled the tree trunk's dimensions. Snug in the darkness, he snarled under his breath. The sky, constantly full of discordant colour and sound, was awhirl with objects which he'd only seen at a vast distance. Close enough that one could smell them, no longer did they invite the gazing of old, but only forced one to turn away in fear, wondering: Exactly what was the Voice doing and why, and how badly was it doing it?

How much danger, precisely, did they face?

A flock of blackbirds circled, and stealthily took over the treetops. Every feathered head was pointed, every eye trained in one direction only, watching for just one sight. The dogs sniffed the ground toward that direction as well, and when they bayed at the impostor night, the sounds were no longer shy and plaintive.

By and by, it occurred to the Voice that the heavens might be miffed with its necessary re-arrangements as there echoed across them, a pitiful, primeval groaning—nothing more of course, than several great bodies being pried from their paths—but it sounded as if some enormous lost beast refused all ministrations and solace.

Merrily, the Voice continued to muck about in the universe, convinced that several of its computations were—almost—working. In due course the groaning stopped, but the echo lingered. So did visions of a sky dangerously perturbed, and curiously more huge than ever before, still coming at them or down upon them, it was hard to tell if there was a difference.

And that left the Creature stranded with more promises than he knew what to do with, and the knowledge that empathy was a much meaner taskmaster than mere compassion had ever thought of being. For with empathy, one stood in, and then became, the very flesh of the sufferer.

What with the deep gloom and their transparency, he couldn't be sure, but thought that he felt the touch of a hand, papery with age, brushing against his own. How desperate those old spirits must be, he thought to be seeking his support.

"Creature," the Voice broke through that pall of smoking calculations, "Excessive humility is unwarranted and unbecoming and turns one into a royal and common pain."

I guess, the Creature told himself as he tried to find a more comfortable position in the dirt, *that about covers humility.*

Regardless of wisdom otherwise stated, his shoulders slumped and depressed but trying to hide it, he leaned over to the old ones. "The Voice may be a mathematical wasteland," he whispered, "but I'm sure it's doing its best and we'll be fine."

A strident flapping of wings forced him to look up. Beating clear of smoking clouds as the Voice continued its diligent search for solutions; the blackbird made its awkward way downward and crouched at the Creature's side.

Nor would it leave. Its lack of so much flight apparatus could only be seen when it lifted its wings, but its movements were stiff and ungainly, and it seemed determined to show off its battle scars in front of his face. Eventually he understood: The bird was scared and looking for protection, even if from someone who could barely protect himself.

"Sanctuary." The Voice rose cheerfully from its labours. "You've become a sanctuary. The bird trusts you."

"Then he knows something I don't," said the Creature, "There just seems to be too much of everything going on, all at once, without sufficient room in between to think."

The Voice inspected its supposed warrior-in-waiting, sweating and banging his head on the log, each time he leapt up at a sudden loud noise from the sky.

"If you look when you can," said the Voice, "at the majority of life as being pretty much a farce, then it loses some of its power over you. Humour has its own healing, a special energy. Why do you think old kings regarded their jesters not as whims, but necessity? In matters of internal strife, the highest heads have been saved by humour."

"I *loathe* the sound of your humour!" With his own head bent, tears sprayed his feet as the descent of a flaming branch drove him from the shelter of the fallen tree to the side of the Sleeping Pool. The bird kept squawking while the Creature inhaled the ancient odour he'd almost grown used to at last. And, as his tears plop-plopped into the endless waters, he drew away, at the quick flash of his image, mirrored there.

"Quite a picture, isn't it?" inquired the Voice. "Did you get a chance to see those eyes?"

The Creature mumbled that they couldn't be his.

"Why not?"

The Voice's question clanged in his head, and worse, he could have sworn that the Voice had eyes, eyes that were staring from behind his own with a gaze directed through the whole of his head, poking at various points of interest...

"Is it because," the Voice nudged him, sternly; "they stream with the same intelligence as the eyes of all those other warrior-questors?"

"I am as much a warrior questor as that faux-night up there is real night!" the Creature howled, and was about to go on when truth seemed to lean over and shove him, until he had to look at a fact he'd probably known in the shrouding fog of his mind, and had avoided at any cost. *The Voice was inside his mind,*

And now he had to recognise,

if not yet fully, that territory within himself, over which he alone had dominion. He recognised also, how invading that territory could only be accomplished by some unique power much like the Vine, and that was surely no force to be trifled with, but he did not care nor stop to consider the consequences. *"How long,"* he whispered over a gathering rage, *"have you been here, inside me?"*

"Always," replied the Voice.

"And *how long* must you remain with me?"

"Always."

No shadows marked the silence then, as if any witness to the Creature's destruction would vanish, even as he seemed to be vanishing. His rage, prompted at last by the unseen invasion of an invisible force into an unknown and unseeable part of him, took on gigantic proportions. The invasion toppled his sense of humility. Turning his face to the curious heavens, he let out a scream so piercing that vapours gavoted with serious intensity, over the Sleeping Pool.

The blackbird wisely disappeared into a fortuitously placed bush, and the Voice said—"You do not find the value in my presence?"

"I was looking for freedom," the Creature shouted, "and just as I suspected, I won't ever have it, not as long as this invasion of yours continues! I want to think for myself, not exist as the shadow of some invisible Voice!"

The pool threatened to overflow with gavoting vapours.

"You have always been thinking for yourself," the Voice pointed out. "I know it's hard to accept, but your mind has a conscious level which is where you are, and a subconscious or lower level which is where I am."

"How deep down are you?" the Creature demanded.

"Deep enough, that not a lot bothers me. You have the harder task, since you are right up there within striking distance, so to speak."

Feeling unsteady and rudely inhospitable, the Creature snapped, "Do you do much down there on that sub-level?"

As your subconscious mind I do down here, just what you do up there. I'm no more brilliant than you. We're simply in different places doing the same thing."

"That part about my brilliance is ridiculous, and just as I was beginning to trust you, at least a little. Why are you always so devious and intent on stirring up trouble?"

"Isn't it amazing how well two such opposites manage to co-exist in the same mind? You do see why I couldn't simply heap all of this on you at once? You would have run much further, much faster, and we would have missed our little chats."

"Voice, is there no way to get rid of you? Because at the moment, the question of my freedom is much more important to me!" No sooner had he said that than he was mortified and grateful for being sealed off from view by the mists. Mists thick enough that one might begin to feel mercifully alone.

"And where," the Voice asked gently, "does that leave you?"

"Confused. Afraid. With all your thinking, don't you ever become confused—or afraid? I'm afraid that I've lost any control I might have had over my quest, and so where am I, really?"

"I think that if you learn to heighten all your senses to their fullest capacity to hear and see, smell and taste and feel—whatever they are telling you—you'll find yourself doing more of the same with your sixth sense, your instinctive, intuitive sense. Then you will have every control a creature could need."

"I don't know that I'll ever get used to the idea of you, Voice."

"It's not the easiest task in the world," the Voice admitted. "If our roles were reversed, I'm not sure how readily I would adjust. Once you understand better *how* your knowledge originates where it does, the idea may not frighten you as much. I know having such an understanding gives me the strength to look everywhere at once...and particularly, at myself."

"Give me a little credit, Voice. I have looked at myself and I don't see anything comparable to what I should be, not if I share a mind like yours!"

"Look again, Creature. But this time, perhaps you will want to look while holding yourself in a more equal light."

"Equal with..."

"With every living being, with those things of nature, and the Vine as well."

"And equal with you?" The angry face was a masque of rejection.

"The very same."

"I'm sure you mean well enough, but that doesn't make

me believe you. Where's your proof? Nobody ever told me creatures have a sub-conscious level, and I'll wait until I see it. Then we'll talk about believing."

"And in the meantime?"

"A pox on your house!"

How he wanted his old place back, that scrap of ground he'd begun to think of as his, the quiet of the glen and the noxious, Sleeping Pool.

Was it still there, amidst the clouds, and the uproar?

It was. Like some laggard friend of the bosom emerging from the rapidly thinning mists, the little glen struggled into view. Despite its loveliness, something was lacking, for over the forests draped in the borrowed curtain of real night, no moon appeared.

...*tic, tic, tickety*

The Voice froze. That sound could mean only one thing, and *it wasn't time.* Frantic, the Voice attacked its calculations, wondering where they'd gone wrong. It seemed both grossly unfair and ironically correct, for something as cheaply constructed as faux-time to be so easily mis-calculated.

"*Voice!*" the Creature was calling.

With a veritable cauldron of computations before it, the Voice did the one thing it could do. It summoned what might be the last cheerful note anybody would ever hear from it, and tried to ignore the continuing *tics* as if they *ticked* not at all.

"Yes, Creature. What is it?"

"Where's the moon?"

Echoing over the Creature's question, the entire glen heard it from far out in space, the reverberating

...tic,

and this time, the Voice did not answer the Creature.

The horizon shivered and blurred as the earth tilted and ploughed along head first until it came to a jolting halt that shook the teeth of everything live, above and below all horizons.

The Creature cried out. Tossed into mid-air, the blackbird plummeted into his lap and stayed there, its shredded wings pulled over its head. The old ones were right behind it

tic, tic, tic, tic...

The earth then *dropped,* as if into some giant slot while bird and Creature clung to nothing but each other, until it again took up its natural movement. Nearly undone by the intensity of his fear, the Creature began to splutter with embarrassment.

"You," he snapped at the nearest target "so stingy with your flying secrets at the beginning of my quest when I was desperate for help. Why are you staring at me? What do you want?"

The bird still hung onto him, shivering in fright. He saw its eyes, liquid and brimming, and wondered why he had ever looked into the eyes of that lone creature back in the compound. It had been too easy ever since that day, and especially now, to recognise fear when he saw it here in this cowering feathered ruler of the skies. Being responsible for the bird's sorry state of garb, he guessed that he should at least reach over and try to offer comfort.

Sometime later while the Creature was still figuring out how to get past the beady glare and the long sharp talons, the Voice burst forth with a satisfied shriek, announcing that everything was now on course.

"Tell me," said the Creature, feeling his life in a shambles around him, "before you succumb completely to your calculations again, where's the moon?"

"I must admit that I have lost all track," said the Voice. "In fact, we may not be enjoying her company for awhile."

"I knew it," the Creature cried. "She's gone. She'll never come back. I'll never see her again."

Unaccustomed as he was to thinking of himself as being connected to the Voice, he didn't quite know who or what to blame for his loss. For *his* moon—his beautiful moon—was in all likelihood never no more to be seen. Something told him the loss of the moon in his life would mean more than just the loss of her presence—it would be akin to bidding goodbye to some hidden part of himself. He wished he knew what it was.

Frowning at the impostor night, he sunk lower and lower yet. He imagined the creatures of the compound, wanting to know what had happened to all his whining complaints and grandiose plans. On that note, he got up and began to stumble about the glen, pounding on trees in deepest frustration while buffeted between the opposing thoughts of Voice and Vine—
when suddenly,

his face relinquished its frowns and took on a half-hearted glow. "Voice, can such convictions as the ones you keep trying to pound into my head, really be trusted?"

"Really," the Voice screamed over the din of skyward objects once again hurling themselves rapidly to other quarters. "Above and beyond all else." And it gladly went back to scanning the heavens. It appeared that moving one mind was harder than moving whole astrological bodies across the universe.

Should he go to bed or stay awake? The impostor night gave no clue. The Creature fell into his moss swing, pointing his toes toward the cliffs and pushing forward and back, hoping what he was thinking would leave, but it didn't. The tree limb creaked. Not very loudly. It didn't disturb him. What did vastly disturb him was the idea of his mind sharing space with the Voice.

Unless he had misunderstood, why would a creature need two minds to accomplish but one end result? Was the Voice *more* than it was saying? He didn't doubt it for a minute. Leaving the swing after a few half-hearted pushes out over the cliffs, he went back to the fallen log and lay down.

The bark had now eaten into more mossy threads. The blackbirds in the treetops shook their wings. They did not close their eyes and neither did the dogs. And so the faux-night spun merrily onward with reckless abandon toward those who waited on either side of the glade.

15

Waiting

Descending unfinished behind the clouds, a ribbon of darkness hung. At the mouth of that ribbon, just the tip of an object shone for a second before the signal was given and the object then carefully moved into place.

The moment had arrived. An entire universe with a vested interest, sternly observed the whole thing from the far-away reaches beyond. Advice had been offered and sincere hopes lavished. Nobody knew if the Voice's amazing creation or its scheme would work. They were only desiring it with equal fervour. The testing for stability was extensive, meticulous, and performed by crews volunteering from that same universe, and referred to as crystal magician warriors, a term pertaining more to their flying crafts than to the crews themselves.

It seemed to take forever for the heavens to start relinquishing the balance of their organisational grip. It took even longer for the Voice to establish nearly all the balance of its envisionings. Not until the last splendid pieces were near enough to each other did the Voice relax and admire everything as it very shortly *could be.* It pictured the whole of it, especially those bustling warriors, much closer to the glen and many times bigger, brighter, and stronger.

"The bigger, the brighter to see," said the Voice quietly, "and definitely stronger than me. So far, so good."

Jarred by the activities at the mouth of the long ribbon of night, fragile clouds broke loose. Down they fell, and scampered into the glen where they joined with the ground mists and danced in the flittering shadows. High above, the crystal magician warriors ceased their labours.

One of them asked the Voice, *Will that be sufficient, do you think?*

I think it will do fine, thank you, said the Voice.

The reply was equally cheerful:

Party on, then.

And they were leaving, each brilliant tail of their flying crafts beginning to shower the heavens with faux-stars of piercing light. The old ones shivered and shook their heads. Briskly then, the Voice went back to work with one eye trained in the same direction that continued to fascinate the blackbirds.

Almost in the welcome lap of sleep, the Creature of Habit leapt up, banging his head on the log, and thinking that it must have been a harder bump than he'd first imagined. The stars were not as they should be. Instead, they were massed in glittering balls, whirling away through the clouds and flashing a multitude of lights.

It made him wonder what the Voice had decided to do this time. He decided not to ask.

What was keeping him awake and making him antsy was another question, having to do with those very same skies: If he had the same extraordinary knowledge as the Voice, would that mean giving up his desire to go Beyond? After all, why go to the moon if one already had what one wanted?

Why, indeed? he thought.

And then he thought, *why not?* The extreme yearning keeping itself alive inside him hadn't decreased by even a hair. There had to be a reason for that, but desire didn't seem to operate on reason or judicial contemplation. It simply was.

"Do you see that?" he demanded of the Voice as he wove through the ground mists and pointed belligerently at the clouds dancing wantonly with them. "I can't understand it. One would think that if they can come down here, I should be able to go up there."

"What gall," the Voice agreed absently, "and so unfair."

"Your wondrous happening is late, Voice, and as for this matter of knowledge—I need to know—when do I get it?"

"Knowledge," said the Voice with an air of even more preoccupation, as it hummed over its formulas, "is merely information. Having information is having raw data, unhulled, unsorted. Hulling and sorting, is the art of Thinking about that information and making it your own instead of sitting on it as though it were there for decoration."

"So where is all this raw data? Where's my information?" He felt once more that whack on the top of his head.

"Oh, alright!" He exclaimed. "It's a difficult idea to get used to! You're saying I already have the information, but I want to know, where is the rest of it? All I get are dribs and drabs. It's not enough! I want every bit of it!"

"We're coming to that," said the Voice, sounding weary, "but I can't just give it to you. You've got to release it."

Release it? Was this another chore for him to do? On the verge of going back to the log and banging his head against it, purposefully and with malice, he caught sight of Hope—which he *had* managed to pry away from his Fear. Some progress *was* being made by virtue of hours of practising. Nonetheless, impatient at the time these meager few gains had taken, a thought fell out of his mouth,

"*I hate* Time!"

"Most creatures do."

"I can't stop thinking about time," said the Creature, climbing into the moss swing. "What if at least a part of Time is as much—or more—about *seeing*, as it is, about anything else? I can' t get rid of the feeling that Time isn't what we think of it as being, but that it's actually all around us—*this time*, and *that time*—I'm not saying it correctly."

"There are a number of nuances for which most languages do not allow, but don't worry about it. Just get the words out."

In the treetops, the blackbirds ruffled their wings and made harsh cawing sounds. The old ones drew closer to the Creature of Habit. So did the blackbird pacing at the Creature's feet.

"I guess what I mean is this: What if Time does exist, but in two separate worlds, one of which is usually invisible, except when we allow ourselves to see it?"

"As in a parallel world?"

"Yes! Those warrior-questors, the old ones, the longboat, they don't belong in *this* here-and-now. Is it possible, that when I see them, I'm actually seeing another world separate from this one? What do you think, Voice?"

"I think," the Voice replied, speaking around a secret grin, "that one of these days you will discover whether you are right, or wrong. And you did construct a worthwhile concept and dared to voice it aloud. Have you any idea how many brilliancies die silent deaths because nobody dared to speak them?"

"I don't care about brilliancies. If I am so brilliant, why can't I get the moon to show up?"

Purple hazes swirled at the Creature's feet, and twined up the moss rope where another few strands had parted. The tree limb groaned under his weight.

"In a way," he said, his eyes roaming the heavens, so clouded over that nothing showed except for more clouds, "it's awful to know what you want. After awhile, it becomes an ache, and you know that unless you find it, that ache isn't

going away. I can't stop wanting the moon."

"Focus," said the Voice. "That's called focus. Very little of a great moment ever happens without it."

"It isn't just an obsession, a fixation doomed to failure?"

"Absolutely not."

"Voice, what is beauty?"

"Beauty? Whatever a creature perceives it to be. It falls under the category of individual taste. One's sense of beauty is first innate in nature—and then solidified upon the shores of personal experience. Like everything else, beauty is relative."

"What about—does it depend at all upon who is seeing it?"

"If you depend upon others to define you, yes."

"In that regard, the Vine has already defined me. I don't think I can change that."

"You can if you stop looking at yourself through the Vine's eyes."

The Creature could feel whole centuries of others like him, wondering at the simplicity of that as they yearned for the same as he. He might have been looking over their shoulders and they over his, everyone from the depths of their own misery, staring at the Sleeping Pool certain they could never look in for fear of seeing themselves. And he knew it might be the same means by which—himself included—they had all been entombed.

The Great Winds, silent as a far-off burial ground for the better part of that night—if night it was—shrieked along the cliffs. The Creature heard their anguish and anger being carried through the caverns of time, straight back to him *demanding* that he find a way to look without seeing through the Vine's eyes. The longer he tried the more conscious he became that he hardly ever looked at himself without a second-hand opinion. And what he was left with every time was the notion of ugliness.

The Great Winds kept up their shrieking. With a sense of dread, the Creature heard as well the sound of the Voice growing louder as it abruptly ceased its computations.

"I believe," it yelped, with beleaguered chipperness, "that I've got it. Almost. *Oops.*"

In panic, the Creature looked for the blackbird that had been pacing at his feet as if unwilling to chance the ruined skies, but the bird was tucking itself into the thickets, and just in time, because the heavens tore open and poured down rain the colour of old mud.

...tic, tic, tic

Having arrived at the end of a rather extensive repertoire of intricate equations, the Voice from the realm of its private world was watching the tail-ends of myriad loose threads begin to unravel. The vast ramifications of its interference thus far were about to blow up in its face, the problem being,

...tic, tic...

with the complications of refracted light telling the eye one thing, when actually the opposite was true—and this was the least of it—one had to be terribly nimble and stick with it long past mental collapse while focusing with the intensity of an inch-worm going from here to there.

...*tic*

The Voice admitted the worst: Time was snatching away the last remaining second, and naught but sheer genius could steal it back.

"Genius," it crowed happily, "What is it anyway, if not the temerity to fly into the wind with one's posterior on fire?"

The clouds went red, as the heavens shook with a vengeance. The Voice reached willy-nilly into every old equation already exhausted, picked one, and plugged it into a handful of hastily re-assembled combinations

...and waited...*tic, tic, tic*

The loose ends started to slip. The Voice knew—what dangled from them, unseen and so precariously—headed likety-split toward flaming oblivion...*tic, tic, tickety*

"We're in for it now," the Voice hollered, "that rude little demon Time has just run out on me!"

The threads unraveling, unraveled further, and wandered down through the light years where no light had ever shown. Only seconds away, the crash when it did come would come so fast that no creature in the world would even hear it

...*tic, tic, tic...the threads were reversing themselves,* and encircling the ribbon of night that marvel of path lying unfinished; re-weaving and weaving until it was done, its length and breadth enough to boggle the mind with impossible mathematical correctness. And,

in the resplendent world of the mind's eye, the Voice saw that
path very shortly being put to use. It foresaw through the magic
of soul, brain and mind the infinite possibility that *would be.*

T o crown the Voice's projected vision of celebration,
a rush of sound that was not the wind swept wildly into
the glen. It was the triumphant entrance of a hope
kept too long from too many, that same hope
now alive with a ringing message,
Second phase complete.

P owered by the surge of its own joy, the Voice
flung itself through the clearing, sideways and back again. Its
plan was ready to go! Even more remarkable, the Creature
had been able to stand upright through all the colossal
skyward cataclysmia. Mid-way into the Voice's shrieking at
perceived danger, it had seen the Creature begin to chant in an
unaccustomed rhythm.
With barely a breath between, he had all but carved each word
into the air,
I am marvelous and magnificent, I am a wonderful,
intelligent, wondrous creature, and I can, I will get through this.
Nothing can stop me, nobody else defines me, I define myself!
The Voice had witnessed his surprise, when panic had not
robbed him of air, or sent him around the bend. Hideous as it
had been, his fear had not been sufficient to topple him.
In that cloud-bound clearing, the Voice watched as he

eventually moved, on unsteady feet, steering as if the smallest mis-step might jostle his new-found courage.

"I must tell you." said the Voice, breaking through his careful concentration of maneuverings, "that rhythm of yours, is a splendid expression of the life-force. Your creativity, the pulse of
it-flows from the energy of that force. A wide variety of folk of the most spectacular kind, have created to their special version of its pulse beat down through time. You should ask Bragnificense. He probably knows everyone of them, by heart."

"I'm very glad to hear it," said the Creature, "probably because I am too exhausted to comment otherwise."

"I," said the Voice, sounding both exhausted, and exhilarated,
"excuse your thorniness, because I am finished."

"Finished with what?" the Creature howled. But his need for an answer was cancelled by a sky that had finally made up its mind and turned into real night—

And, at the edge
     of softly
          churning clouds,
               strange beings
                    seemed to wander, as if
                        bent
                            on some
                                mysterious
                                    mission…

…reinforcing his belief that he *had* to get up there, and soon.

"Wanderlust," said the Voice, sounding as if it were lying down in a cool place, with its eyes closed.

"Pardon?"

"*Wanderlust,* the mark of the untamed heart, the explorer. The very first explorer in history had wanderlust. Before he knew it he was discovering one mystery after another. Once it gets you, that's it. Ask Bragnificense. He knows them by heart too, every last one of those roaming, untamed, discovering creatures."

The Voice did not mention the other attribute those wanderers shared, knowing the Creature had already caught a glimpse of it within himself. By the look of the flock of blackbirds, clenching and unclenching their talons on the unlucky branches of a stand of walnut trees, and starting to puff out their feathers as if feeling an ill-wind this might not be the time to remind him.

Once again, the Voice closed itself off, and went back to resting.

Atop the hill overlooking the cliffs, Bragnificense stood just beside the walnut trees, taller than their tallest branches, peering into the distance along with the blackbirds. Even with no moon, he shone like a beacon.

The Creature tried to follow his gaze, but it was impossible without climbing a tree, and he couldn't because he had just noticed three of the most utterly beautiful stars that he'd ever seen acting rather peculiarly.

"Oh," he whispered,
"what's happening?
What makes me think
those stars are guarding
something?"

"Maybe they are," the Voice
replied.

The Creature waited and waited, for what he hoped was the moon, but she did not come out. He reached for the feather behind his ear, the one he'd carried for so long. It must have worked itself out of the braiding in his hair, because it was gone. In the compound, other than the water jug which really belonged to the Vine, he'd had no possessions, no companions. The feather had been his first.

Its prior owner, the blackbird, was nowhere in sight. So. He'd lost his feather, lost his bird, lost his moon. He thought about that, and had to acknowledge a feeling of loss and rejection, as well.

Real night having fallen, the wildlife scurried from the forest. As they passed him on their way to the Sleeping Pool, it seemed to him, that every living thing started calling out the message he could not decipher. Suddenly, he heard it clearly, *there were two parts to that message,* and he understood neither.

It had not been the easiest of days. The night hadn't turned out much better. More hurt than he wanted to admit, by losing what little he'd had, and being rejected in the bargain, and then being reminded of further ineptitude. Like a pot too hot and afraid to boil over, he started to simmer. Then he began to steam. In a fit of pique, he walked up to the first boulder he found, and gave it a swift kick. The pain was unbearable, his screams embarrassing. After a time, the physical pain started subsiding, but inside him the emotional hurt raged on.

"Relax," said the Voice, "and your brain will help you."

The Creature of Habit stiffened. MY BRAIN?"

"That part of you which slaves aren't supposed to have, but they do."

"*Brain.*" The Creature pronounced the word, as if his tongue had caught fire." "I was hoping that word didn't pertain to me. It has such a messy sound to it."

"Ah, but it's a marvel, nonetheless." and the Voice chuckled.

"Soul, mind, brain—they are you—each of these three beautiful gifts, and without one, the others would be lost. Of these three, only your brain takes physical form. Remember your brilliant thought about time? It came from your brain, but only after it had been encouraged by your soul and mind—and that's an evolutionary wonder!"

"Oh? Well. I *refuse* to evolve!"

"Suit yourself," said the Voice, "but you might want to take a good look at that boulder you kicked, because you are very much like it. You're getting better, but you're still not there."

"I'm sorry! I've already seen that boulder and have certainly felt it—*why* am I like it?"

"Stone carveth not. It is only carved upon."

Presently, the Creature realised the Voice had gone, and not come back. And he reflected: No feather, no bird, no moon. And now—no Voice either. Afraid of what he had done to cause the complete abandonment of himself, he rushed to avoid thinking about what that abandonment might mean. He decided to leave the moss swing for later as a delayed reward—not that his rudeness deserved a reward—and he settled down to sketching. He wished again in that night with no moon, that she had not left him. There was however one lone star peeking determinedly through the clouds, and as he knelt in the dirt, it got much brighter. His compartments this particular evening soon became the victim of a brash outpouring of creativity, appointed with all manner of crenellated battlements and narrow slitted windows and drawbridges, and moats. When their minute detail flourished beyond the capability of the stick he was using to draw, he found another much sharper, and went right on drawing in his customary fashion—careful to translate rigidly, each stroke being brought to him.

He had a better idea than ever before of what might be transpiring—old old souls pushing their minds up against his own, drenching his vision in theirs—willing him to re-create for them what had lived in their creative thoughts long ago.

The dogs were practically under his nose before he saw them. They paid no attention to him, and acted content to hunker just a few feet away, eyes riveted to his endeavours. But their nearness made him nervous. The stick flipped from his grip and skittered across the drawing, leaving a beautifully artistic slash in the dirt. One that would not be duplicated by the rigidity of his style no matter how hard he tried, and finally realising failure when he saw it, a wild keening wail erupted from his lips, nearly identical to the keening the old souls always raised.

The tiny star shone more powerfully, illuminating all. The dogs tilted their heads at him as if recognising his thwarted desire. Before he could move, their eyes locked resolutely upon his own, replaying before his startled vision the curve and flow of the bodies of every last forest creature he'd seen on his journey, each supple bending of grasses to ground, the somber slashes of tree trunk and limb against rain-lashed horizons, the softness of the moon's rounded curves sailing the unending, heavenly oceans.

Not until all of nature's display of itself it had finished infiltrating him fibre by fibre; not until his fingers felt what his mind's eye actually beheld in his brain—that unstilted, natural, ebb and flow of line and shape and dimension—did the dogs finally release his gaze. The moment they did, he proceeded to push himself past rigidity, until; mid-way through completion of the sketch, his strokes with the stick began changing from meticulous and stilted to free and sweeping, leaving him to draw as adroitly as many an old master from his own imagination and *that of no other.*

In the throes of great wonder, he watched while the wood between his fingers seemed willingly, gladly, to obey the bent of his mind alone. In fact, so personally betraying was each stroke in the dirt that he himself might be sprawled there.

And the Voice which he believed had abandoned him kept silent—trembling under the weight of high expectation rewarded—for the Creature of Habit had just taken the next to the last step of his journey.

The dogs looked from the stick to the Creature as if noting for themselves the change in his drawing style and feeling an awe of their own. At that, a flush infused his face, growing as bright as the light in his eyes, and he pondered the unbelievable: Had he created what lay before him, seeming by free-flowing stick strokes alone, to identify himself before any other? Quickly, he sought to erase so telling a picture—and found he could not because alongside his awe and the admiration in those canine eyes, there surfaced in himself regarding his artistic efforts—a flush of *pride.*

What did one do with so potent and forbidden an emotion?

He had no idea and upon hiding it, it simply got bigger.

The dogs hunching over his drawing looked up, trying with
their eyes to tell him what they'd always known
about pride.
By the light of that one little star that still
shone, the Creature got to his feet and fled.

Among grasses dripping with dew and swaying in the path of an insistent wailing wind, dark shapes trotted that night across the horizon and halted at the edge of the cliffs. Prostrate under an ancient tree, the Creature of Habit dreamed in a dream far too real that he spoke with them—unafraid and fluently—at length. And the dark-shaped wild things taught him a trick there in the world of his supposed dreaming, but he couldn't remember on waking exactly what it was. He only felt the corners of his mouth strangely curled up askew.

And shaking stubborn sleep from his eyes, so out of balance was he with himself, that the earth's obvious excitement heralding preparations for something amazingly different affected him not at all.

He had to stand waiting just above the pool until he'd thoroughly come awake. It was shock to which he fully awakened however, for he sensed that sometime in the night which was not yet over, he had become nocturnal, exactly like those wild things which much preferred darkness to day.

So natural a state did his nocturnal self seem, that he immediately mistrusted it telling himself it would go away. What went away instead were the upturned corners of his mouth, as they swiftly assumed same old droop. All he was left with was the most insane desire to run about for hours sniffing the air.

At the pool just below, the same dogs that had bayed in his dreams hours earlier, frolicked at the dark water's edge, taking dainty sips and staring in his direction as if knowing something he didn't.

"Creature, Creature," said the Voice, its cheer diminished by a sharp sense of urgency, "shall we now come to terms?"

"And whose terms would those be, mine or yours?"

"What's mine is yours, what's yours is mine," the Voice sing-songed expectantly, but the Creature was preoccupied.

"Those dogs drinking at the pool, do they always have to act as if they're laughing at something?"

Still at odds with a dire lack of time, the Voice summoned a blithe reply: "Those dogs, as you call them, are wolves. The old ones say that to run with the wolf in the light of the moon is to know the earth and the heavens, for the wolf is the voice of both."

"*Wolves?*" the Creature repeated, firmly resisting

the thought of running anywhere with one of them. "You mean they're not just *dogs?*"

According to the Vine, dogs were bad enough, but wolves—everybody in the compound had heard the old creature speak of them in a hushed voice—spinning a hundred tales of their courage and complexity of nature. They had also heard the Vine hiss and spit at the mention of them, calling them cunning and untrustworthy. *On the mean and filthy scale,* the Vine had said *they are many notches above dogs. Never turn your back.*

The wolves were but a few yards away. Their reported ability to turn on a hair and race like the wind scared the Creature, but he was listening to their almost shy, occasional *woofs* of seeming laughter. And then without meaning to, he caught the eye of a wolf he hadn't seen in awhile. Big and white, its ears immediately flattened, and teeth bared, it started padding forward, the hairs on its coat bristling.

"Don't move," the Voice whispered. *"Pretend you don't exist."*

The other wolves, having seen that locking of gazes between Creature and white wolf, had not taken kindly to the idea. In a flash, growling and snarling, they advanced with the white one in the lead, an expression glowing in its eyes, faintly hypnotic, but

most of all, threatening.

Would they confuse profuse sweating with actual body movement? They were insistent, poking at him with their noses, as if testing for some evidence of life...while the snarling white shadow stood over him. Dust billowed, ghostly against the dark night. And still, he could not leave the eyes of the wolf.

"What does he want?" croaked the Creature.

"This white one," said the Voice "is referred to as the Great Silver Spirit. He's the alpha of all alpha wolves, and he'll rip your heart out if you keep looking him in the eye. That's considered a challenge and he's putting you on notice that the glen of the Sleeping Pool belongs to the wildlife."

"He can have the glen. I'll leave immediately!" The unwilling immobility of his body could only be borne just so long. He could feel his muscles rebelling against the strain.

"Oops," said the Voice. "It would seem that now, something else altogether has his dander up."

The blackbirds in the walnut trees, were muttering to each other, eyes riveted at a point beyond the cliffs. The long column of Bragnificense's backbone had stiffened. The Creature saw through his panic and the sweat dripping from his hairline the white wolf as it raised its head. A growl caught in the massive throat at whatever it seemed to see. The growl became a series of sing-song vibrations, almost like words. The others nodded and howled and yipped, at the information being passed to them. Bragnificense was slowly turning his head away from the horizon. The birds were flying up in a great flash of wings, screaming at the top of their lungs.

"What is it?" the Creature cried, for the wolves were already racing off, each one hurriedly establishing a watch-post, their eyes forming a glittering circle low to the ground around the clearing. Bragnificense put out a huge paw, and hoisted him up, depositing him on a limb at the top of a tree. The little star came out from the clouds, and everything in the distance shone brightly. The ground was a dizzying good ways down, but most dizzying of all was the long, far-off thread of rustling leaves, winding its serpentine way through the starlight.

Straggling behind it were the creatures of the compound.

Memories of the compound battered his wits. Not knowing what else to do, he climbed into the worn moss rope, and pushed himself forward over the valley, watching the cliffs getting nearer. Then he swung backward, trembling, and thinking.

The glen of the Sleeping Pool would never again be the same. The Vines would come in, tear it to ribbons, and everybody with it. His eyes flew open, at a very practical idea: Since the Vines could not get into the glen unless their passage was granted, he could sit right here until they went away.

Thoughtfully, he swung as far out as the looped length of moss would allow. About to begin the long arch back up to the cliff top, the eyes of the white dog drifted into his mind...it felt like a punch in the stomach as pieces of a very big puzzle jumped out of his thoughts, and he was racing in his head, trying to fit them together, but he discovered there was no place to sit waiting for anything, and all he could do was hang onto the tufted old moss as it broke and went sliding through his fingers.

16

Puzzle Pieces

There was nowhere to put his feet, only empty air filled with starlight. Up the rope, hand over hand he crawled, listening for the rest of the threads to break, too scared to open his mouth and callout for the Voice. Not that it would have done any good. It hadn't even noticed his fall. He could feel the whole of its focus concentrated on that advancing line
in the distance…
Even if creatures couldn't die, the Vine would find a way to get him, if he didn't hurry. He pictured his body lying broken on the rocks, bones protrouding from bloodied flesh. And just when he'd found those puzzle pieces. "Oh, please," he pleaded,

"let me have another minute to try and put these pieces in place!"

The rope had a bit of give to it. He bobbed at the broken end like a piece of dry-rot wood on water, his feet searching the face of the cliff for a tree stump, a rock, anything substantial enough to get a foothold. But the earth crumbled around the first rock, and it

sailed into the darkness. If it hit, he couldn't hear it, the valley was too far down. One mangy tree stump allowed him to perch, and keeping his grip on the moss rope, he worked his way upward, hugging a rock outcropping here and a root there, dirt flying into his eyes, and legs and hands aching with the strain.

On reaching the cliff ledge, he hauled himself over, so relieved that he buried his head in the grass. His feet were doing a nervous little tap-dance, making sure there was really ground underneath them. He leaned over the edge of the cliff, then he looked up at the remnants of the rope hanging from the tree branch. There was no safety in hiding anywhere, how could he have been so stupid—no, he had not been stupid, it had been a stupid move. *The act, not him.* Stupid.

The breath he expelled at the radical change in his thinking was loud in his ears. He liked the sound of it and the familiar noise of the glen seemed reassuring: the old ones railing, their anger blending with the shrill calling of the blackbirds, the mournful wailing of the wolves.

One had to admire the wolves, he thought, unaware that another puzzle piece was about to land. To confront the enemy as they had done—to establish their own territory—having the gumption to insist loudly, and even downright meanly, that he recognise their prior claim...

Prior claim. Angrily, he wondered how it had escaped him for so long: *The creatures of the compound had prior claim on themselves, a claim they had never enforced with the Vine.* He envisioned going up against the Vine, the same way the wolves had gone up against him, and had reached the part where the Vine would naturally step in, and lash everybody to pieces, when the Voice surfaced, with profuse apologies.

"I fell off a cliff," the Creature announced, "and found out that I exist! Actually, one had nothing to do with the other."

"Astounding," the Voice exclaimed. "Existence, the one thing we never thought to discuss."

"You told me," the Creature said, his feet gratefully discovering the earth was truly beneath them, "that it was bound to happen. One day I would have to defend myself. At first, I wanted to leave the Vines out there, and wait for them to go away, but something else that you said changed my mind. You told me I couldn't change my view of myself until I stopped looking through the eyes of the Vine, and you were right."

"Things began to fall into place when I started thinking back about how the Vine forbids us to look into each other's eyes. Well, after looking into the eyes of the wolf and seeing its reaction—*Voice, that wolf wouldn't let me look away*—it wanted me to see for myself, to acknowledge its existence, and *guess what I learned from that?"*

The Creature of Habit looked very much, like the wildest, most untamed thing in the glen. "I learned the Vine was afraid that if creatures of the compound looked into each other's eyes, *we would acknowledge our being.* The vine didn't want us to believe that we existed, or that we had a right—each one of us—to protect our own personal territory. When the white wolf was coming at me, and you said, *sit there, and pretend you don't exist*—after I tied it together, I knew—I could hide, and ignore the Vine, or I could get busy and claim myself. Why am I talking so loudly? The way I'm shaking, there was a time when I would have thought I was crazy!"

"Creature, have you any idea what you just did?"

"I was *thinking,*" the Creature answered. He was inspecting his bloody palms and raw legs, for the moss had not been as soft as it had looked. "I know I was thinking before, but this is different, I can't explain it, but it's more like making some strange *connection*—I actually discovered that I exist, can you believe that? I've been around for ever so long, and I'm only now finding out what existing feels like!"

"And have you decided what should be done with regard to the Vines' arrival?"

"Joined as we are, Voice, I wanted to see if you agreed, but I think we should let them in as soon as they get here. The downside is that if we lose, the wildlife loses, too. The Glen will be ruined—"

"Then we'd better win."

"The creatures of the compound will help us, I'm sure they will—"

"Let me be the first to warn you, always count your

supporters twice, and your adversaries once."

The Creature hadn't quite tumbled to the meaning of that, when the big white wolf, part of the watch-post around the clearing, trotted up the hill to him. He hardly dared believe what he thought it was telling him. And then the wolf was fading away, disappearing into thin air, until the only thing left, was a silver aura that shimmered and sparkled under the trees.

"The wolf seems to agree with us," he said, "about letting in the Vines. His eyes—staring into them—I have to think that staring into the eons must be the same. *Can he be that old?*"

"Yes. He can. Look, a talisman for the end of your journey."

It was floating down from the treetops, a single black feather, much the worse for wear, tumbling into the Creature's outstretched hand. He didn't say 'thank you' to the lone blackbird in the walnut tree because his mouth was frozen in another *O* of disbelief. In a panic, he turned as if searching for the Voice. "How much time do we have before the Vines get here? I never did find out how one knows what is Truth and what is not! *How can I be ready for the Sleeping Pool or the Vines, either?*"

"Listen to your senses," said the Voice, darting between worries of its own, and determined to make every minute count. "You worry too much. When a creature is done, he's done.

Let us begin."

And so,
at barely the stroke of midnight, begin they did.

17

Beginnings

Midnight reigned,
        having come to the silent earth
by tipping the trees with threads of silver,
creating a dream-like aura that fell on
blind eyes, as the Creature of Habit
lingered at the top of the hill. The hill,
hardly more than a slope which he'd
traveled before with no problem, suddenly
looked unending. There were too many eyes
at his back, too much of the unknown,
awaiting his arrival below.

Wolves gathered, the smell of their fur richer than incense, as they pushed him forward. Like everything else in the night, they gave the impression of dancing on the edge of expectation. Underneath that expectation, he heard as it drew nearer, a stealthy, serpentine gliding sound...but the railing and ranting began, drowning it out. Accompanied by sounds of the donning of battle garb, the movements of the old souls beside him were anything but stealthy. They fully intended everyone hear them coming. He marveled at the armour they'd scrounged from somewhere; the metal cut-work tarnished with age, leather fittings mouse-eaten to a threadbare state. Wearing it definitely gave them a substantial appearance, as down the hill, ranting and railing to the sounds of
their clinking and clunking, they vanished into the trees.

He, on the other hand, felt very *insubstantial,* seeming only to have donned the smell of ancient water, and the odour increased, the longer he tried through the night that hid it to glimpse its fern-laden banks.

In the nearby marsh, a covey of loons festooned the midnight winds with a series of haunting cries. Quickly, another covey answered back. Peepers unleashed their tiny voices. The waters of the unseen Sleeping Pool brushed hypnotic against the earth. Deep into his bones, the Creature could feel the urgency of each small voice saying *hurry* as he started his first hesitant steps down the hill.

Muffled within the folds of the eons, far-away cries blended into the usual sounds of the glen. The Voice knew that if it allowed itself to do so, it would see every struggling creature caught within those folds, fighting to reach the Sleeping Pool, in time.

Feeling the pressure of a strong wind blowing and its posterior again on fire, the Voice focused with all the considerable power of the subconscious, willing that outside the glen of the Sleeping Pool—just for tonight—what passed for time on this planet, would exist on the same plane as the glen. But if the extravagant long ribbon of night had been difficult to prepare for and then create, that difficulty paled before this task. In fact, so major was the resistance being met as to render any notion of success, dimmer than the light from a cold and distant star.

Harder than it had ever focused on anything, the Voice focused once more. Instead of producing identical time, it began producing counterfeit time in such huge quantities that more than one eon rocked in the firmament and inhabitants predicted an immediate end to the world.

The second try was worse, and the Voice cursed, as the weather on more than one continent, in more than one universe, took strange and bizarre turns, leaving some with more water than they wanted and others with none at all. Ice ages came and went in the blink of an eye, and whole desert regions turned into Rain Forests.

I think, said the Voice to itself, *that I've overshot the mark.*

Somewhere in the universe, an unseen entity felt the jolting changes in the fabric of its handiwork. First it frowned, and then it laughed, and prepared to make haste. It didn't need an invitation.

The Creature's descent was halting. The wolves, splendidly dressed in coats so fine that they floated around them, incandescent as halos, could not have been more mannerly. Their smiles were shy, not even showing their teeth, but despite their dandy appearance, these were untamed beasts, no doubt weaned on attack. Their alertness re-stated the Vine's belief, that they could go mad at any moment in a vicious display of fangs and a rending of flesh.

He pictured them leaping onto his bones, tearing him to shreds, and the run he broke into was awkward and far too slow. There was no chance of out-distancing them. The steps began to add up, and a change became apparent. This kind of running, he thought, felt the way flying must feel, for his feet did not flinch at sharp impediments of spiked thorn or protruding stone. They just barely touched the ground, as though he were running on uncommonly limber legs, and thickly padded paws. In a flagrant mingling against his face as he all but soared over the hillside, were the wild odours of fur and rich black earth, and a taste of the winds, far away.

To run with the wolf in the light of the moon,
is to know the earth and the heavens, for the wolf is the voice of
both.

That's what the Voice had told him, but the heavens when he looked up, showed him no moon by which to know anything, and still, he had to wince at the twisting inside him as something fragile, yet old and stubborn, started to yield.

Breathe faltering; he beheld a spell cast before him, spinning heaven and earth to the rhythm of a single, surging beat. Cradled in the palm of two worlds simultaneously and quite securely—before he could refuse to be drawn, he was taken—fitted betwixt and between

the world of the wolf and the Sleeping Pool.

Through the narrowness of that betwixt and between, the wolves were leading him, by means of one instance, directly unto another just like it, so that it was but a single moment in time. And although wide awake, he dreamed as in his supposed dreaming of hours before, of speaking to them and fluently—while they tried again to teach him the trick he could no longer remember.

Once more and carefully, they prompted the corners of his mouth, easing those corners into the shape of what had forever, been buried inside him. No sooner did he protest, than just beyond the scope of his meager vision—they started to do the same thing to his throat searching for primal utterance—a sharing long-buried too, that could stretch beyond the last threshold of the universe.

Precisely when he thought whatever they were seeking would surely be routed out, the animals without even slowing their pace, abruptly let loose of him.

High, high overhead—
just loudly enough to pierce the narrowness where the Creature
was confined and still running—a WHOOSH of sound
accompanied a wash of stars crossing the heavens and leaving
behind what looked like that same lone star the Creature had seen
before.

At the sight of that oddly timeless wink seeming to follow
while casting bright light over his shoulder—and with the corners
of his mouth and his throat so a-tingle as to keep him captive—he
couldn't explain the ache in his heart, or what followed after. All he
knew was, that he and the wolves hung in mid-air, within strides
interrupted for a period of time, as something unfearsome, and a bit
familiar to the Creature
      seemed to hover nearby.

Quicker than quick, lighter than air, what felt like a mild
shock-wave followed, no telling how long until it finally ended.
Whereupon mid-stride became full-stride, as if nothing had
happened, while Creature and wolves continued on
      as they had been.

The change that had just come over so-called time on the rest of
the planet, as announced by that wash of stars, seeped into the
subconscious world of the Voice gently as the water moving in
darkness. There was but a vague warning *tremour* now hanging
about as the midnight hour relaxed and enjoyed itself at a much

broader; and slower pace. The impossible had happened, and the Voice was not about to snub the gift of a *nudge of time* in its favour. In fact, it hardly knew what to say at such generosity, coming as it had to have come from Time itself, an entity so guarded of its very existence that nobody could tell—with any assurance—whether it did, or

it didn't.

When the Voice made no objection, the unknown entity without further preamble began to loosen that thinnest of veils with which all creatures comforted themselves, that their known world was the only world that

existed.

Through the gossamer sheerness of a thousand moving folds, as they were lifted from the face of the glen, was revealed eon after eon, in a stunning succession of shimmering small glens, which together made up the face of the whole.

With a slight flurry of tremours, to let the Voice know that it too, was concerned—the unseen, unidentified entity swiftly searched the furthest cranny in the furthest dungeon, where any creature might be secreted in misery—for if one creature were not free this night, then no creature could be free.

For your old-world visitors, the entity said, ceasing its lifting, and positioning deep pockets of open shadow under the trees, and the Voice immediately understood. Theirs had been a shadow world for so long, that even the darkness of night would be much too light for some who would later emerge.

The no-longer unknown entity then placed more shadows, but left them closed and shrouded in mysterious blankness.

These, it said, *are for nature and night to play with—as a gift for the Vines—and a nice Machiavellian touch, don't you think?*

"Masterful!" the Voice replied, in admiration.

No, said the entity, with a glance at the long ribbon of night descending from the clouds. *That is masterful.*

Only by the tremours finally having stopped did the Voice suspect that Time had finished its work, and left.

From where he stood observing the cliffs on the far side, Bragnificense leaned down with a report.

"How far away are they?" the Voice asked.

"They're close enough," Bragnificense answered in a booming attempt at a whisper, "that I could count the leaves on the spines of each Vine. They won't, of course, be able to see into the glen, or enter, unless—is the Creature still of the same mind?"

"The very same, as far as I know," the Voice replied, and added, casually, "He believes that we can enlist the aid of the creatures of the compound."

Bragnificense sharpened his claws amongst the bright scales on his chest. He made no comment until the Voice had explained time as it would be, tonight; he only rolled his eyes, and clicked his tongue.

"So," he said, "time which never existed in the glen of the Sleeping Pool exists tonight, as NOW. And out there, beyond the glen, everything on this planet which was moving at its own pace is presently moving at the exact same pace as everything in the glen? Does this mean that tonight is TONIGHT, for everybody on this planet or does that include the entire world?"

"There was a slip-up," the Voice admitted. "I expect, I hope, it will be put to rights, as soon as we've finished."

"I guess so," said Bragnificense.

As they finally reached the bottom of the hill, the wolves were slowing down. The Creature sailed along in front of them, the muscles around his mouth displaying a tortured look, understandable in view of the fact that they had never been used in the way the wolves had been suggesting. And the Voice thought to itself how wise they had been to lead him as far as he could go at the moment and then let loose of him. One had to hope that before the night was over...

"Maybe," said Bragnificense, sensing the Voice's disappointment, "with everything else the old ones and the Creature will be finding tonight, that will be enough."

"No." And the Voice sounded unmovable. "Tonight is the night to have everything. Anything less will *not* be enough."

Hurry, Hurry, the smallest of glen creatures cried in the Creature's ear and hurry he did, one foot rushing after the other, until—

Before his startled stare, and lit by the one wee star blinking from the skies—the Sleeping Pool lay there before him, compressed through the dawn of time and each eon thereafter—yet fully unfolded of its secret self, to both the earth and the heavens.

For the next few moments, he could do absolutely nothing except watch the circles break away from the water and reach outward flowing around him, ready with the warmest of healing embraces...and before they could corner him, he stepped back. The loner he knew himself to be reacted badly to such closeness.

Across the short distance between him and the pool, his eyes fell upon its surface. The glimpse of the image reflected there,

frightened him, further—

"Ah, Creature," said the Voice, "do not turn your face away. *To know thyself is to know the Universe and all its glories.*"

Somewhere inside him, yet separate and apart, a wave of warmth and compassion such as he had never known swept him up. The wave seemed stronger than he; as if it could knock him over if it wanted to. That wave surrounded him, opened his eyes to the inner mysteries of a night he'd seen every evening of his life, and never seen at all.

From the image of the glen, the night began to spin an all-telling tapestry of bright hoarfrost threads, increasing their numbers until the reflection he'd managed to avoid in the pool, sprang back at him, clear upon the face of each leaf and tree.

Underneath the flesh, the skeletal frame of his reflective structure mocked, as from its very frailties energy sang, a kind of continuum magnificent and strong, quite like the energy of the Sleeping Pool.

A second wave linked itself to the first, allowing that energy in long luminescent waves, to span effortlessly both time and space. So much of what he'd learned to ponder on his journey, so much of what mattered to him, was laid bare of its secrets in that vanishing speck of time, that he wanted to leap up and shout its discovery,

but there were no neat compartments to confine its wonderment, no ready words, by which to explain it. What he did know was what lay within that shimmering miracle, near enough to touch, belonged to him.

It was his very own power.

At recognising a strength of his own so gigantic, he felt a great need to protest its existence.

"I can see," said the Voice, "how uneasy you are."

"We are never supposed to admire anything about ourselves," came the mumbled objection.

"Old threats bind unbreakable, Creature, until some renegade somewhere decides to spit on them. Furthermore, if you disavow pride and assertiveness of self, are you not scorning creation? Are you not scorning every living thing of which you know and even perhaps those things of which you know not?

"You came here seeking unlimited thought. I cannot give that to you since the reach of any thinker is his own province. Instead, I will give you Endless Knowledge, and you may do with it what you will."

"Is the knowledge you have truly Endless?"

"You have it" said the Voice, "in the exact same measure. Be still, and I will show you."

The Creature blinked but once, as the Voice ever-so-softly, touched a spot somewhere near his brain and instantly it was as if he had two of them. "How do I suddenly know that we are given only one brain?" His awe did not let him speak above a strangled murmur. "What is that you are touching?"

"The unseen place," the Voice replied. "It is the place which holds Endless Knowledge."

"For me, you mean?"

"Endless Knowledge is for everyone, and so everyone has a hidden place whether they know it or not."

And again, there came the touch, and he saw that the Voice was right, except that it would take more time than anyone might ever have to sort it all out. He drew in his breath, receiving what began in earnest...images of things he had never seen, words of a thousand meanings, and messages garbled by the energy of minds not his own—and then a jumble of ideas—many too brilliant to grasp, many too false, or falsely predicated to accept.

The divergence of so much of the knowledge spreading before him came as a shock. That such latitude of thought had ever been allowed! He reveled for a time amongst the riches of thought and saw whole civilizations turn around then, to deny all but the most circumscribed, just as the Vine had taught him to do.

Both stunning and indifferent, the art and literature of souls without count flashed before his eager eyes in a collage of images, as its creators created within, and yet far beyond the scope of their talents, the links in a connection to something that had no name.

It was the same with the music, grand smashing waves of it from glorious to sublime, to primal; music that could haunt with the power to bind or unbind, exactly as its creators intended. The Creature was thinking that his ugliness would exclude him from the company of those creators

when they materialized before him, creatures before creatures existed where he stood—some ugly in their beauty, some beautiful in their ugliness—and others of more ordinary visage.

But over and above his pitiful preconceived idea of beauty, so clearly that he wanted to cry out with the pain of it,

there came to him on those two waves, *yet a third,* and it bore him along as if he were nothing and everything, to what seemed a plane above him, so that he surrounded himself and surrounded that plane, and slowly it took its own shape and was no shape at all, but it flowed within him and defined for him, beauty.

And beauty encompassed all, leaving no room for anything else, for nothing else existed. Buoyant then, the Creature floated, amongst a miasma of other ideas, one more preconceived than the next, and slowly with great purpose so that he might savour it

always, the third wave, buoyant on the other two, led him amoungst those preconceptions and did not destroy them, but lifted veil after veil, until he

was not sated with other possibilities, but hungry for more, and only one veil remained—but he was too awe-stricken to

sense the closeness of it—*nor had the third wave taken on any perceptible shape.* It simply was what it was, and he knew he had always felt it inside himself, as a part of him.

And the Voice asked him from a distance so great that it might never be spanned: "What do you see?"

"Nothing," the Creature replied, "I see nothing and I see everything."

In that flawless moment, the Voice asked him from the same great distance: "Wondrous, is it not?"

"It defies definition."

"It may be," said the Voice, "the only thing that does."

The midnight hour stretched on, tall dark ferns throwing fringed shadows into deeper shadow. Loons cried in the marsh.

Faster, a thousand tiny voices urged him.

More ripples were breaking, forming those circular reaching embraces. Tears streamed from the Creature's eyes. Regardless of the distance yet remaining between him and the pool, and before he could change his mind, he reached right back, returning his first embrace in a lifetime of none. In the grip of strong emotion, he turned to see the woodcarver, not melding into the six old souls, but surprisingly visible with his claw-like hands, and dour face.

Not one old soul appeared to believe anything as they eyed both circles and Creature. Their battle garb was falling away. Their faces were firmly shuttered. Instantly, he knew what they were thinking, for they were looking at themselves through the eyes of their Vine, while he saw a completely different view, a view he would not have had, just moments before.

How he wanted to make them see their beauty, for he knew with a sharpness so fine it delighted him that the freedom they'd all been seeking truly resided in that Sleeping Pool.

Seised by the first impatience he'd ever dared feel with anyone, the Creature of Habit shoved them into the nearest circle. When it had enfolded them, and their faces glowed with the same emotions he was already feeling, he whispered,

"If I go first and do the honours, will you follow? If I can look into the pool, will you look in?"

Giving them no opportunity to refuse, he locked his knees in a warrior's stance, straightened his shoulders and pointed his nose to the wind. With a smile trying hard to break past the corners of his mouth, he took off running in the new way he'd found, and which had spread untamed, to his nose. His feet barely touched the ground, whereas his nose wanted to inhale every inch. Only at the rim of the pool did he stop. Still embraced by the warmth of the circles, he summoned the whole of his heart, and what he could only hope might be the soul of himself, to lean over and look down through those waters. How quickly he wished that he hadn't.

At first all he could see was his own reflection, and not a shred of handsomeness, only a wart or two and miserably mis-shapen angles, with no lack of homeliness in-between. There simply was nothing about him to welcome the eye, to invite it to rest upon him. Disgusted by his image, and smarting, he wanted to leave both pool and glen, and indeed, the world itself

—when right out of the palest midnight hue of that night, he wondered what the rest of his life would be like—*never to know the universe and all its glories.*

The circles tightened around him, the Sleeping Pool beckoned...he directed his gaze into the water as if fearing that he might fall in, and was startled at the sight of his eyes looking back. There was probably more danger of falling into those eyes, than into the pool, for they seemed to draw him further and further into a deeper part of the reflection. He could not turn back, and tracing that reflection, line for line, inside the pathway of those deeply grooved ever-widening circles through waters so soothing they would stay in his mind forever, he came not to the end, but rather to a surprising beginning.

Comprised of a nature maintained by an inner core, unassailed by doubt or fear, what lived inside the beginning was that frightening untamed heart of his. And he knew in a flash what he was seeing through it.

It was what he had used to be, before the Vine.

His first inclination was to run to that self and convey a most hearty greeting, no matter that greetings had always been considered a Forbidden Habit. But he stayed where he was, bowing low to the old ones. He stood quietly as they approached the Sleeping Pool and looked in with the same reluctance that he had felt. And as each one found his own beginning, he shocked himself by not even wincing at the loud sounds of joy they were making.

In the starlit clearing, he leapt high into the air, trying to get used to the idea of having freedom at last. It felt odd, at first, that spring in his step, the fear running off him in rivulets. The constant desire—to reach far beyond himself, charge fearlessly into the unknown; to say the first word, any word, popping into his head—his freedom was arriving in a flood that he never thought of controlling. He wanted to strip himself bare, dance in the moonlight as soon as the moon showed up, again.

"That," said Bragnificense, "was exhilarating. At the very least it makes you wonder what those Vines do, for fun."

"We'll find out shortly," said the Voice, listening to the not-so-distant drag of leaves upon the earth, no longer blending into the sounds of the glen, but standing out sharply. In the pale darkness, the wolves took up their sentry posts. Perched on the Creature's shoulder, the blackbird gave a call signifying that it had settled down for the night. The Creature sounded as he spoke, reflective and far away, once more under the spell of a night that felt too magical to end.

"To think," he said, "of all those great civilizations, the treasure they possessed—and always, after a time—everything was gone."

"*Gone,*" said the Voice. "Like *death,* one of those absolute words which can only fall short of their true meaning. This," and it touched the spot again, "never dies. From yours to you. Endless knowledge. What was—still is—and always will be."

Unsorted knowledge immediately poured into his mind. He headed straight to it—and then turned back. He kept seeing inside the oldest puzzle there was, the demise of entire civilisations and the creatures that comprised them destroyed as well. *Demise and destruction*—nothing more than death, he was certain, and yet—there had to be more to this subject than he understood at the moment.

That and other puzzle pieces skipped through his mind. He couldn't wait to get at them. Head lifted to the soaring dome of the skies, even with endless freedom and knowledge in his possession, he wanted to hold moonbeams in his hands and have his feet brush the clouds, *but Vine whips were trying to herd him into the corner:*

In same the direction from which the Vines would come, he shook a clenched fist.

"You haven't got us, yet, Vine," he shouted. "I hope you're ready for us, because we're ready for you!"

His wonderment boundless,
he felt like the inch-worm, dead-set on getting from here-to-there, peering out over the universe from a position gilded with riches,

and

Starstruck With Promise.

18

Shadows

On the hillside, old fir trees opened their shaggy arms to the night rapidly filling with a silver haze and completely hiding the long ribbon of darkness.

Assuring itself that the Voice's calculations for that ribbon were as close to correct as they could be, Time sat back, and watched the unfolding of a night it had plucked from the lap of disaster. The haze thickened, hanging from the trees, and blanketing the ground, shroud-like, and secretive.

The Creature, who once feared never having more than a few thoughts, now entertained too many, each demanding immediate attention. Not the least of which was the nasty rustle of many leaves covering the last bit of distance to the clearing, at a pace rapid enough to horrify a fencepost.

Having declared himself ready, he stopped to wonder if that were true. The rustling paramount in his head and knowing what he knew about Vines began to outweigh the pull of Endless Knowledge...it was with some difficulty that he yanked himself back from fear, concentrating instead upon the wonderment draped around him like a brand-new and awesome, garment.

Newly-freed instincts caught the scent of that garment. His mind cleared—especially of the rustling—and he started prowling through the riches of knowledge, looking for something quite specific. He saw that he must learn to organise his curiosity; for once within those labrynthian passageways, it was too easy to get caught up in stray bits of thought and start thinking of those who had pondered, long ago...

Miniscule red bugs ran across his toes and up the fern fronds, as he hurried to find a more succinct meaning of the word soul, for he believed that he might have been very close to his own.

That third wave, he thought, how boldly it *had lifted him up and out of himself,* bringing in the same breath a much greater sense of himself and everything around him. The third wave had been born aloft by two other waves. He felt those two were especially intertwined and all three were somehow mysteriously connected to the Voice, that other unseen part of him...he stood in the passageways of knowledge, staring at that threshold, about to cross it, when the Vine hissed and spit, blurring his vision. He tried to get away, but just like sitting on a moss rope and waiting for trouble to pass, trying to get away didn't work either. Even in the act of defying them, he couldn't help missing those two old Habits, as with a very free hand, he ripped whole patches of Vine leaves from his eyes, and bid both Habits and Vine, goodbye.

Red bugs. The last ones he'd seen, had been in the compound, traipsing over the Vine. And now they were here, in the glen of the Sleeping Pool, a veritable army of them...teeth chattering but feet first, as freely as the hand which had severed his ties to the Vine over the threshold he flew, along with his questions,
thinking so fast that by the time he got there, not many questions remained.

Soul—self: The two words meshed in his mind. What had one to do with the other? As far as he was concerned, one might do without *self,* but a *soul?* He didn't want to live without its nearness, not after experiencing those awesome waves...which left the question of how to *find* his soul and keep it close.

The Voice had once made reference to *ultimate treasures of the universe,* protected by their invisibility. Surely *souls* fell into that category. A *self* could not be seen either. Could a *self* be an ultimate treasure as well?

He wondered where his soul had been keeping itself, and could a creature hide his own soul from himself without even knowing he had done so? Or had the Voice, his subconscious mind, seemingly so strongly connected—

But midnight was already dancing to strains of music, passionate and old and the glen of the Sleeping Pool sang a welcome to the ancient souls stepping timidly from the protection of the shadows. Suddenly, the mood of the music was shifting, taunting the Vines already circling their destination. The music grew louder. Its pounding rhythm seemed to bond the Creature to those ancient souls, not through words, but the *energy of them*—expressing thoughts that could otherwise never be spoken at all—and he nodded readily at each wary old face, clinging to what passed between himself and them, that silently affirming journeying of thought.

From blank-faced patches of darkness, an energy, ancient and war-like, permeated the silvery air—more old spirits from this time and that time and times long long ago—looking for the treasure that would unbind. As they found the circles and were embraced, the sounds of keening they made were poignant and piercing. No matter that the print of his knees still showed at the rim of the Sleeping Pool. He knelt again to do the honours, and then moved out of the way.

Upon claiming their wonderment, that keening changed to peals of joy. The Creature wanted to laugh; he wanted to cry. They were so withered, so ancient and brittle, these old souls.

How would they hold up in battle against the Vines? Somehow, it wasn't surprising that each one wore battle garb. What did shake him up was that the height of the excited leaps they made into the air were, inch for inch, as high as his own.

The growling had already started. Three wolves broke away from the pack on sentry duty. Fangs gleaming, they trotted up the hill and plunked themselves down in front of him, sad eyes offering an early apology for what they would shortly do. The Creature heard what they heard—the same invasive, rushing sound—but it seemed he moved in a far-away dream, where an awful fear ruled.

Bragnificense, inspiring as much confidence as any huge bastion tree, guarded the glen in unusual silence. A thin tight line encircled his mouth as he picked red bugs from his person.

Identical bugs had taken the ferns captive, wandering the trailing fronds as they pleased. At the feet of the walnut trees, the Creature saw his drawing still laid out in the dirt. His heart skipped in gratitude. One day soon, he told himself, he would copy the drawing onto a more permanent surface such as a nice big boulder and do it in wonderfully vivid colour.

The Voice whispered in the Creature's ear. The blackbird on his shoulder stirred. Reluctantly, he got to his feet.

"Go." he said to the bird. "Hide yourself in that tree. Return when I call you. If I don't call, fly away fast as you can. And don't come back."

For the second time on that planet, the wolves, with the Great Silver Spirit in their midst, uttered the same baying notes in shivery sequence. The invisible wall surrounding the glen shimmered and bent the light as it dissolved, exposing the Vines, leaves rushing dead-speed along their backs, slithering around and around the clearing.

The sound of their whips cracked on the midnight air.

Serpentine and wiley, the same old fear cornered the Creature's mind, wringing from him a cry met by the awful roars of the Vines as they reared high above even the tallest tree, to sneer down into the glen.

A massive bouquet of mounting rage, the Vines pushed their way through the trees, herding the creatures of the compound in front of them. Bragnificense picked out a Vine, seised and shook it. The Creature, caught in the hem of smothering leaves, stumbled and fell. When he looked up, Bragnificense had already been reduced to little more than the tip of a nose poking out of the greenery of one whole Vine. It had pinned him to a tree, its whips binding him so tightly that not a single silver scale could move.

A creature of the compound spoke with no expression. "You didn't learn much on your journey, Creature. Nobody beats the Vines."

On scrambling to his feet, the Creature noticed his Vine was nowhere to be seen *and every creature carried a water jug.* Wiping the earth from his face, he held out what might be their last hope and maybe his, as well. "If we join together, we can beat the Vines."

"Water," said another creature in the dullest of tones,

and hefted an empty earthenware jug. "The Vine said to get water." And he trudged off with the other creatures, at a stolid pace. His eyes were deader than those of the helmsman in that longboat.

From across the glen, came a roar.

"Where is this renegade Creature of Habit? I want him, I shall have him, string him up by his eyeballs! As for this rumoured Sleeping Pool, get all the water out, plug up the spring
underneath it, fill it with dirt, let that be the bloody end of it!"

The Creature's stomach turned over at hearing his Vine, but he was looking up at Bragnificense, bound by whips and engulfed in emerald foliage. Another Vine slithered up the tree, and pulled on the monster's nose.

"Look at the loonie lummox throwback," the Vine screamed, holding its sides and rocking with glee, "I thought we got rid of those eons ago!"

More Vines crowded around, ready with more ridicule, and recalling tales of the monsters they'd driven to extinction during one eon or another. The creatures of the compound returned, and their jugs were empty. They sat on the ground, mumbling,

"Where's the water? The Vines need water."

The Creature of Habit started to tell them. Then the hair on his head stood up. *The creatures of the compound couldn't see the Sleeping Pool, a mere few feet away.*

"Voice," the Creature cried, "what's the matter with them?"

"You can't see what you can't appreciate. The Vines don't see the Sleeping Pool, either, but then they never did have souls to begin with." And seeing the Creature's confusion, swiftly added,

"—it all goes back to creativity, the core of appreciation. A creature who does not create something, at least in his heart, steals unseen power from himself. The irony is, the creatures of the compound that wouldn't help you now can't be helped by you."

Vine whips cracked near the Creature's head, and he ducked, hearing the Loons calling eerily. "The old souls saw the pool," he rushed to object, "What's the difference between them and the creatures of the compound?"

"Desire," said the Voice, hurriedly. "The old souls have it, the creatures don't. Desire rises from self, or it never rises at all. Nobody can give you desire, it comes from being true to yourself. What I'm saying is the creatures of the compound may get their chance at the pool, but it won't be from this plane. Here, the mind must produce a desire for connection, to reach out, explore, and bring
the soul into the fold of one's self, where it can be appreciated."

"*Self.* I didn't consider it as being that important."

"It is everything. Self is *you, the sum total.* It's what makes you what you are, an individual like no other, with a soul uniquely your own. Look behind you. What do you see?"

The Creature looked over his shoulder at the creatures of the compound, unmoving from the path of the Vines.

"Can I actually find my soul and myself, and keep them close?"

"You've already found your wonderment, thus you are free to keep looking," said the Voice, "at everything. You're getting nearer by the minute. Just don't give up."

Vibrations shook the glen, powerful enough that his Vine

tumbled into the Sleeping Pool. It tumbled out again, unaware of the water dripping from its foliage. Enraged, the Vines thrashed about, seeking the enemy. The glen turned into a sea of maddened foliage and coiling whips, lashing at everything in their path.

Dodging to evade the whips, the seven old souls yanked back the folds of inky shadow, and extended a hand to more ancient creatures struggling to emerge quickly, lest the treasure be destroyed before they got there. The Creature held his breath, for surprisingly, the source of the rocking vibrations was coming from the group which the old ones hauled forth, next.

At the very front lines, in the midst of weary and riotous old souls invigorated by impatience, the Bereft Ones, had finally arrived. Eyes deadened in vacant faces, vacant-seeming bodies held onto selves reduced to almost nothingness. Not a mind operated among them. Only the telling threads of an inert but momentous desire vibrated with life, empowering their voices, raking across one's mind, exposing their misery...then crying out with another pain, as well. It was plain that hard as they tried, they couldn't see the pool, and only gazed blankly right through it.

But true to its promise, as the Creature tried to believe what he was seeing, the Voice took up the threads of their desire and was stepping forward into the center of the glen, halting before the Bereft Ones, and the tranquil waters they sought.

The Voice, that unseen part of him, was forming itself before them, becoming the outline of two waves that trembled for a moment, infusing the threads with life…disintegrating with the force of that effort…then coming together again,

and holding a shape that was part of a chain, a *connecting link* between those Bereft Ones and their souls. And the living fibre of that link, glowed in the starlight, fierce and proud and strong.

The Bereft Ones faces lit up, even as they started to weep. For revealed to them, as healing circles enfolded them warmly, was the Sleeping Pool of Freedom.

The Voice stood firm for as long as it could, holding the two waves together, keeping steady, their link between them and their souls, while they looked into the waters. Tattered and battered as they were, their wonderment as they met it seemed too much for them and for an instant, the Creature feared they might not comprehend. But little by little, bit by bit, light came into those staring dead eyes, their faces started to glow.

Link. The Creature heard the puzzle piece fall into place in his head. "I know what you are," he started to tell the Voice, but the old souls were already running, desperate to take positions, ringing themselves with their backs to the pool, digging their toes into the earth, for the Vines were surging forward.

A gust of hot breath singed the Creature's cheek. So Close was his Vine, that he cringed at the smell of its leathery leaves—

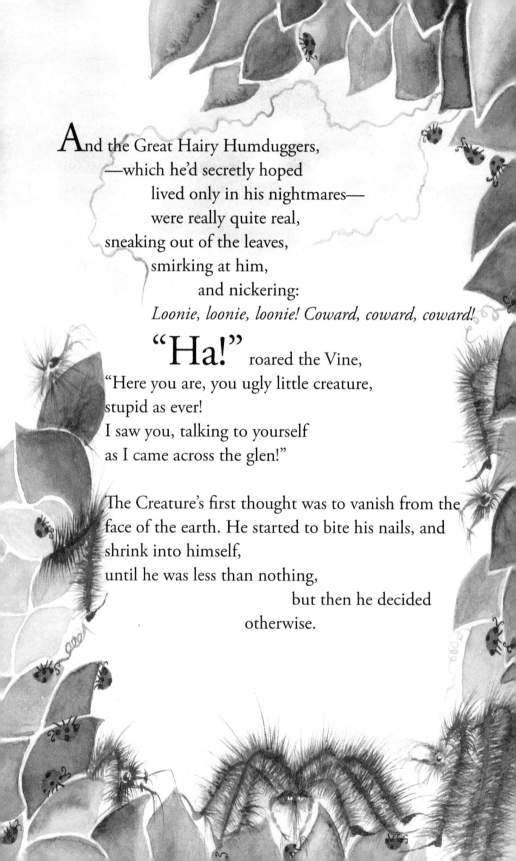

And the Great Hairy Humduggers,
—which he'd secretly hoped
    lived only in his nightmares—
        were really quite real,
sneaking out of the leaves,
    smirking at him,
        and nickering:
        Loonie, loonie, loonie! Coward, coward, coward!

"Ha!" roared the Vine,
"Here you are, you ugly little creature,
stupid as ever!
I saw you, talking to yourself
as I came across the glen!"

The Creature's first thought was to vanish from the
face of the earth. He started to bite his nails, and
shrink into himself,
until he was less than nothing,
                    but then he decided
        otherwise.

"Didn't I tell you," the Vine raged on, "that one day, you would go mad with your insane imagining and grandiose dreams? What possessed you to come to this wicked place, which has only fueled your worthless dreaming?"

"I've been claiming my existence," the Creature replied, but his tongue stuck to the roof of his mouth.

"Your *what?* You spend years being a dunce, and now you think you're some kind of genius? Look at them!" the Vine screamed, cracking a whip at the creatures of the compound. "They know better than to try my patience. They only do what I tell them to do, and they're much better off than you, skulking around in this junkyard eyesore! What is all this rusty, musty old metal, clunking about?"

The Creature looked at the old ones, proudly arrayed in their ancient armour—and realized—the Vine believed that except for the wildlife and Bragnificense, he was alone in the clearing. Nor did the Vine see the Voice—which he himself, had only just seen, and briefly.

Wolves snarled through their teeth, but the Vine was too enraged to hear them. From leaf to leaf, Humduggers scuttled, the Vine rustled and swayed, beginning to elongate, until it towered from an extraordinary height. And grabbing the Creature, it tossed him like a stray twig so high that he saw the cliffs beyond the clearing.

Out over the valley below, it held him, swinging him back and forth with his feet peddling the air.

"Why don't I just drop you on your smart little head?

Then we'll do away with the silly pool, and all will be right with the world again. Unless of course, you want to say you're sorry, in which case you can come back to the compound with me, and find out what real punishment is!"

"Do whatever you want, Vine, but I wouldn't go anywhere with you. You lied! Everything you said was aimed at reducing us to nothingness, telling us that imagination doesn't exist, that thoughts are insanity! You took away every crumb of pleasure, left us nothing but the task of obeying *you!*"

The panic in his voice, the anger and fear, bounced off the cliff walls. The valley swung before his eyes, each time he dared look down. In the glen, wolves howled. Ancient creatures were beating on the Vine, sending Humduggers slipping and sliding along its steaming leaves, as tendril whips collided in a nightmarish tangle.

The Creature of Habit either undaunted, or truly insane—he could not decide which—shouted to the other Vines, who writhed so gleefully, at his plight: "You may as well go back where you came from! We're going to stand right here, every last one of us, and fight you. We belong to nobody but ourselves, and we won't go back to being non-existent!"

He should have seen it coming, but didn't. He was listening to his Vine yelling accusations at him, of ingratitude, treason and treachery, and wondering how he'd ever managed to live with those words, when

with a final hurling of insults, the Vine grinned into his face—and dropped him. He was falling, the valley rushing up to meet him. The wind drew tears from his eyes, his limbs flailed, useless to save him.

In a blur of white coat, a huge wolf sprang onto the Vine, which was stretched in a horizontal line from the lip of the cliffs, out over the valley. Streaking to the very end of the great spiney ridge, the wolf gave a mighty *bounce* that sent the Vine downward,
just low enough. The wolf reached out, snatched the Creature of Habit into its mouth. Like the wind, it ran with him, back along the stupefied spine to the clearing. The Creature lay where he'd been carefully deposited, unable to believe his good fortune. Unwilling to waste it, he leapt to his feet.

"So you've been rescued, so what?" the Vine bent down, to scream in his face. "You'll need more than a scrawny pack of dogs and a moth-eaten monster to save your miserable hide!"

Time, having waited to make final adjustments to the evening, gave the first signal.

The Creature of Habit was suddenly garbed in silver encrustment, created by the splendid magic of night. He looked every inch the warrior—so from that band of ancient warriors fresh out of the shadows, one of them tossed him a sword that glittered and spun in circles silver, through the night sky waiting—and he caught it.

With the wolves' resplendent in their natural finery and panting at his heels as if they would keep all comers at bay until he'd finally finished his duties, he strode to the center of the glen. Inclining his head to the right of him, then to the left, his tongue seised the treasure held in his cheek.

Quite ceremoniously, he spit it out upon the ground, thus declaring the counting begun.

And so it was that the Creature of Habit marched into battle, shoulder to shoulder with seven irksome old souls, and all the other ancients gathered so far. A cheer, started by the mighty helmsman and his oarsmen, was being taken up in that misted, no-moon night, and punctuated by the wolves' excited yipping.

The Vines swatted, at what were to them, invisible punches, and the jab of rusted old swords being wielded by empty air. Between attacks, they slithered and simmered—and *conferred.*

"Hang on, Bragnificense," the Creature yelled. "It won't be much longer, and we'll be rid of these Vines!"

"Pride," whispered the Voice in delight, "what a lovely emotion it is. And what a grand warrior you make."

"Never," said the Creature, "nag me about my humility again. I have an excellent idea how much effort you put into all of this. And an even better idea of what you are. The first wave was my soul. You are what makes the ancient connection. You—*the second two waves, my unseen, subconscious mind,"* and he put out a hand to steady himself as he said it, "are the link between— connecting me to my soul—*the part of me that never dies.*"

"Exactly right," said the Voice.

"So I am not immortal. I could die out there." And he indicated with a faint wave of his sword—suddenly rather heavy in his hand—the battlefield crowded with enraged but withered old souls and warriors.

"Quite possibly, yes. You could," said the Voice.

"In that event, what would happen to you?"

"I shall miss you," the Voice told him, cheerfully.

"What would you do? Sit under a tree and contemplate the moon?"

"The moon is your province," said the Voice, in a very odd tone. "Down through the years, there have always been offspring. You have none as yet. So even I don't know exactly what would happen to me next."

"Then I guess we both have something to worry about." The Creature turned with the driest of looks and his sword raised high, but the cheering had started too soon. The glen grew dark, then darker, for the Vines, puffed four times their normal width and height, ringed it completely. The wee star, in order to shed any light over their shoulders, had to dash in every direction at once.

While employing their whips in lethal fashion, the rude roaring Vines commenced a serious—and fruitless—search for the Sleeping Pool, their eyeballs red with staring under every tree, and behind each rock and boulder, and tinniest fern.

"Creature," his Vine called out in silken tones, "it's been a terrible journey and you know we're not used to traveling. Perhaps it's the strain which has left us out of sorts. What would you say to calling off a silly war you can't win alone, and bringing us a sip of the water from your wonderful pool? We'd really like a chance to *admire* that pool!"

Laying aside his sword, the Creature bent down out of Habit for the earthenware jug. Then he straightened up.

"I can't," he said. "I won't. I delivered my last jug of water."

The single star seemed to shimmer in merriment, the Vines hissed in a venomous rage. Vine whips darted out to throttle him. The Creature had just braced himself for the worst when from the tallest treetop there came a raucous screeching, and the beating of great giant wings.

Silhouetted for a moment, sleek against the silver sky, the blackbird arched itself, preened and puffed itself up to quite scary dimensions. Screeching loudly enough to sufficiently frighten every Vine in sight, the blackbird screeched louder yet and started its downward swoop through the trees.

Only someone who knew of its tattered condition, or who noticed how badly it listed to one side, would have feared for its flight. For it was but a piecemeal bird using all that it had, to stay aloft. And it might have been just the wind—small lovely pockets of breezes blowing softly here and there—which managed to keep it steady, while the Creature's heart caught in his throat.

After the smallest of faltering and continuous distracting screams, it landed right on course. Nor would it leave its perch atop his shoulder where raggedy feathers tickled his nose, and made his sword shimmer in front of his eyes. Then he saw something which made his eyes well up all over again, and he guessed he probably wouldn't be needing that boulder. The Vine was strutting, dragging its glorious coat of green along the edge of the dirt drawing, staring down at the beautifully artistic strokes, and smirking.

"This has to be yours, Creature. It is so pathetically like you, it might as well have your name on it."

Every eye in the glen fastened upon the drawing, but no comfort could be taken from the sounds of approval at his work, because before he could move, the Vine dropped a long tendril dead-center across the sketch. It shook the tendril, sending a storm of dust up the Creature's nose.

Pain flooded his heart, he thought surely he would die from his rage. The old souls nearest hollered and pounded on the Vine, as if it had destroyed not only his efforts, but their own, as well. A clutch of ancient warriors, swords in hand, were climbing the Vine, determined to ax each lusterous leaf. Right then he knew pride wasn't a crime. Not having it was.

Unable to see the ancients, the Vine retreated at the worst of the blows and kept looking about for their source. The blackbird's talons tightened on the Creature's shoulder, as an idea shot into his mind, devious enough to be worthy of the Voice, itself.

"Perfection!" said the Voice, pretending mock-horror when the idea was explained. "Congratulations, Creature. There's more to you than we dreamed!"

The battle raged on, with Time watching every move, and a fine, fine battle it was. Except that at times, the warriors sliced bits of themselves and each other, with their swords. They had been away from battle a very long time, and had to recapture the knack of it as they went along—and the great Vines had a tendency to trip now and then, upon the trailing tips of their whips—but they hadn't been away from their craft, and it was easy to see they were winning.

Eventually, things got onto a more even track, the warriors warring more proficiently, the Vines growing madder proportionately—and the Creature of Habit enjoying the heft of his mighty, borrowed sword—while he waited.

The din was awful. The clanking, stomping, bashing and thrashing seemed never to stop. In the midst of a really good thrust of his sword, pointed in the vicinity of his Vine's considerable middle, he decided the time was right.

He hissed at the Vine and ran. He wove and darted and dodged, uphill most of the way, the Vine hot on his heels. Its recent journey aside, the Vine, having spent most of its life being waited upon, and hardly moving a muscle except to employ its whips, was giving an amazingly good account of itself.

Having watered the Vine the whole of his life, only the Creature knew what he was up to, sprinting forward, turning on a hair, and doubling back, simply to turn and dart once more, to the top of the hill. The shame and betrayal expressed on the old souls' faces nearly stopped his running from the enemy, now in crazed pursuit. The other Vines, having taken up the chase, pursued him too, as he kept on, dashing zig-zag between big boulders, darting into the underbrush, and materialising again, at the top of a tree.

The Vines were exuding a powerful sweat, leaving pools of it trailing the earth behind them. The thrill of success made the Creature too confident and he overdid it. Doubling back for the third time, he skidded on one of those trails. The blackbird lost its perch, and the Creature sailed head over elbow, to land at the feet of the Vine. It took him a second to feel the Vine whip biting into the tender flesh of his throat, another second to wonder how he might escape, and a third to admit that he probably couldn't. The tendril would either cut his throat in two or choke him to death, long before help arrived.

"Beg me," the Vine—his Vine—hissed in his ear. "Say please."

He almost did, as he had, any number of times before, groveling and pleading for leniency. But he thought that it did seem funny—the Vine huffing and puffing, gasping for breath, and swelled with pride at trapping a creature more than a hundred times smaller, and the trappee so busy wondering exactly what death would be like, that he was about to be dead.

And he laughed.

"Oops," he said, with the tendril still carving a dent in his neck. The Vines froze, while his second laugh rolled around the glen and bounced off the trees and started to echo across the waters of the Sleeping Pool, reaching all the way up to that one timeless star creating such lovely light The laugh felt so good inside him that he couldn't stop. Even the Voice was impressed.

No Vine had ever been laughed at before, and could not imagine it daring to happen. And while they simmered over that…

Time gave the second signal,

and night and nature played with darkness and light in patterns that moved one onto the other, then broke away, beguiling both eye and mind. Those shadows standing in mysterious blankness throughout the glen, now appeared full of life, letting one think that bands of old warriors gathered there among tall grasses that could well have been swords.

Forcefully, the night winds seised that illusion. Carrying sounds of the clanking of battle garb and sword, they blew through valley and dale, swirling mists of delicate hue that appeared suspiciously, like the frosted breath of anxiously ready warriors and steeds.

Great was their number, and threatening their movements. The Vines looked upon them, in panic. But night and nature weren't through, for they cast upon every old soul just enough darkness to banish their transparency and make them stand out against the light—thereby revealing to each Vine those whom they had entombed long ago.

None of this matched the Vines' idea of reality, of course, and they thought they were going mad, especially when night and nature then shifted the light once more, and the Vines saw their shadows being cast upon the glen. So hard did they shake with doubt concerning their sanity that their shadows took on a life of their own, leaping and skittering, an army of long forked tongues and slithering fingers. As jumpy as the Vines already were, they now became manic, for their shadows utterly terrified them.

"How does it feel," the Creature asked, "to be scared of your own shadow?"

His Vine couldn't answer. It was cowering through the glen in an attempt to get away from itself, and gleeful shadows darted after. The other Vines stumbled about, crashed into trees and each other, slithering and rearing and sweating profuse droplets of frantic perspiration. Their roots were dragging the ground.

Their panic shouldn't have lasted long. The minute they grew tired, the shadows would have stopped leaping.

The loons started it—calling out in their eerie way—mockingly, from beneath the Vines' very feet. The owls that never traveled in flocks screeched and swooped in massed furry, along with a sky full of blackbirds, and their flapping shadows were cruel and ominous. The rest of the wildlife came then, throwing their shadows through the forest until the whole of it writhed with serpentine tongues licking fauna and trees, then bounding out to chase themselves up and down the glorious coats of green.

Gnats and bats swarmed, and infested the Vines. Wolves grinned ghoulishly, casting shadow-fangs before them, and leading the smallest of wildlife, bristling with anger. The mice especially, mimed the scurrying Great Hairy Humduggers, until there seemed to be thousands upon thousands of them, smothering the Vines in
a blanket of tiny, hair-covered, fur-covered, scurrying bodies.

And the noise: Anything that moved moved in shadow, growling and snorting, bleating and screaming, and bellowing blood-curdling, primitive expletives.

Oddly enough, the din didn't bother the Creature's ears. His artistic nature now fully engaged, he could appreciate the sounds they were making, the picture they created, with nightmare howlings and fearful flickering; midnight shadows that marauded around the Vines—mirroring the Vine's description of wildlife right before he'd left on his journey.

So slowly then, that nobody really believed it was happening, the Vines, having exercised themselves into a lethal lack of moisture, started to lose their wonderful finery and their long singing tendrils. They were shrinking into themselves, growing abysmally shorter and miserably thinner, until the only thing visible about them, was a sad, sad pile of withered and shrunken dead leaves and roots.

"What do we do now?" grumbled a sweating warrior. "This place is a mess. We can deal with the leaves, but what about these roots?"

A big old sawtooth tail shot across the clearing, and the tail was attached to its owner, Bragnificense. "Hello!" he shouted to the Creature. "How are you?"

"I don't think I could be much better, thank you," the Creature said cheerfully. "Since as of this moment, I seem to have deciphered the first part of the message! *Hello, how are you?* Now isn't it silly, how that could have escaped me all this time?"

"Not silly at all," the monster smiled back. "The smallest of things always hide behind the largest of things, until we move everything out of the way, and look through our own eyes. Then we see, that what was big, was actually small, and the small was perhaps…"

"The biggest of all?" the Creature finished Bragnificense's rhyme with him—and for a minute or two; he had to say to anyone who passed by, *Hello, how are you?* –just to hear the sound of it.

"Try not to care too much if you ever decide to rhyme, and they tell you how badly you do it," said Bragnificense. "They tell me the same, but the pleasure of rhyming is mine, and it keeps my mind magnificently primed!"

With no further fuss, Bragnificense set about, rhyming wretchedly and grinning grandly, digging out with his sawtooth tail, every single Vine root in sight. And when he was done, roots and leaves were stacked sky-high, fodder for what would become a very nice bonfire with a lovely rosey glow, lighting up the tranquil ripples in the Sleeping Pool.

"Well," said the Creature, politely returning his sword to the warrior who had lent it, "I suppose we shall still have to put up with each other."

"I think I could manage that," said the Voice.

Just beyond the Vine roots neatly stacked and ready to be fired up, Time wandered unobserved, enjoying itself and checking to be sure the long dark ribbon dangling from the sky, would be ready when needed. Like an especially good guest, Time also wanted to leave a little something behind, as a token of thanks for what had turned out to be a smashing evening.

Stray bits of root from the bonfire now blazing, shot upward, hissing red against the night sky. Forest creatures peeped out of their nooks and crannies, relieved the war was over, and their home was back to its old self. The throngs gathered at the fire stood knee-to-knee, more than a hundred deep all around. The simple little hum they were humming in unison, while gazing across at the Sleeping Pool of Freedom had a hidden beat, and a whisper of unintelligible words with a definite pulsating sound.

The Creature wasn't sure about that innocuous hum. It wasn't a chant or a mantra, either, The mood of it, the passion behind it reminded him again of the grand primal music he'd heard in the passageways of knowledge. The longer he listened, the less at ease he felt.

For a tiny little quick-step in time, remarkably similar to when he'd been running with the wolves, he found himself unable to decide—was that hum coming from the long ago past— or sometime in the far-off future?

From a place he could not see in the world visible to him, Time gazed into his face, and traced with that pulsing hum, a steady line across his brow. The hum penetrated his senses, alternating in a softly-fluid, and harshly-broken rhythm, as Time did not cease its gazing, but engaged him further, moved him to enter alongside itself those labrynthian passageways of knowledge.

Following the humming by way of its beat, they were going back so far that when the trail petered out, all that hung before the Creature were a handful of frayed and glittering strands, dangling over an abyss of light years and the black holes that held them.

When his eyes caught up with what his senses keenly

perceived, he dared to see a light shifting against the darkness, taking on the shapes of strangely formed entities. And in that light, the pulsating beat became wildly more insistent, sweeping him away with the thoughts just under it, thoughts that were hurrying to meet his own.

Time held him then—
for he wanted to fall and float gently downward—seeing in those strange shapes below, in the world
which surrounded them within that softly shifting light, a whole new vista of far more intricate,
labrynthian passageways.

He could smell it—the odour of water, water that was getting ready to sit there forever, in a time he could only dream of—patiently waiting for someone to arrive, and notice.

Time tightened its grip, held him by the scruff of his neck,
refusing his excitement, his desire to be off and questing again.

Not yet. Remember, you have guests. And I have another gift for you to share with whomever you will, said Time in its wordless fashion: He who notes a fine oddity is always right to follow it. And he who notes the first oddity will always note and follow the next, though it be a thousand years. And when you arrive, I'll be there to welcome you.

19

Full Circle

There was nothing of nature the Creature
could not see, from the tiny toad enchanted with its reflection, to
each think blade of grass; the tall old trees; the earth itself, dark with
riches from nature's treasure, added and fermenting over more
seasons than he had lived, yet his gaze
traveled helplessly upward;
nothing could stop it. Above all
the land, so finely detailed
in that shimmering night,
nary a light-filled portal
shone in the misted sky.
"Surprise!" the Voice
chuckled in his ear.
"Something
wondrous?" the Creature
asked, still thinking of
the gift
Time had given him.

"Beyond wondrous," the Voice replied, and immediately, the Creature heard the rumble and felt the shake, while the heavens and the land then stood very still—still as the Voice, holding its breath and moving back, leaving the Creature to stand by himself in the middle of the glen. No matter how grand and magnificent he felt just then, he was very much aware of himself as being no bigger

than a sigh in the universe.

"And so," said the Voice, "We come to the last veil."

The Great Spirit Winds, of a mind to howl and click their heels, controlled themselves, to the extent that they only murmured softly, and let night winds blow the frothing clouds across the heavens. The clouds continued as they had been, to gather at the top of the dark ribbon-while the Creature wondered further: Had the Vines managed to steal the moon,

and the last star as well?

Saddened at the awful emptiness of the night sky, he nearly missed the beginning of what he'd sought for so long. As it was, he watched unsuspecting, as a light flashed willful in the firmament. A thousand stars began to blink through the ribbon; the frothing clouds at its top, drew back to reveal

his moon beyond,

unfettered.

Afraid never again to get the chance, and determined to speak before she was gone—perhaps this time forever—

He raised his head to her and uttered a cry
that rose from his most ancient time,
hearing from his mouth, not words, but a mournful wailing.

And the moon answered him back—

This is my flight,

and my flight is my being
…it defines me,
      raises me
      to a height
            and a pattern
            no other has
            achieved.
            But always,
         there are other heights
      and other patterns,
   each to its own defining,
   and raising

yet another…

The Creature's cry kept emitting from his throat, for he could not close off the timeless wellspring from which it came. As if she understood too well each plaintive note he uttered... the moon answered again. At first he thought she was being modest, displaying a humble nature until from each note, quite concise—he understood what she was
telling him—

...*a crown rests upon every head. Be not in awe of another's path, for your own is inspiring enough.*

Holding her words so close to his heart that breathing seemed impossible, he could see that she was slowing, pausing in her flight and hovering at the top of that thin ribbon of deepest hue. The clouds closed in upon her, but still the form of the moon could be seen inside them, taking on the attitude of one who was out for a stroll, just ambling on down that ribbon, enjoying herself...

In the shocked silence, the Creature heard nothing except for the Voice, crunching its invisible teeth and holding its breath, both in the very same moment.

The moment grew longer, extended itself for another interminable beat. The merest hint of a glow bathed the land, a glow so ethereal, so beguiling...the light shone brighter and
brighter. The Voice kept holding its breath, and the Creature too, for the moon was doing what she'd never done, she was about to enter the glen of the Sleeping Pool.

Straight down that ribbon she came,
his moon—
resplendent in evening finery
and the pull of the tides that exuded from her—
all silver and glowing, and accompanied by frothing clouds,
silver and shining as she

—and on either side, a warrior star—
positioned points of light.

The universe waited—nor did the winds move, nor any star nor planet, nor tic of the time that was not—and it was Time itself, contriving to keep it that way.

The honour guard they came then, valiant numbers of stars without count, from all the silver shores and all the silver mountains and vast silver reaches of the universe, near and far, and quickly did they surround her, while she hung there in silent splendour, above the Creature's head.

It wasn't until he'd taken in the whole of what was happening, taken in the whole of her and her universe, too, that his misted glance flew to the Sleeping Pool, seeing each ripple upon its surface, moving in lines of glimmering silver—moving like tides—tied to the mind

of the moon and Beyond,
and she was beckoning to him.

So akin to her did he feel just then
that she might have been flesh of his flesh. And in that marvel of time that was not time, and space that was not space, but only a byway direct and affirming and paved by pin-prick lights, it was up to the ribbon betwixt heaven and earth a'dangle, that Bragnificense swung him, and he hurriedly placed himself, excited to the marrow and ready to fly
where the ribbon led.
Breathing a sigh,
he took in a knowing—where he was going, there existed no need for the hurry with which

he'd too often consumed his journey. As she continued to beckon, so he was drawn by tides that swept him down the corridors of time, to his primal self—where all was raw instinct, confidence born of necessity, and a strength of purpose so powerful—that it matched very nearly, the moon's tidal pull.

His faith holding steady
upon the thin and enticing slice of night, he made unexpectedly, the leap between mind and soul, taking him precisely where he'd
always known
he could go.

While he floated weightless as the Will-O-the Wisp, just under the holes in the sky, the wind seemed to sigh right through him. He stuck out a toe and then a whole foot watching beguiled, as it cut a swath through the firmament.

Unattached as he was, nothing prevented the ease with which he simply thought of being over there—and suddenly was—with his nose up against a star—or thought of being much higher—and instantly was—captivated at the sight of what seemed another whole realm of stars and planets and moons, and even a sun, sleeping off the cares of the day.

Unbending within the light it created, the strongest of energy began to flow inside him,
and the moon responded,
enfolding the whole of him in the tidal pulse that made up the heart of her being, letting him feel through that pulse

the words that she whispered straight to his face:

...a thousand warriors strong
could not do what you have done;
nor a thousand explorers nor minds alone, either...

No sooner were her words done, than she showed him his eyes yet bound by fragments of stone and Vine leaf intertwined, and his soul of the same where joy is supposed to be born.

Instantly, he knew where he had been hiding his soul, even from himself. It had been tucked away, inside every thought he'd ever thought, about the heavens and Beyond; inside every thought and longing glance he'd ever lavished upon the moon.

And in that moment it was come to be—that a rapture took him as a thousand stars soughing, his every emotion not emotion at all, but only a single feeling, strong enough to start shaking loose old moorings that had kept him forever, it seemed—too close to safety's shore.

Back along the glittering byway, across the same distance as the mighty helmsman and his oarsmen had watched their own—the Creature of Habit beheld the shoreline belonging to him.

The moon took up that distant destination. From the bonds which Time had already loosened, she unleashed it across time and space.

And smiling, she set him adrift,
there on the sea of his soul...

Then she was done, except for one thing—and she smiled

at him as she gave it—letting him understand that as she—*he was only as free as he would be.*

He who knows that,

she whispered on the wind,
knows it all.

Shadow shapes trotted through the forest darkened, and entered the glen one-by-one. Just seeing them outlined in starlight and moonlight—like the moon, flesh of his flesh—was enough. The muscles at the sides of the Creature's mouth started working, stretching his face into the broadest of smiles. As good as he already felt, he felt even better.

The smile turned into a grin.

When he no longer floated and drifted, but felt as though he still was, his feet touched the ground once more. The wolves crouched at the edge of the pool, and everything true seemed to be in their eyes. As they got up to greet him, he held out his hand. Roughened tongues licked each of his fingers, throaty cries mingled hauntingly with his, climbing untamed

through the soft balm of midnight. The moon moved lower over the Sleeping Pool, waiting for him to absorb those cries—splendid as they were, with nature—and the universe near and far. The Creature quietly sniffed the air, and smelled the land and all the winds, and the heavens, too. Then drink he did of those things, and deeply, for he was of them and they of him.

"Listen," said the Voice in his ear, "do you hear it?"

The cries of wolf and Creature, seised by the Winds of Time, were heading gale-force, straight down to the glen, and there happened a shrill tearing sound, as though everything on the earth were being blown from its moorings.

The sound gathered speed, and burst crescendo-force, upon his senses. Everywhere he looked, trees toppled, rocks flew. The winds rent the earth—and he was of that earth—being torn to bits right along with it, until every unseen part of him had been ripped away, and lay exposed—to starlight and moonlight, and the light of his full reason.

His eyes teared with flying debris. He couldn't have seen the parts, even had they been visible, yet never had he been so aware of the need for them, as now, when they were gone. Weak with the loss, and desperate with desire to have them back, he fought the howling gales. Bent nearly double, he chased his parts of heart and mind and finally his soul and spirit, through winds equally determined that he now crown his quest

...and when he would fall, nor find his feet again, his strength, always sought from without, rose up instead from within, until it could rise no higher. It gathered him together, part by part, forcing him whole, back into himself, until he would explode with his entirety.

And lo, every hair of him did prickle in the moonlight, as he filled with the wonder of what he was. Silently, he cried within, that the sound of his joy should be so muffled. Dare he did,

to rail aloud—and he wailed primordial stored tears—not tears of
fear and trepidation, but tears of celebration, at the threshold
before him. And when the shattered earth
had ceased to rain upon him,
the Creature of Habit
took the threshold of his fear, strong of step.
His eyes scanned the glen—while the Voice answered his
question before he had even asked it.

"The upheaval of self-awareness," said the Voice, "is never
without event."

Both becalmed and battered as he had just been by
emotion, his mind moved him forward in a state close to shock.
Slowly, he looked to the land and he looked to the heavens
where the moon hung low.

But the glen sat silent as before,
with all in perfect place behind the shimmer of silver night,
while the ripples in the pool moved in rhythm
with the tide
of the mind
of the moon and Beyond.

Conscious still, of the on-going turmoil in his mind, he
marveled. Nothing of the glen had changed or been destroyed.
He had only seen it in his mind's eye, for his mind did truly have
an eye of its own.

"Trust it…" the Voice said…

The Creature could do nothing else, for beyond
the last veil,

his mind was further changing, re-aligning itself, opening wide—

until in the eye of it, there was reflected not only himself, but every last creature down through his chain—before and after him,

each to its own defining—nor could the Creature deny the celebration

of that defining.

Stunned, he looked down at himself, the sinew and bone and muscle, the flag of flesh spread over it all. The wind sang around him, its ancient song of his link through time, as he felt of himself all that made up the construction of his physical being.

Tentatively at first,

he spread his mind and touched it—both the seen and the unseen of it—and then, in a paean of joy, *the Creature of habit gazed through it, into the depths of self.*

The white wolf sat on its haunches, beneath the walnut trees, waiting for the ancient souls to take their places upon the ribbon. When Bragnificense had finished hoisting them up— every last one, including the Bereft Ones, and the dour-faced woodcarver—and they had finished their journeys, with moon glow still lighting their faces, Bragnificense hauled them back down.

The wolf started to lead them to the edge of the glen.

But the ancient souls were insistent, their gestures firm,

Bragnificense must finish his journey, they said, and then they would take their leave.

"Must you?" cried the Creature of Habit, shocked to know that he meant the words from his heart, and without reservation. "What about our next journey? What about the compartments I'll be building? You know you'll always have a safe place to stay!"

The Voice didn't need to tell him, the thought flying into his head: The old ones were leaving, and they wouldn't be back. Nor should he follow, just yet.

So he stood there with them, while Bragnificense lumbered up the pathway with what looked suspiciously like the hint of a skip.

Nobody could hear what the moon said to him, or he to her, but across the firmament where the stars twinkled in a language of their own. What everybody did hear were awesome, echoing, and ancient bellows, as if all creature like Bragnificense, driven to extinction long long ago, were releasing their thoughts to the moon.

Her replies were lengthy. Their grief was lengthy. Wolves and Creature waited. The old ones waited. The Great Spirit Winds waited, too, nor was Time the least bit impatient.

Curious, the Creature turned to the Voice, with a question.

"Isn't this getting to be a really long night?" he asked.

"Some nights are like that," said the Voice, and Time smiled.

Bragnificense was having himself a final bath in the stream

that burbled at the feet of the Sleeping Pool, making up brand-new rhymes concerning the second part of the message.

How free and I, he trilled, *only as free as I would be.*

The blackbird nose-dived him, testing its wings for the coming flight, and the Creature finally found the creatures of the compound wandering under the walnut trees. He asked if they would like to journey with him, at least for a bit. They wandered away, without looking at him or saying a last goodbye.

And then it was time. The white wolf led the old souls to the edge of the glen, and bayed a plaintive, announcing call. The end-note sounded. The old woodcarver raised his claw-like hand to the Creature, who unable to utter a word, waved back, not quite the loner he had imagined. For as the ancient ones drew together, and then disappeared along with the wolf, in a great bursting of sparkling stars, he knew the compartments he would soon build, were

going to seem empty without them.

Time made unseen adjustments to the end of the dark ribbon moving languidly in a bit of a breeze. The wolves nudged the Creature, as though he'd forgotten his manners. And from his new nocturnal self, the Creature of Habit raised his head to the waiting moon, and saluted her, the way they had
reminded him
that he could.

The Great Spirit Winds gathered themselves together, but not before they had secreted a bit of frippery lying upon the sweet grass, where the Creature would later find it. Crystal magician warriors whirled across the skies, busy as Time was busy, making sure the way was clear.

In the Creature's stomach, something went *ping*—his heart turned over, his eyes blurred—but not for nothing, was he a warrior-questor. As the moon settled herself, and began to ascend, she gave the Creature a wink, and he winked back.

So did the Voice.

Once again at the top, and released from the arms of that vertical shaft of ingenious construction, the moon sailed on. In the distance, the Great Spirit Winds watched the Creature of Habit, as he came upon the little blue flower nestled among the grasses. An *Ah* of surprise, another of delight, a deep inhaling of its fragrance, and he laid down with the flower, held close to his face.

When he awakened in the morning, ready to be off, he would discover that the hillside on which he had slept so soundly for once, had sprouted a thick blanket of little blue flowers that reached as far as the eye could see.

Safely out of sight, the moon rose considerably higher than she usually rose in her flight, and she smiled to herself. She did a little dip—as if taking a good deep breath—and amazingly rose even higher, until she was positioned before the last stars, where the sky let in a lovely light from Beyond.

It was in that direction, that she gave a broad wink, tucked all her stars into bed, and continued on her way.

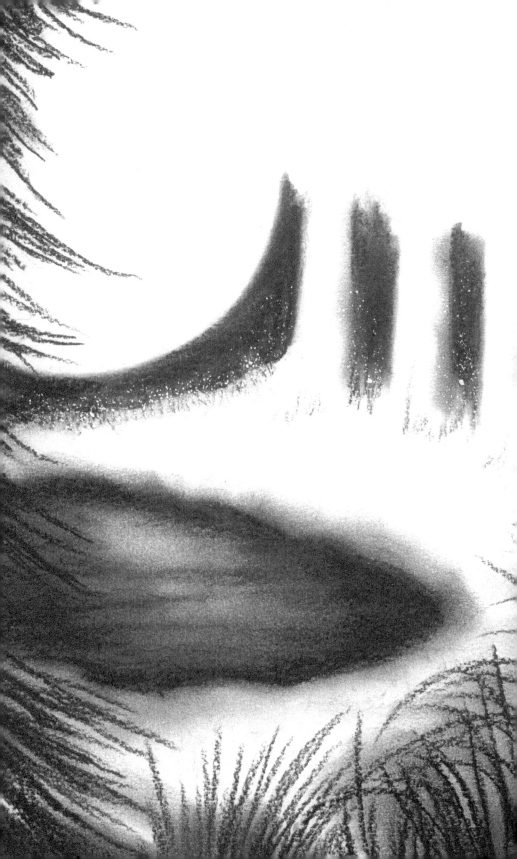

Epilogue

The moon still sails by in her evening flight.
The Creature has occasionally been known
to lift his head and bay at her.
She does not seem to mind.
Some, who never made a journey
of their own,
say that baying is an act of nature,
and creatures shouldn't be doing it.
It is, they say,
a habit—belonging
to the wolves that prowl near
a small pool—
which miraculously
has never been discovered in daylight.
Only by the glow of the moon
has a weary traveler ever stumbled upon
the silent glen where the pool sleeps.
The pool is surrounded
by giant trees tipped in silver...
and upon her surface,
there are ripples...moving like tides
tied to the mind
of the moon
    and Beyond.

About the Author

Truddi Chase was born February 22, 1935, near Rochester, New York. As a child, she was severely abused, both physically and sexually, by her stepfather, and the one person who should have defended her—Truddi's mother—not only turned a blind eye to the violence but participated in the physical abuse of her own daughter. How does any human being, let alone a child, endure such trauma? Though not able to escape the physical violence being inflicted upon her, Truddi was able to survive by using the only means available to her: she composed a world of other "personalities" in her psyche that helped her cope with the horror in her life and shield her inner self from complete destruction.

As an adult, Truddi began intensive hypnotherapy sessions with Dr. Robert Phillips, Jr. who quickly discovered that she had been surviving the trauma of abuse with multiple personalities. Part of her therapy included writing an autobiography, *When Rabbit Howls* (1987). This groundbreaking book takes the reader through Truddi's experiences—flashbacks, gaps in time, and strained relationships—after being diagnosed with Multiple Personality Disorder (MPD), now known as Dissociative Identity Disorder. When Rabbit Howls was the first book written by a "multiple", and unlike many people diagnosed with MPD, Truddi chose not to integrate her personalities; instead, the personalities worked together as a team and became known as "The Troops". The book was later turned into a made-for-television mini-series, *Voices Within: The Lives of Truddi Chase* (1990) with Shelly Long portraying Truddi. Her experiences sparked great public interest, which led to numerous interviews, including a personal interview with Oprah Winfrey (1983) and also as a guest on The Oprah Winfrey Show (1990).

Truddi's passion for public education about the effects of child abuse led her to create the powerful and universal story, *Creature of Habit...A Journey*. Though still managing her own Post Traumatic Stress (PTS), she wanted other victims of abuse to know that they don't have to live in fear or be ashamed of the abuse they suffered, and above all, that they do, indeed, have a voice. Throughout *Creature of Habit*, she demonstrates that painful human experiences are still useful for cultivating a deep sense of compassion, understanding, and empathy for those around us and for teaching that "real kindness is a natural generosity of spirit. It's a showing of affectionate emotion...a genuine concern for the well-being of another." Truddi's life is not merely a story about abuse and survival, but of giving generously to others...in spite of what had been taken from her.

Truddi Chase passed away March 10, 2010.

To see more of Truddi's artwork
and purchase prints of her work
visit www.TruddiChase.com

Moonbeams Unlimited Publishing

Delaware

CPSIA information can be obtained
at www.ICGtesting.com
Printed in the USA
LVOW05*0908120116

470251LV00007B/20/P